Entrepreneurship Education in Asia

Entrepreneurship Education in Asia

Edited by

Hugh Thomas

The Chinese University of Hong Kong

Donna Kelley

Babson College, USA

Edward Elgar

Cheltenham, UK • Northampton, MA, USA

Published by
Edward Elgar Publishing Limited
The Lypiatts
15 Lansdown Road
Cheltenham
Glos GL50 2JA
UK

Edward Elgar Publishing, Inc.
William Pratt House
9 Dewey Court
Northampton
Massachusetts 01060
USA

A catalogue record for this book
is available from the British Library

Library of Congress Control Number: 2011932873

MIX
Paper from
responsible sources
FSC
www.fsc.org   FSC® C018575

ISBN 978 1 84980 947 4

Typeset by Servis Filmsetting Ltd, Stockport, Cheshire
Printed and bound by MPG Books Group, UK

Contents

Contributors

Note: for fuller information on contributors' affiliations and positions, see the first endnote in each chapter.

George Abe, University of California Los Angeles, USA.

Peter Adriaens, University of Michigan, USA.

David Chang, University of California Los Angeles, USA.

Du Guirong, Harbin Institute of Technology, Shenzhen Graduate School, Shenzhen, China.

Vathana Duong TE, Yonsei University, Korea.

Timothy Faley, University of Michigan, USA.

Guan Sisi, Beijing Institute of Technology, China.

Donna Kelley, Babson College, Massachusetts, USA.

Bonjin Koo, KAIST Graduate School of Management, Korea.

Huo Lingyu, School of Information, Beijing Wuzi University, China.

Joosung J. Lee, KAIST Graduate School of Innovation and Technology Management, Korea.

Jonathan Levie, University of Strathclyde, Glasgow, United Kingdom.

Liu Lijun, Beijing Institute of Technology, China.

Alicia Coduras Martinez, Instituto de Empresa Business School, Madrid, Spain.

Priya Mohan, University of California Los Angeles, USA.

Takeru Ohe, Waseda University, Japan.

Rognvaldur J. Sæmundsson, Reykjavik University School of Business, Iceland.

Thomas Schøtt, University of Southern Denmark, Denmark.

Siohong Tih, National University of Malaysia, Malaysia.

Wang Ying, Beijing Institute of Technology, China.

Karen Wilson, World Economic Forum, Geneva, Switzerland.

Xu Lei, Harbin Institute of Technology, Shenzhen Graduate School, Shenzhen, China.

Yu Jinquan, Harbin Institute of Technology, Shenzhen Graduate School, Shenzhen, China.

Acknowledgements

The editors thank Tom Byers and Tina Seelig of the Stanford Technology Ventures Program who set up and foster the Accel Roundtable of Entrepreneurship Education (REE) conferences. Your energy and encouragement have made a real difference in promoting entrepreneurship education throughout the world. We also thank the professors, researchers, staff and students at the many universities throughout the world who promote and support REE each year. REE Asia 2009 was made possible by our co-organizers and supporting organizations, whose names are listed in the REE Asia 2009 conference proceedings.[1] Special thanks go to Mr Chien Lee, Member of the Council of The Chinese University of Hong Kong and Director of the Lee Hysan Foundation, our conference's first sponsor, who expressed his wish that we record the deliberations of REE Asia 2009.

The papers which correspond to Chapters 3 through 6 and 8 through 11 were selected from 40 papers submitted for double blind review. We extend our sincere thanks to all of those who submitted and presented papers and who attended the conference. We also thank the professors who helped us in the review process: David Alstrom, Kevin Au, Florence Ho, Kaman Lee, Leung Kwok, Janny Leung, Louis Leung, Liu Sun Wing, Lo Wai Shun, Thomas Man, Maurice Tse and Yang Jun.

We thank the staff of the Center for Innovation and Technology and Center for Entrepreneurship, especially Professor K.F. Wong, Rosanna Lo and Samuel Tam on whose shoulders it fell to organize funding for and organizing of REE Asia 2009, and to Eric Leung who assisted in preparing this manuscript.

Without the support of Tim Williams, Publisher, and Alan Sturmer, Editor, Edward Elgar Publishing, this book would not have been possible. And finally we would like to thank Joanna, Larry, Kira and Jada for their patience and support. You make it all worthwhile!

Hugh Thomas
Donna Kelley

NOTE

1. Thomas, Hugh and K.F. Wong, *Global Entrepreneurship: Proceedings from the Roundtable on Entrepreneurship Education Asia 2009 Hong Kong and Shenzhen October 2009*, Center for Entrepreneurship, Chinese University of Hong Kong, 2010.

Foreword

Tom Byers*

As stated in my own textbook,[1] entrepreneurship is a vital source of change in all facets of society, empowering individuals to seek opportunities where others see insurmountable problems. For the past century, entrepreneurs have created many great enterprises that subsequently led to job creation, improved productivity, increased prosperity, and a higher quality of life. Entrepreneurship is now playing a vital role in finding solutions to the huge challenges facing civilization, including energy, environment, health, security, and education. With the importance of entrepreneurship and innovation in mind for the future growth of civilization, East Asia is arguably the most exciting and compelling place on the planet to examine the subject at this moment in history.

Furthermore, education has always been a great enabler of peace and prosperity. It follows naturally that we should create and share knowledge about entrepreneurial behaviors, skills, and processes for the benefit of all students enrolled in higher education. During our founding years of the Stanford Technology Ventures Program in the 1990s, this is why we created the first Roundtable on Entrepreneurship Education (REE) conferences (http://ree.stanford.edu). Since that time, almost 40 have been held on five continents in partnership with outstanding universities. Few have been as robust and exciting as the gathering in China during 2009 at The Chinese University of Hong Kong and Shenzhen University. Stanford University was very proud to be part of that historic and timely event.

Professors Hugh Thomas and Donna Kelley have now expertly assembled and organized a collection of thought leadership from this 2009 conference. Why and how should entrepreneurship be taught to the current and next generation of students in East Asia? This book provides answers relevant to educators and policymakers, corporate and non-profit leaders, entrepreneurs and their teams, and anyone interested in fostering a global entrepreneurial economy and society.

NOTES

* Tom Byers is Professor (Teaching), Buzz and Barbara McCoy University Fellow in Undergraduate Education, Stanford University, Academic Director, Stanford Technology Ventures Program and an Affiliated Faculty of the Woods Institute for the Environment.
1. Dorf, Richard C. and Thomas H. Byers, *Technology Ventures: From Idea to Enterprise*, 2nd edn, New York: McGraw Hill, 2008.

Introduction

Hugh Thomas

Entrepreneurship Educators in East Asia share a common quest with our colleagues in all countries: inspiring and equipping the next generation to create a better world, one enterprise at a time. In October 2009, over 200 educators, researchers and practitioners from 50 universities and 19 countries discussed this quest at the Roundtable on Entrepreneurship Education (REE) 2009 in Hong Kong and in Shenzhen. Jointly organized by the Center for Entrepreneurship of The Chinese University of Hong Kong, Shenzhen University and the Stanford Technology Ventures Program, the conference investigated how educators, particularly those at universities, should teach and promote global entrepreneurship – the ceaseless search for potential value creation and the organization of businesses to create that value. This book is distilled from the deliberations of that conference.[1]

Most people are not – and probably should not be – entrepreneurs, if by "entrepreneurs" we mean those who start a company. But all people can see problems as opportunities to create value through problem solving. And they should be trained to improve their ability to create value. In this broader sense, all people can be – and should be – entrepreneurs. Entrepreneurship education is a lifelong process that should promote entrepreneurial skills, attitudes, and behaviors to all ages. It should include socially marginalized and disadvantaged groups as well, thereby confronting the ills of modern society.

Our first chapter, "Educating the next wave of entrepreneurs", is a comprehensive review of effective entrepreneurship education approaches. Written by Karen Wilson for the World Economic Forum (WEF) Global Education Initiative, with advice from experts at the WEF's Entrepreneurship Education Technical Advisory Group, the chapter takes a global perspective, defining entrepreneurship broadly to include not only building for-profit and social ventures but also taking an entrepreneurial approach to problems in established organizations.

Companies (the chapter mentions AMD, Cisco, Intel, Microsoft and the Goldman Sachs Foundation) can organize conferences, forums, business plan competitions, training courses for entrepreneurs and faculty, accelerator programs and online tools such as videos and games to practice corporate social responsibility and mentor new value creation. Government policymakers can increase recognition of the importance of entrepreneurship education and encourage cooperation among multiple partners to deliver effective programs. The chapter encourages public and private sector leaders to equip people with the ability and inclination to start businesses and to improve their cultural and institutional infrastructures to support their efforts.

Chapter 1 encourages us to take a variety of approaches. Higher education should focus on growth and opportunity-driven entrepreneurship. Social inclusion should encourage the poor, social minorities, the disabled and other marginalized groups to engage in productive economic activities. Education programs should promote practical innovation and creative problem solving. This means that teaching has to be hands-on, project-based and multidisciplinary. The authors also emphasize the importance of promoting innovation, developing entrepreneurial ecosystems, cultivating effective educators, and engaging with businesses.

While Chapter 1 draws conclusions for educators from a review of the supply side of entrepreneurship education, Chapter 2 looks at its demand. A reprint of the *Global Entrepreneurship Monitor Special Report: A Global Perspective on Entrepreneurship Education and Training*, the chapter surveys the people who have received entrepreneurship education and training, the types of training they have received and the relationship of this training to entrepreneurial attitudes and activity. The chapter is based on random telephone interviews of the adult population in each of 38 countries, with at least 2000 adults surveyed in each country. Additional evidence is presented from a survey of 36 experts (entrepreneurs, policymakers, debt and equity providers and entrepreneurship educators and trainers) in each of 31 countries. Previous GEM research has rated entrepreneurship education as the most problematic factor influencing entrepreneurship in an economy, a finding which motivated the study. Entrepreneurs need external assistance in starting their businesses, so practical entrepreneurship education is important.

The chapter distinguishes between voluntary and compulsory training on one hand, and between formal and informal training on the other. More than one-fifth of the working-age population has received training in starting a business – the average is 21 percent and ranges from 10 to 30 percent, even among countries at similar economic development levels. Around 80 percent of those receiving training have been trained as part of their formal education, showing how important schools, colleges and universities are in providing a foundation for entrepreneurship. Self-study was the most frequent source of informal training.

The chapter reports a high overlap between formal and informal training. This suggests that formal training provides a foundation for developing attitudes and abilities. Formally trained individuals may subsequently go on to seek specific knowledge and skills informally, whether they start a business or solve problems in existing organizations using entrepreneurial mindsets. These observations reinforce Chapter 1's emphasis on entrepreneurship training as a lifelong pursuit.

Trained individuals are more likely younger, wealthier and more highly educated. Men opt for training more often than women. Training is associated with early-stage entrepreneurial activity more in developed economies than in less developed economies. Training is more accessible and effective for wealthier individuals in developed economies. To achieve equity as well as to further economic development, training and a concomitant emphasis on developing other enabling factors is needed in less developed economies and the less advantaged sectors of developed economies. This conclusion supports Chapter 1's prescription to increase entrepreneurial training among socially excluded groups. Entrepreneurship training – broadly defined – should be made available to the individuals that need it most.

Chapters 3 through 11 present nine papers from different authors describing entrepreneurship education in East Asia. Four of the nine chapters concern entrepreneurship education in China, reflecting China's importance: it has a fifth of the world's population, a quarter of the world's entrepreneurs and over half of the world's entrepreneurs who plan to grow their enterprises rapidly.[2] The Chinese boom in entrepreneurship has been a major force behind the high economic growth rates in the Chinese economy. And the privately owned economy now accounts for 40 percent of gross domestic product (GDP) and 55 percent of the industrial output. China has the second-largest economy in the world, and will most likely become the largest, in real terms, within the next decade.[3]

The relationship between entrepreneurship and education in China is complex. Entrepreneurship is a negative function of academic attainment: those with postgraduate degrees are only one-fifth as likely to be an entrepreneur in China as those without.[4] The Chinese tradition dating back millennia and reinforced through most of the years of the current regime is to study to achieve job security – either in the government or in large companies. Starting a company – or "diving into the sea" as they say in Chinese – has usually been viewed as dangerous and often as morally suspect.

Yet this tradition is under attack. On one hand, the level of status and respect given to entrepreneurs is rising rapidly.[5] On the other hand, the number of graduates from universities has gone up fivefold in the last decade, at a time when the demand for educated untrained job entrants has increased far more slowly. Today, while there are frequent shortages of trained workers in the traditional manufacturing regions of China, there is glut of untrained university graduates. The need for students to learn how to become job creators in addition to job seekers was voiced by President Hu Jintao in late 2008 and again, more strongly, in January 2009: entrepreneurship education and practice should be promoted in universities, and college students should be encouraged to start companies upon graduation.[6]

These political calls reinforce a trend started in 1998 when Tsinghua University introduced China's first new business plan competition, and continued the next year when the State Council first mentioned entrepreneurship education. Programs were implemented on test bases in subsequent years and business plan competitions became more popular. But it was not until 2004 that the Ministry of Education made strengthening entrepreneurship education for teachers and students, and encouraging them to start high-tech enterprises a part of its policy.[7]

In late 2008, the Minister of Education, Zhou Ji, called for the strengthening of entrepreneurship education: increasing business startups by student graduates, providing funding for these startups and giving them access to local incubators in economic and technological development zones and industrial parks. He also asked for universities to provide integrated approaches to entrepreneurship education and to stimulate the spirit of creativity and entrepreneurship through teaching, research, student placement and student activities.[8] This policy shift is currently being implemented through individual university initiatives, which include developing steering committees, incubators, centers, departments and even faculties of entrepreneurship. Measures include increasing interactions with successful entrepreneurs, case analyses, simulations and student projects involving real companies and markets. This movement merges with offering introductory business education (not only entrepreneurship education) to non-business students.

Chapter 3, by Du Guirong, Yu Jinquan and Xu Lei gives an overview of a decade's-long development of entrepreneurship education in China. They report low rates of student entrepreneurship in the face of cultural and institutional constraints. They describe the surge in research on entrepreneurship in general and student entrepreneurship in particular. And they analyze the effects of the most widely publicized entrepreneurship education platform in China, the National Entrepreneurship Plan Competition for University Students – also known as the "Little Challenge".

The next three chapters come from a team at the Beijing Institute of Technology, grappling with the problem of implementing entrepreneurship education for science and technology students. In Chapter 4, Huo Lingyu, Liu Lijun and Wang Ying compare the Chinese experience with the American one. Notwithstanding the differences – China is less advanced in the integration of entrepreneurship across disciplines but is emphasizing labs, incubators and science parks to a greater extent than the US – readers will be struck by the similarities in obstacles to entrepreneurship education: a passive approach to employment, a resistance to interdisciplinary subjects, a lack of funds, and little room in established programs for new entrepreneurship electives.

China's problems in implementing entrepreneurship education – shallow content, few qualified teachers, immature curricula, insufficient grounding in practice – are further investigated by Wang Ying, who presents her solution in Chapter 5: an integrated platform for entrepreneurship education tailored to Chinese requirements. The reform she suggests is fundamental, involving redesigning the curriculum and inserting major components of real-world practice into the classroom. This builds on programs currently being implemented in China, integrating them onto a single platform.

Chapter 6, by Liu Lijun and Guan Sisi, gives detailed plans for a specific entrepreneurship education program, largely for postgraduate engineering and science students, which they entitle the "Three-Stage Open Process Intellectual Entrepreneurship Program". Emphasizing that their reforms are not antagonistic to traditional professional education, they outline program structures that they believe can be implemented in the short to medium term.

As China has yet to formalize entrepreneurship curricula, academics and pedagogues, including those featured in Chapters 3 to 6, are mapping creative solutions in collaboration with colleagues, government policymakers and industry practitioners. They are also learning from foreign practice, be it Asian, American or European. The second decade of the 21st century is a truly exciting time to be shaping entrepreneurship education in China.

Entrepreneurship in Japan is as old as entrepreneurship in China is young. As Takeru Ohe describes in Chapter 7, family-based business values – thankfulness, diligence, innovation, thrift and social contribution – stimulated and guided Japanese entrepreneurs in an unbroken history from antiquity to the present day. Yet as Japan becomes the first post-industrial society on earth to experience natural population decline, traditional entrepreneurship has waned. The influence of family traditions on Japan's young has yielded to modern education, the electronics revolution and an increasingly global culture. Formal education, while it helps young people enter established companies, counted for near nothing in stimulating entrepreneurship during the second half of the 20th century. The stage was set for the birth of entrepreneurship education amid Japan's lost decade of the 1990s. Ohe discusses recent programs, in many of which he has played a substantial role. Common themes of experiential learning, learning by doing and integration of business into education run throughout these successful experiences. He suggests that Japan's leading position in many technologies forms a comparative advantage for its all-too-few young entrepreneurs, but only if they adopt global niche development strategies.

The combination of experiential learning, direct contact with businesses, creativity and a global perspective is central to the programs implemented and described by Ohe and his co-author, Siohong Tih of the Universiti Kebangsaan Malaysia, in Chapter 8: "Consulting-based entrepreneurship education: regional cases". Conducted in Malaysia, Indonesia and Vietnam, the programs bring undergraduate and postgraduate university students to local small and medium-sized enterprises (SMEs) as trainee consultants, complementing the standard internship programs already offered in many of the region's universities. Under the supervision of a university professor, each team of student consultants analyzes the business of a participating SME, drawing on field interviews with the company owners, employees and customers. The program is appreciated by the SME entrepreneurs, who expand their business horizons, and students, who improve their practical knowledge of business while increasing their interest in entrepreneurship and refining their analytical and communications skills. Entrepreneurship education and community thus combine for mutual benefits.

Chapter 9 continues the theme of fusing community and entrepreneurship education. Bonjin Koo, Vathana Duong TE and Joonsung J. Lee of Yonsei University in "Developing an interdisciplinary social entrepreneurship curriculum" describe how the Korean government has been promoting social enterprise: employing business principles and taking risks to improve society. Social entrepreneurship, they maintain, should be stimulated by problem-based learning from the unique societies of each country and region.

Sustainability, which crucially distinguishes social enterprise from charity, requires the entrepreneur to implement innovative business models. Students can study successful models implemented elsewhere in the world to stimulate their social innovations but the implementation must be community-relevant, typically differing from society to society. For example, one Yonsei University project reintroduces wholesome play into the lives of computer-addicted, socially isolated Korean children, while another applies information technology to improve marketing and credit for farmers in rural Cambodia. The authors report that the students appreciate the importance of being taught business principles in class before applying them to social problems. But the same students overwhelmingly view the community, not the lecture hall, as the best venue for learning social entrepreneurship.

How can a university implement community-based entrepreneurship education on a global scale? In Chapter 10, George Abe, David Chang and Priya Mohan describe how two microfinance field study projects, one in Vietnam and a second in northwest China, were conducted as part of the University of California Los Angeles's Applied Management Research Project, a mandatory two-quarter, Masters thesis-equivalent, 20-week, group-based project, involving over 100 postgraduate projects per year. Social entrepreneurship (including microfinance) accounts for about one-sixth of their projects, and are treated no differently from for-profit entrepreneurship projects. Projects come from the students themselves, or recommendations from faculty members (either individually or through research centers) and alumni. Students are responsible for selecting their topics and forming their own teams. Each team invites its own faculty advisor, with whom it scopes the project. In these projects, like those described in Chapter 8, students provide consulting to the businesses, so having an advisor experienced in corporate consulting is critical to project success.

The entrepreneurial revolution is not only propelling formerly impoverished societies into plenty, but is also exposing the contradiction between traditional capitalism's model of boundless consumption growth and a world with a finite, vulnerable environment. China is the world's number one polluter [9] and the rest of the developing world is emulating its example. But society's truly big problems are, to entrepreneurs, the truly big opportunities.

Peter Adriaens and Timothy Faley, in this book's final chapter, "Teaching entrepreneurial business strategies in global markets: a comparison of cleantech venture assessment in the US and China", identify China as the current world leader in the deployment of renewable and clean technologies. They describe China's movement up the technological value chain and the burgeoning research centers of the Suzhou Industry Park, much of it devoted to cleantech. A critical link in that value chain is venture capital investment.

The entrepreneurship education program described in Chapter 11 combines coursework for MBAs at the University of Michigan and the Suzhou Institute of Sichuan University in which students assess the deployment of specific new competing technologies and business models. The program combines a US focus on early-stage technologies with a Chinese urgency for deployment and growth. The authors discuss how their teaching modules may start from either the entrepreneur's or the investor's perspective, but must always come back to how value is generated by the technology users and how that value is captured by investors in the enterprise.

The themes in this volume are remarkably consistent. University educators, if we are to be relevant to the needs of today's students, must accept the challenge to teach broadly defined entrepreneurship. Yet we do so in organizations ill equipped to foster entrepreneurship. Our hope for success is to break the confines of the classroom and academic specialization. Innovation, multidisciplinary learning and knowledge transfer from the university to the rest of society and from the rest of society to the university are critical. At its heart, entrepreneurship involves understanding consumer problems and solving those problems to create value. This process is inherently project-based and multidisciplinary. The challenge for university educators is to create effective entrepreneurial ecosystems, with our allies in established corporations, government departments, and non-governmental organizations (NGOs) as well as with entrepreneurs – social and for-profit.

NOTES AND REFERENCES

1. Center for Entrepreneurship, *Roundtable on Entrepreneurship Education Asia 2009 Proceedings,* The Chinese University of Hong Kong, 2010.
2. High growth expectations entrepreneurship is the percentage of the population starting companies who expect their enterprises to employ over 20 persons in five years. In 2009, China had 24.2 million high expectations entrepreneurs; India had 1.5 million and the US had 1.3 million. See Thomas, Hugh, Kevin Au, Louis Leung, Wilton Chau, Bernard Suen, Mingles Tsoi, Florence Ho, Wang Weili, Shi Jianling, Zhang Jun, Tian Huan and Yan Lina, *Global Entrepreneurship Monitor 2009 Hong Kong and Shenzhen*, The Chinese University of Hong Kong Center for Entrepreneurship, 2010.
3. Assuming a 6 percent per year differential between the US and the Chinese nominal GDP growth rates, current US and Chinese GDPs of $14 trillion and $5 trillion respectively, a service economy that is 68 percent and 42 percent of the US and China economies respectively, goods economy price identities between China and the US and that wages are the only factor in determining the differences between nominal and real service economy output, the Chinese economy's real GDP will exceed the US's in 2020 if US wages are greater than or equal to 2.25 times Chinese wages. Currently US wages are 10 times Chinese wages.
4. Thomas et al., *op cit.*
5. In 2005, 66 percent of Chinese thought that those successful at starting a new business have a high level of status and respect. By 2009 that figure had risen to 79 percent. Ibid.
6. Hu Jintao Address to the 17th Party Congress in October 2008. In the address he said that the strategy of increasing employment would be carried out in part by "encouraging

entrepreneurship to increase employment". See also PRC State Council "Notice on Strengthening Employment of College Graduates", January 2009.
7. Ministry of Education, *2003–2007 Action Plan for Invigorating Education,* 10 February 2004.
8. Zhou Ji, "In-depth study and implantation of the scientific concept of developing a full employment of college graduates in 2009", *Government Statement*, December 2008.
9. Kahn, Joseph and Jim Yardley, "As China Roars, Pollution Reaches Deadly Extremes", *New York Times*, 26 August 2007.

1. Educating the next wave of entrepreneurs: World Economic Forum Global Education Initiative Executive Summary[*]

Karen Wilson

1.1 INTRODUCTION

Entrepreneurship has never been more important than it is today in this time of financial crisis. At the same time, society faces massive global challenges that extend well beyond the economy. Innovation and entrepreneurship provide a way forward for solving the global challenges of the 21st century, building sustainable development, creating jobs, generating renewed economic growth and advancing human welfare.

When we speak about entrepreneurship, we are defining it in the broadest terms and in all forms – entrepreneurial people in large companies, in the public sector, in academia and, of course, those who launch and grow new companies. Now more than ever we need innovation, new solutions, creative approaches and new ways of operating. We are in uncharted territory and need people in all sectors and at all ages who can "think out of the box" to identify and pursue opportunities in new and paradigm-changing ways.

> My greatest challenge has been to change the mindset of people. We see things the way our minds have instructed our eyes to see. (Muhammad Yunus, Managing Director, Grameen Bank)

Entrepreneurship education can be a societal change agent, a great enabler in all sectors. Not everyone needs to become an entrepreneur to benefit from entrepreneurship education, but all members of society need to be more entrepreneurial. The public sector, private sector, academia and non-profit sectors all have roles to play in facilitating the development of effective ecosystems which encourage and support the creation of innovative new ventures. We need to create the types of environments that are conducive to encouraging entrepreneurial ways of thinking and behaving.

Much has been written about the impact of entrepreneurship on

1

economic growth. If we are to attain the Millennium Development Goals of reducing poverty, we must develop human capital in all countries and societies, in remote regions as well as major cites, and in all sectors, to address both the opportunities and major challenges we face in the world. While the context around the world varies dramatically, entrepreneurship education, in its various forms, can equip people to proactively pursue those opportunities available to them based on their local environment and culture. We have seen a number of waves in entrepreneurship education, starting a century ago, developing in phases and now expanding exponentially. By making entrepreneurship education available to young people and adults alike, we are preparing the next wave of entrepreneurs and entrepreneurial individuals to enable them to lead and shape our institutions, businesses and local communities.

> What we need is an entrepreneurial society in which innovation and entrepreneurship are normal, steady and continual. (Peter F. Drucker)

The time to act is now. There is tremendous movement on the entrepreneurship front in countries around the world. As evidenced by the numerous recent reports and initiatives focused on entrepreneurship education, there is also sufficient buy-in for action. While many of the reports point in common directions, most initiatives have been at the local, regional or national level. With the current momentum, now is the time to take these efforts to the next level – to move from words to action as well as to address entrepreneurship education in a comprehensive manner at the global level. The WEF's effort in this area can be the catalyst to bring together actors who have been involved in numerous initiatives around the world, encourage a bias for action and build concrete next steps for implementation.

1.2 PURPOSE OF THE REPORT

The full report consolidates existing knowledge and practices in entrepreneurship education around the world to facilitate sharing and scaling as well as to enable the development of innovative new tools, approaches and delivery methods. It provides a landscape of entrepreneurship education practices across youth, higher education and social inclusion, providing not only examples but also recommendations across these segments as well as for various stakeholders.

The report has been developed by a core working group of authors and through consultation with the WEF's Entrepreneurship Education

Technical Advisory Group and other experts. The Steering Board of the WEF's Global Education Initiative has played a critical role in launching, supporting and providing guidance on the project as it has evolved during the course of 2008. In addition, several of the Global Agenda Councils of the WEF (specifically those on Technology and Education and Entrepreneurship) have highlighted the importance of entrepreneurship education.

> Only by letting thousands and millions of entrepreneurs try new ideas, to innovate, to create businesses that put those ideas to work in a competitive and open way, only by doing those things are we going to be able to tackle some of the world's big problems. (Angel Cabrera, President Thunderbird School of Global Management, Chair Global Agenda Council on Entrepreneurship)

1.2.1 Why This Report? Why Now? More Importantly, Why Should You Read It?

Our goal is to raise awareness about the importance of entrepreneurship education for developing the skills to solve global challenges, increase understanding about current approaches, build acceptance of entrepreneurship's rightful role in education and provide a platform for action to take the necessary next steps for mainstreaming entrepreneurship in education.

The report is geared towards high-level policymakers and leaders from the private and academic sectors who can work together to develop high-impact solutions through multistakeholder partnerships for embedding entrepreneurship education within their countries and regions.

Entrepreneurship is a global phenomenon. The future, to an even greater degree than in the past, will be driven by innovation and entrepreneurship. It is time to more adequately develop entrepreneurial skills, attitudes and behaviors in our schools systems as well as outside formal schools systems, to reach across all ages as part of a lifelong learning process. As we have seen through initiatives such as Global Entrepreneurship Week, which took place for the first time in November 2008 and will continue on an annual basis, activities and initiatives around the world are growing rapidly.

1.2.2 If There Have Been So Many Recent Reports, How Does This One Differ?

First, in this report we use a broad definition of entrepreneurship to include the pursuit of opportunities, whether they are to create start-ups, spin-outs or entrepreneurial activities in larger organizations (private or public) or social ventures.

Second, this is the first time entrepreneurship education has been considered in such a systematic manner throughout the lifelong learning process of an individual – starting from youth, continuing into higher education and including informal education systems which reach out to those socially excluded. Entrepreneurship has taken many different forms in communities across the world. There have been many successful initiatives focused on enhancing entrepreneurial skills and training in developing and developed countries, as well as programmes targeted towards youth. However, as yet, there has been little attempt to draw on these findings in a systematic way to move beyond classic stereotypes and develop a wider understanding of the key issues involved in implementing entrepreneurship education in different countries and communities.

Third, we have attempted to address this topic on a global basis. Clearly, the full report is not meant to be a catalogue of initiatives around the world; rather, it is meant to give a flavour of the types of activities that exist and to serve as a basis for further discussion and research. The report is intended to provide the foundation and starting point for a series of further discussions and the development of locally relevant action plans in regions across the world.

1.2.3   Definitions and Views of Entrepreneurship

A key theme surfacing throughout the development of the report is the varying views and definitions of entrepreneurship around the world. In a number of countries around the world, the role of entrepreneurs is unclear and can even be viewed negatively. In some countries, entrepreneurship is not often rewarded but rather penalized. The multidimensional benefits entrepreneurship provides to society need to be illuminated.

In addition, there is a need for clarity on the definitions of entrepreneurship. There are many working definitions, but for the purposes of the report,

> entrepreneurship is defined as: The pursuit of opportunities beyond the resources you currently control. (Howard Stevenson, Professor, Harvard University)

Entrepreneurship is a process that results in creativity, innovation and growth. Innovative entrepreneurs come in all shapes and forms; its benefits are not limited to start-ups, innovative ventures and new jobs. Entrepreneurship refers to an individual's ability to turn ideas into action and is therefore a key competence for all, helping young people to be more creative and self-confident in whatever they undertake.[1] As HM

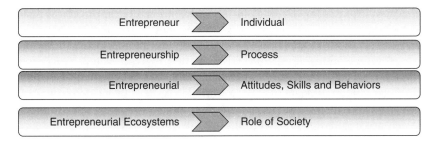

Figure 1.1   Forms and meanings

Queen Rania of the Hashemite Kingdom of Jordan stated at the Global Education Initiative private meeting in Davos 2007, society faces a strong need to encourage people to "practice at believing the unbelievable, using imagination, courage and tapping into the inner entrepreneur".

There are many other words often used as substitutes for entrepreneurship including enterprise, innovation, small business, growth companies, etc. To fully capture and understand the entrepreneurship phenomenon, we need to take a broad and inclusive view; otherwise we will miss important components and trends in this rapidly growing movement. In addition, there are many forms and meanings of the word entrepreneurship (Figure 1.1).

1.2.4   Overview of Recommendations

The recommendations in the report are divided into two categories. First, there is the "Call for Action" for policymakers, with the goal of raising awareness about the importance of entrepreneurship education and the need to address it through multistakeholder partnerships.

Second, there is a menu of more specific action items in the recommendations sections for all key stakeholders, including those from the public, private, academic and non-profit sectors. While the report lays out a variety of steps which can be taken to develop and embed entrepreneurship education in formal and informal education systems, the authors and members of the WEF's Technical Advisory Group for Entrepreneurship Education encourage public and private sector leaders to take a revolutionary, not an evolutionary, approach.

Entrepreneurship education is needed to build entrepreneurial human capital for the society of the future. We need more to encourage a more entrepreneurial culture and develop the necessary skills, attitudes and behaviors to prepare young people and others to pursue entrepreneurial opportunities. In addition, we need more entrepreneurial institutions and societies. The danger of not doing so is that we maintain the status quo. In this time of economic crisis, we simply cannot afford that. It is time for rethinking systems and taking bold and decisive actions that will benefit society today and in the longer term. We need to leverage the power of innovation and creativity to guide our way to a healthy and prosperous future. Entrepreneurship empowers people, in all societies and at all levels, to take their own destiny into their hands. It creates opportunities which not only contribute to economic growth, but also to personal and professional development.

1.2.5   Call to Action

Transform the educational system
Entrepreneurship education is essential for developing the human capital necessary for the society of the future. It is not enough to add entrepreneurship on the perimeter – it needs to be core to the way education operates. Educational institutions, at all levels (primary, secondary and higher education) need to adopt 21st-century methods and tools to develop the appropriate learning environment for encouraging creativity, innovation and the ability to "think out of the box" to solve problems. This requires a fundamental rethinking of educational systems, both formal and informal, as well as the way in which teachers or educators are trained, how examination systems function and the way in which rewards, recognition and incentives are given.

Academia needs to work with ministries of education as well as other ministries, the private sector and other stakeholders to rethink the educational systems in their country with the aim of developing entrepreneurial societies. Embedding entrepreneurship and innovation, cross-disciplinary approaches and interactive teaching methods all require new models, frameworks and paradigms. It is time to rethink the old systems and have a fundamental "rebooting" of the educational process. Incremental change in education is not adequate, especially in today's rapidly changing society. We need schools, colleges and universities that are entrepreneurial in their approach to preparing individuals for the future.

Build the entrepreneurial ecosystem
Entrepreneurship thrives in ecosystems in which multiple stakeholders play key roles (see Figure 1.2). Academic institutions are central in shaping young people's attitudes, skills and behaviors; however, actors outside of the education systems are playing an increasingly critical role in working with formal and informal educational programs as well as reaching out to

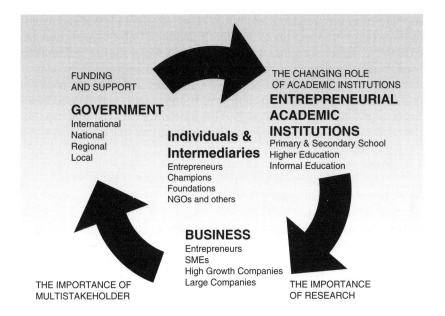

Figure 1.2   Entrepreneurial ecosystem

underserved and socially excluded target groups. This requires collaboration and multistakeholder partnerships.

First and foremost, entrepreneurship education requires close cooperation between academia and business. Past barriers to academic collaboration with business need to be broken down and outreach both encouraged and supported. As demonstrated later in the report through the case studies, companies and entrepreneurs play instrumental roles in promoting entrepreneurial endeavors by providing knowledge, expertise, mentoring, social capital and financial support. In addition, businesses that foster an entrepreneurial culture contribute directly to the entrepreneurial education process themselves by providing employees with the opportunity to cultivate entrepreneurial skills and aptitudes at work. Policymakers at the international, national, regional and local levels all have important roles to play in setting the appropriate legal and fiscal frameworks to encourage entrepreneurship and in filling market gaps as necessary. Higher education institutions have a critical role to play as intellectual hubs in entrepreneurial ecosystems by serving as an incubator for innovation and research as well as a focal point for collaboration among researchers, students, professors, companies and entrepreneurs. Foundations, non-governmental organizations (NGOs) and other organizations can play an important

facilitation or intermediary role, often helping to link various stakeholders. Most important are the champions (often serial entrepreneurs but also
educators, staff or students) who leverage their social capital and serve as
catalysts for building the entrepreneurial ecosystem.

As illustrated by the WEF's Global Education Initiative, the need for
multistakeholder partnerships is critical for education and even more so
for entrepreneurship education. There is a need for capacity and capability building within the entrepreneurial ecosystem and this is best done
through partnerships and a "portfolio" approach, not through "one-off"
initiatives.

Strive for effective outcomes and impact
The purpose and goals of entrepreneurship education need greater
clarity. They should be based on a broadly defined set of outcomes,
not only on narrow measures such as the number of start-ups created.
Entrepreneurship education is about developing attitudes, behaviors and
capacities at the individual level. Inherently, it is about leadership. It is
also about the application of those skills and attitudes which can take
many forms during an individual's career, creating a range of long-term
benefits to society and the economy.

Developing a broader framework for assessing entrepreneurship education is necessary to capture a richer and more nuanced set of outcomes.
Measuring intangible outcomes is difficult; however, applying only simple
measures of the potentially wrong things can result in falling far short of
the intended outcomes and impact. Even worse, anecdotal stories of "best"
practices could lead to the replication of programs which actually are not
working, resulting in wasted time and money for little to no impact.

To measure effectively, better data is needed. While there have been
many studies and research projects on entrepreneurship, to date, there
have not been enough empirical research on entrepreneurship education itself and its impact. Longitudinal studies are not easy to design and
implement, but they could provide better evidence of the impact of entrepreneurship education. Internationally comparable statistics and data
collection is imperative as well.

Leverage technology as an enabler
Throughout the report, the role of technology in delivering entrepreneurship education is evident, particularly in terms of creating greater
access and scalability for entrepreneurship education. While the development community has struggled with the challenges of social inclusion,
poverty alleviation and interventions to overcome barriers to progress,
the information technology and telecom industries have entered the fray

and created dramatic changes in the landscape of opportunity and social inclusion. The growth of the Internet and the use of computers and mobile phones has also made a huge impact, particularly with small businesses and education.

The role of the media is also important for raising awareness and creating role models. Mass media in the form of radio and television has grown across the world, especially after satellite television. This parallel development of information and communication technologies (ICTs) and media has created new infrastructure and opportunities and changed the landscape. The ICT industry has been proactive in working with users, content developers, educational institutions, policymakers and others to frame a set of opportunities that can be disseminated to those who would benefit most from them. Those in the entrepreneurship education field tend to be early adopters in leveraging the latest technology. The full range of implications for enterprise and entrepreneurship education needs to be further developed, particularly in developing economies where scaling is critical:

> Education is the clearest path to individual opportunity and societal growth, and entrepreneurship education is especially vital to fuelling a more robust global economy. Entrepreneurs bring new ideas to life through innovation, creativity and the desire to build something of lasting value. Therefore, we must continually foster educational cultures within our companies, governments and communities to keep the entrepreneurship pipeline filled for generations to come. (Dirk Meyer, former President and CEO, AMD)

1.3   STRUCTURE AND SCOPE

Given the various forms of entrepreneurship both across and within regions and countries around the world, the report looks at three types of entrepreneurship: youth (with a focus on disadvantaged youth), higher education (with a focus on growth/opportunity entrepreneurship) and social inclusion, outlining the differing types of education approaches needed for each. In each of these areas, the report identifies opportunities and challenges, highlights existing entrepreneurship education tools and good practices and develops recommendations for multistakeholder support of the development and delivery of effective educational programs for entrepreneurship.

While the first two forms of entrepreneurship education are self-explanatory, the third is more complex. Entrepreneurship for social inclusion seeks growth by allowing more people (especially marginalized ones such as the very poor, women in many contexts, minorities, disabled

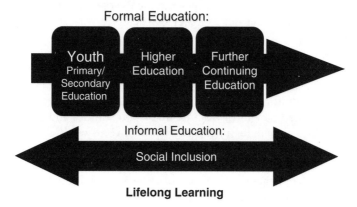

Figure 1.3   Educational lifespan

and disadvantaged) to engage actively in productive economic activities (Figure 1.3).

There are commonalities about entrepreneurship education across all three of the focus areas. However, there are also distinct differences that merit this particular segmentation. It is important to look at all of these key communities to develop a comprehensive view of the landscape and recommendations for next steps. It should be noted that each of the three types of entrepreneurship exist in most countries across the world, although some are more dominant in certain regions than others. Addressing entrepreneurship education requires working with existing education systems to incorporate the necessary changes as well as launching new initiatives outside of current structures.

The purpose of the report is not to identify and highlight all practices but to provide some examples. Because the field is moving and growing extremely rapidly, it is difficult to create a "catalogue" of all practice. Nor is the report a data-driven research piece. Rather, it collects the views and examples to date on these topics to be used as a platform for further discussion.

1.4   KEY FINDINGS OF THE REPORT

Can entrepreneurship be taught or, more importantly, learned? It's an age-old debate. It is clear that education plays an essential role in shaping attitudes, skills and culture – from the primary level up. Entrepreneurship

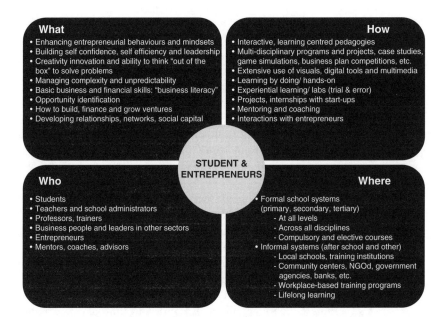

Figure 1.4 Key areas to maximize the learning of the participants

education provides a mix of experiential learning, skill building and, most importantly, mindset shift. Certainly, the earlier and more widespread the exposure to entrepreneurship and innovation, the more likely students will become entrepreneurial, in one form or another, at some stage in their lives:

> Most of what you hear about entrepreneurship is all wrong. It's not magic; it's not mysterious; and it has nothing to do with genes. It's a discipline and, like any discipline, it can be learned. (Peter F. Drucker)

The three core chapters of the report focus on different segments of the educational lifespan or system from youth to higher education to those socially excluded. Each chapter highlights opportunities, challenges and current practices. However, there are many common approaches and key success factors across the chapters. Outlined in Figure 1.4 are some of the key areas in terms of what, how, where and who to teach entrepreneurship, to maximize the learning of the participants.

1.4.1 Youth

This section highlights the findings from the report chapter on Entrepreneurship Education for Youth, defined as ages 6–24.

Context and importance

- Young people around the world have a right to entrepreneurship education. Every individual has the right – as part of his or her personal understanding and exploration – to be exposed to the possibility of ownership that benefits the community and to the habits of thought that lead to socially responsible wealth creation. These rights are grounded in the individual's entitlement to the ownership of one's person, labour, time and ideas, and the individual's obligations to community and broader social goals.
- We propose that every school system offer entrepreneurship education. Mainstream pedagogy will have to change, leading to the hands-on, project-based, multidisciplinary approaches that entrepreneurship education requires.
- We aim our proposals – our call to action – at senior policymakers. Change must occur primarily in the public systems of education and youth development. Senior policymakers must foster the growth of an entrepreneurship ecosystem that is itself entrepreneurial, that liberates the innate creative abilities of youth and that gives everyone access to ownership.

Existing practices
Below are some promising practices within youth entrepreneurship education that foster and reinforce 21st-century attitudes and skills.

- Celebrate the entire range of a learner's talent. Entrepreneurship education celebrates each child's entire range of talents and aspirations, and does not reduce anyone simply to a grade point average or test score or intelligence quotient. Entrepreneurship education rewards the diversity of approaches that emerge from individuals working to meet the needs of others.
- Focus on fundamentals:
  - Joy of business, responsible wealth creation and ownership, always stressing a commitment to community and service to others.
  - Market opportunity recognition and research.
  - Empathy ("walk in your customer's shoes").
  - Comparative advantage.
  - Laws of supply and demand.
  - Marginal utility ("economics of one unit").
  - Return on investment and break-even calculation.
  - Compound interest ("Rule of 72").[2]
  - "See One, Do One, Teach One".

Entrepreneurship is reflective action, so no amount of book-based learning on its own will allow the student to progress in this field. One cannot just study a chart of the dance steps to learn a new dance. And there is no better way to confirm and demonstrate that mastery exists than to teach a skill – especially a new-won skill.

Pedagogy
The curriculum for most successful youth entrepreneurship programs includes many or all of the following activities, typically with clear learning objectives tied to textbook themes, usually with pre- and post-reflective sessions and evaluations, and frequently taking place outside the classroom:

- Simulations and games.
- Interactive teamwork and group activities.
- Direct, action-oriented market research (students need to recognize market opportunities by observing and interviewing potential customers, identifying needs in their own communities).
- Student buying and selling events, using real money (grants or loans from the school or program).
- Field trips to local businesses, especially entrepreneurial ventures.
- Entrepreneurs or venture funders as guest speakers in class.
- Business plan competitions, with business people as judges.
- Student-run businesses, using real money (including in-school stores).

Visualize and plan for business
Students need to create and present a business plan. Leverage technology/ use multimedia: digital tools (including games, simulations, animation) offer particularly rich learning possibilities.

Work closely with entrepreneurs
No entrepreneurship program can succeed without close interaction with entrepreneurs. Find, train and support the right teachers: entrepreneurship education demands an entrepreneurial teacher. Retooling for successful youth entrepreneurship education means selecting and promoting teachers who are able to engage young learners in the necessary experiential activities:

> Preparing today's students for success and eventual leadership in the new global marketplace is the most important responsibility in education today.... Entrepreneurship education is an important tool to achieving these objectives

[and] . . . should be universally available to provide all students with opportunities to explore and fulfil their potential. (Stephanie Bell-Rose, former President, Goldman Sachs Foundation & Thomas W. Payzant, Harvard Graduate School of Education)

1.4.2 Higher Education

This section highlights the findings from the report chapter on "Entrepreneurship in Higher Education".

Context and importance

- The demand for entrepreneurship programmes, courses and activities in higher education is increasing globally.
- Typically, skill-building courses in entrepreneurship education entail creativity, new venture creation, business idea development and opportunity recognition, business planning, leadership, entrepreneurial marketing, entrepreneurial finance and growth management as well as soft skills like negotiation or presentation competences.[3]
- Courses in innovation and innovation management are essential ingredients of an entrepreneurship program or curriculum. Delivering innovations in the form of new products or services and building rapidly growing enterprises requires specific leadership competences and social responsibility by pioneering entrepreneurs.
- In terms of the methods, there is a need for more interactive, interdisciplinary and proactive learning approaches, with teachers acting as moderators rather than lecturers, fostering team-based, participant-centered and interactive learning.
- Information technology is a valuable enabler for developing individually tailored e-learning modules, business simulations or virtual project communities with participants from different countries or disciplinary backgrounds.

The entrepreneurial university

- A number of universities are striving to become "entrepreneurial universities" making entrepreneurship part of the core mission of the institution.
- For an entrepreneurial university, it is a prerequisite that cross-disciplinary, cross-campus initiatives and courses are integrated in such a way that all students can be reached and introduced to entrepreneurship.

- According to Clark,[4] the core elements of an entrepreneurial university are: a strengthened steering core with a clear vision and mission, boundary spanning structures and mechanisms to interact with the "outside" world (external stakeholders), a diversified funding base (less state funding), inter- and multidisciplinary activity and an integrated entrepreneurial culture.
- Gibb[5] further suggests that the entrepreneurial university embeds entrepreneurial learning outcomes in the way it designs and delivers its educational opportunities that more accurately reflects the essence of an entrepreneurial culture in society. It requires a new paradigm for entrepreneurship not founded on a traditional business model that aims to develop entrepreneurial lives and careers.
- Leading entrepreneurial universities and colleges chiefly distinguish themselves from average institutions by taking on a commitment for scientific excellence as well as for maintaining academic values and following ethical guidelines.[6] The commercialization of inventions or innovations which evolved from these institutions is then achieved on the basis of an ethical value system with an aim of creating value for society.
- These leading entrepreneurial higher education institutions differentiate themselves through a marked performance orientation as well as a clearly recognizable profile based on their scientific strengths, often leading to the commercialization of inventions and innovation.
- At the same time, experiences in many countries illustrate that there is still a considerable challenge in the process of establishing entrepreneurship education throughout the university sector.[7]

Stakeholder actions

- An extended perspective on entrepreneurship is necessary. This perspective should also address students as future opinion leaders and stakeholders of new enterprises (e.g. as investors, bankers, journalists or policymakers).
- The introduction of entrepreneurship into national (or regional) education systems at all levels of education is critical to raise the level of knowledge about entrepreneurs within the group of future leaders.
- The integration of entrepreneurship into the curricula of all faculties is critical, as is the involvement of entrepreneurs and (local) enterprises (especially high growth enterprises) in the design, running and promotion of these entrepreneurship courses.

- Action should be taken at all levels (national, regional and local) to improve the framework for entrepreneurial learning and activities, especially in higher education institutions and their surroundings, taking into account in each case the different, specific local conditions.
- The design of adequate framework conditions by universities and governments should not only serve to support entrepreneurship education and the recognition of credible entrepreneurial opportunities, but also to establish the further entrepreneurial "support chain" of technology commercialization and academic spin-off activity in higher education contexts.
- Governments can play a vital role in creating funding mechanisms for programs, activities and initiatives associated with entrepreneurial education. There are many direct and indirect funding options. In addition, public authorities can support national and international entrepreneurship research and education networks to expedite their sustainability and reach.
- Entrepreneurs play an important part in the motivation of students by serving as role models. In this respect, alumni can play a key role and by engaging them, the university is also tapping into a potential source of future funding and support.
- The potential for collaboration between established companies, universities and their spin-offs should be nurtured further. In addition, private enterprises and entrepreneurs should be cultivated to finance entrepreneurship chairs, institutes and centers.

An entrepreneur is a person who is willing and able to convert a new idea or invention into a successful innovation, simultaneously creating new products and business models largely responsible for the dynamism of industries and long-run economic growth. (Joseph A. Schumpeter)

1.4.3 Social Inclusion

This section highlights the findings from the report chapter on "Entrepreneurship Education for Social Inclusion". By that, we mean those outside of the formal education and/or employment systems.

Definition

- For the purposes of the report, social inclusion is defined as a term that applies to those people who are defined as being at the "bottom of the pyramid", based on CK Prahalad's seminal work in mapping

out the world's aspiring poor, comprising 4 billion people who are joining and actively participating in the market economy.[8]
- We narrow this definition further for practical reasons to include: illiterate and unemployed, semi-literate and underemployed, those with secondary and university education but who remain outside formal employment, and society at large.

Context and importance

- The most fundamental reason for thinking about entrepreneurship at the grass roots is to find sustainable solutions to overcoming the injustices of poverty, which are evident in most countries and captured in the Millennium Development Goals of the UN.
- There are many key drivers for societal change, demanding increased capability in terms of entrepreneurial human capital. The visible injustices of poverty have meant there has been a growth of social enterprise as a response to the lack of fairness in trade, access to markets, resources and opportunity.
- Much of employment in the developing world is generated by the informal sector. It is therefore important to focus on grassroots, innovation-based entrepreneurship. This has implications for the role of NGOs and curricula with respect to emergent horizontal supply chains, markets and much more (local) knowledge and innovation-based enterprises.
- However, there is still much to do, and the missing piece seems to be a form of education that can be applied for self-improvement in more direct ways than current education systems provide.

Current approaches

- There are arguments about how and what to do at this level of society in terms of entrepreneurship education. At the same time, there have been many solutions to alleviating poverty and practical projects and programs that go by descriptions and titles other than entrepreneurship.
- Much is being done, albeit in ad hoc projects, sometimes without the benefit of real understanding on the supply side, an apparent disconnect between policy ambitions and grassroots realities. In addition, some of the so-called education in entrepreneurship is nothing more than business planning, book keeping, regulatory compliance training or strategy-made-simple forms of training.

- Fortunately, there are highly interactive programs that are run in many countries, which are practice based and provide for simulations and real-world experiences that can be replicated and scaled up if supply-side constraints can be dealt with. Some of these programs start at an early age, with the potential to be connected later to life-learning programs.
- These programs highlight the characteristics of people who are entrepreneurial in terms of behaviors, self-confidence, creativity, ambition and the ability to build social capital, as well as other group cooperative behaviors that are needed to succeed.
- Highlighting these programs can help create a clearer understanding of what constitutes entrepreneurship education for social inclusion and provide a platform for building on some of the successes that exist around the world.

Scale and sustainability

The deliberations that take place as a result of the report development should move towards creating a powerful commitment for entrepreneurship education that can enhance social inclusion. If the agenda is to achieve scalability in entrepreneurship education, there is also going to be a need to increase the quantity and quality of people on the "supply" side, finding and training enough people with the skills, knowledge and practitioner experience to act as tutors/trainers and enablers of entrepreneurship education. Beyond the actual tutors, there is a need for those in the wider stakeholder community – the "ecosystem" – who also understand entrepreneurship so that their role, regulations, support and infrastructure can be more effective.

Such a grand scale also cannot be achieved on short-term, project-based funding. New models need to be found where this form of education is funded in the longer term as a discrete activity and/or as part of an integrated activity in other programs for education, health, water, credit schemes and the like. Creative solutions that are long term and sustainable need to be found to ensure that entrepreneurship education is available in society for a long enough period to make a difference.

The main challenge is to ensure that there is clarity about the objectives of the entrepreneurship education provision and thus to design measurements for those achievements. The challenge is to better understand what does or what does not work in terms of the efficacy of entrepreneurship education.

Over the next five years, Goldman Sachs will support partnerships with universities and development organizations that will lead to 10 000 women receiving a business and management education. These innovative certificate programs will help open doors for thousands of women around the globe whose financial and practical circumstances would otherwise prevent them from receiving this type of education.

1.5 LESSONS LEARNED FROM GEI STEERING BOARD CASE STUDIES

As part of this project, a series of interviews was conducted with several companies serving on the Steering Board of the WEF Global Education Initiative to learn about their programs and experiences in entrepreneurship education. The organizations interviewed included AMD, Cisco, Intel, Microsoft and the Goldman Sachs Foundation. These organizations have launched a range of activities including organizing conferences/forums, initiating business plan competitions, developing training courses – for both entrepreneurs and faculty, creating accelerator programs and labs and developing course materials using online tools such as videos and games.

While each company has taken various approaches to addressing entrepreneurship education, there are a number of common elements:

- Focusing on raising awareness, changing mindsets, developing both hard and soft skills.
- Connecting business, technology and other disciplines.
- Using technology as an enabler for delivering entrepreneurship education.
- Building cross-border linkages.

At the same time, there are many common challenges which were identified through the case studies:

- Changing mindsets is a long-term goal; it is difficult to "move the needle".
- Entrepreneurial attitudes vary across regions/cultures.
- Need to localize content to fit the local context.
- Challenge of building serious student interest in launching high growth/tech companies (depending on the region/culture).
- Necessity of building the proper internal and external systems or infrastructure to implement the programs.
- Need effective short-, medium- and long-term measures of program outcomes.
- Making sure the programs are sustainable.

There were also a number of common lessons learned including:

- The need to address the ecosystem/all parts of the value chain:
    - Cannot be done in isolated manner – have to partner with others.
- The importance of multistakeholder partnerships:
    - Local, regional and national governments.
    - Other companies.
    - NGOs.
    - Schools, universities, training centers.
    - Student and entrepreneur organizations.
- Need for critical mass:
    - More than one-off initiatives.
    - Need to scale/link programs.
- Importance of getting out there, getting feedback and then modifying approach:
    - In essence, being entrepreneurs.
- Activities are more powerful if they leverage the core competencies and human capital/people of the firm.

The full report contains the detailed case studies (Table 1.1) outlining the programs and activities of the companies. We congratulate these companies, as well as the other Global Education Institute Steering Board members, for their significant investment in entrepreneurship education as well as their leadership in spearheading the WEF initiative in this area.

1.6   OVERALL RECOMMENDATIONS

The role of education in society is changing. No longer are schools and universities expected to stay within their ivory towers. New forms of education are emerging both within and outside of formal education systems. After-school and community programs, workplaces as well as TV, Internet and media are playing increasingly active and important roles. These multiple channels provide many opportunities to build effective approaches to delivering entrepreneurship education.

Below are a set of approaches which, through the work on the report, have been found to be agreed upon approaches for entrepreneurship education. In addition, key success factors and current challenges are outlined.

Table 1.1   Entrepreneurship education initiatives of Global Education Institute Steering Board

Steering Board Case Studies

Company / Activities	Forums/ Events	Training/ Mentoring Students & Entrepreneurs	Training Faculty	Business Plan Competition/ Awards	Accelerator/ Incubator Programs	Centers or Labs (Physical Virtual)	Curriculum Content	Online Education Tools
AMD							✓	✓
CISCO		✓	✓	✓	✓	✓	✓	✓
INTEL		✓	✓	✓	✓	✓	✓	
MICROSOFT	✓	✓		✓			✓	
GOLDMAN SACHS	✓		✓	✓			✓	✓

1.6.1   Approaches

Across youth, higher education and social inclusion, there are a number of approaches which are being effectively utilized and which support the call to action to "mainstream" entrepreneurship education.

Developing leadership and life skills

The clear priority of entrepreneurship education is to focus on developing entrepreneurial attitudes, skills and behaviors. It is about developing the leaders for the society of the future and providing them with the life skills necessary for navigating in the rapidly changing world. Effective entrepreneurship education programs focus on building the self-confidence and self-efficacy as well as developing the practical skills necessary for students to initiate and pursue ideas, and provide them with experience in building the necessary teams around them to implement projects. Entrepreneurship education should not be limited to a focus on start-ups, which is often the case in current programs around the world, but should be focused on shifting mindsets and developing skills which can be applied in many forms and entrepreneurial settings. Always important, but perhaps more so in today's environment, is the inclusion of ethics – helping students understand the importance of being responsible leaders:

> Entrepreneurship in education means developing personal qualities and attitudes as well as formal knowledge and skills: Personal qualities and attitudes that increase the probability that a person will see opportunities and act upon them. Further creativity, self confidence, resourcefulness, willingness to take risks, the ability to see the consequences of one's own actions, and the willingness and ability to come up with new solutions all help to develop an entrepreneurial attitude and conduct. Such qualities and attitudes will be useful in any work situation and in society in general, and knowledge and skills related to what is required to establish a new enterprise and how and why we succeed in developing an idea into a practical and well-structured activity. (Strategic Plan, Norwegian Government, 2004–2008)

Embedding entrepreneurship in education

Access and exposure to entrepreneurship within educational systems at all levels is important as it is the outreach to target audiences outside of traditional educational systems. In both respects, the role that technology can play in delivering entrepreneurship education is essential. While most students do not start or join a new business upon graduation, many do so during later stages of their careers or will contribute as an entrepreneurial employee within an organization. Therefore, exposure to entrepreneurship as well as practical training in starting and growing companies is important. Many recent reports support the call for making opportunities available to students at all levels and in all settings. At the same time, the level and background of the students, as well as the local context, needs to be taken into account in shaping the programs and curricula.

Institutional culture, practice and policies often get in the way of developing an entrepreneurial spirit and environment within educational systems. Entrepreneurship champions play critical roles but there must also be a strong commitment from the school leadership. Traditionally, schools and universities have been focused on ensuring students can secure future employment. Today, both formal and informal school systems must prepare students to work in a dynamic, rapidly changing entrepreneurial and global environment.

This requires a complete paradigm shift for academia, including changing the fundamentals of how schools operate and their role in society. It requires encouraging and supporting our educational institutions to become more entrepreneurial.

Taking a cross-disciplinary approach

The world is not divided into functional silos, so the educational process should not be either. In an increasing number of schools and universities, entrepreneurship is treated as an integral part of a multidisciplinary education process. Students are encouraged to take courses and engage in projects with students from other disciplines, enabling them to draw upon expertise from across the institution – engineering, science, design, liberal arts and business. Minimizing the institutional barriers to this cross-fertilization, these institutions can provide a more creative and innovative learning process. There is no discipline whose students will not benefit from such an approach. In most countries, the majority of entrepreneurship courses are offered in business schools or programs. Entrepreneurship needs to be expanded across disciplines, particularly to the technology and science departments, where many innovative ideas and companies originate. Even on campuses with less of an interdisciplinary approach, entrepreneurship programs are increasingly linking traditional business courses with those offered in science and technology programs. This allows for the sharing of expertise and knowledge between the business and technical students, sparking greater innovation and facilitating technology transfer.

Utilizing interactive pedagogy

A greater emphasis is needed on experiential and action learning with a focus on critical thinking and problem solving. The pedagogy should be interactive, encouraging students to experiment and experience entrepreneurship through working on case studies, games, projects, simulations, real-life actions, internships with start-ups and other hands-on activities which involve interaction with entrepreneurs. Schools and training programs provide a safe environment for encouraging students to stretch and test themselves, to experiment and develop an understanding of risk-taking and the ability to turn ideas into action. It is important that students have the opportunity to experience both successes and failures – and to learn from both experiences. Most importantly, they need to learn to try, even if they fail, and then to start over and try again. Active and learning-by-doing methods integrate elements of practice into the learning process. This highlights the importance of actively engaging entrepreneurs and other professionals in both course design and delivery. These individuals also serve as role models, particularly if they are alumni of the school, as well as coaches and mentors. They also enhance entrepreneurial spirit within the university and create stronger links between the university and the local community.

Leveraging technology
In today's environment, technology plays an increasingly important role in the educational process. Many leading ICT companies, including the members of the World Economic Forum's Global Education Initiative Steering Board, are ahead of the curve on this trend, already working with school systems and teachers to leverage technology, both as a delivery channel and a teaching tool. For entrepreneurship education, this is particularly important. Not only can technology help reach larger audiences, including those who previously might not have had access to entrepreneurship education, but it can also help in the development of interactive and locally relevant programs and materials.

1.6.2   Key Success Factors

Across youth, higher education and social inclusion, there are a number of key success factors which enable effective entrepreneurship education.

The entrepreneurial ecosystem
Entrepreneurship thrives in ecosystems in which multiple stakeholders play a role in facilitating entrepreneurship. Policymakers at the international, national, regional and local levels all have important roles to play in setting the appropriate legal and fiscal frameworks to encourage entrepreneurship and to fill market gaps as necessary. Educational institutions, at all levels (primary, secondary and higher education) have a critical role to play in developing the appropriate learning environment, utilizing relevant learning methods and developing educators to teach using interactive pedagogies. Higher education institutions, in particular, have a critical

role to play as intellectual hubs in entrepreneurial ecosystems by serving as an incubator for innovation and research as well as a focal network for collaboration among researchers, students, professors, companies, venture capital firms, angel investors and entrepreneurs:

> Intel believes that entrepreneurship is crucial to building local innovation capacity. It brings new technologies to market, and supports economic development through building strong local and regional economies. Both the public and the private sectors have important roles to play in advancing entrepreneurship around the world, including through enabling effective entrepreneurship education. (Craig R. Barrett, Chairman of the Board, Intel Corporation)

Developing effective educators

Despite the rapid growth of interest in entrepreneur education, there is still a lack of critical mass of entrepreneurship educators in schools and universities across the world, not to mention in the informal educational systems. The current pool of entrepreneurship teachers should be expanded. Growing the base of experienced educators not only means providing the necessary training and education, but also requires expanding the definition of educators beyond professors to include entrepreneurs, alumni, business professionals and even students. Entrepreneurs and others with entrepreneurial experience should be allowed, encouraged and trained to teach. They not only provide great value in the classroom, but they also enhance entrepreneurial spirit within the institution overall and create stronger links with the local community and ecosystem. Using active learning methods is more complex than traditional teaching methods. It requires engaging students' feelings and emotions in the learning process and developing the creativity, innovation and critical thinking skills of individuals.

Educators/facilitators therefore must be able to create an open environment of trust in which students develop the necessary confidence to take risks by learning from trial experiences with both successes and failures. The proper incentives, assessment, rewards and recognition must be put in place to encourage educators to try these approaches.

Curriculum development

The proliferation of entrepreneurship programs around the world has been positive in terms of validating interest in the field, but more depth and rigor is needed to ensure that entrepreneurship courses, materials and research are of high quality. Research and curriculum development are of particular importance in helping to ensure entrepreneurship's rightful place among the academic disciplines. This requires curricula that focus on learning "for" rather than "about" entrepreneurship. Students also need to learn how to manage and grow enterprises, not just how to start them. Entrepreneurial learning must be deeply embedded into the curriculum to ingrain a new entrepreneurial spirit and mindset among students. In many countries around the world, entrepreneurship tends to be offered in standalone courses rather than being integrated in the content of courses in other departments or disciplines. Entrepreneurship also remains primarily elective or extra curricular at many schools and universities.

Outreach (engagement of business)

Entrepreneurship education should be very closely linked with practice. Educators should be encouraged to reach out to the business community and integrate them into the learning process. Outside speakers and case studies provide role models for students considering an entrepreneurial career path. This is an important part of creating entrepreneurial drive: if students see that people "like themselves" were able to successfully create companies, it helps to demystify the process and make that option more feasible.

More local case studies, featuring entrepreneurs discussing their successes and failures as well as challenges they faced in the process, need to be developed and shared broadly. This is particularly important for those outside of formal education systems. More could also be done to profile these entrepreneurs in the media to create a broader exposure to such role models.

In most countries, universities are government funded and, in many cases, lack the incentives to initiate proactive outreach with the private sector. Government funded universities tend to have very traditional structures, making it more difficult to integrate new approaches. University-business collaborations are an essential element of the entrepreneurial university and are founded on mutually beneficial relationships. This is a major policy thrust of the European Commission and is a new government approach in the United Kingdom, where university enterprise networks are being established.

Advancing innovation

Innovation and research and development (R&D) spur economic growth, competitiveness and employment, notably in high-tech, high-skilled and high-value areas of the economy. A number of institutes and universities around the world provide some of the finest engineering, technology and science training; however, the commercialization of R&D is still in its infancy. More needs to be done to encourage links between academia and the private sector, as well as the sharing of best technology transfer practices.

To foster technology transfer, scientific and technical institutes and universities should include modules on entrepreneurship; these would enhance awareness within the research community of the opportunities and modalities that exist to commercialize innovative R&D. Links with business school students and faculty as well as with the business community should also be encouraged. Venture capital firms can and are beginning to play a more important role in working with technical universities to structure and fund spin-outs. Nurturing centers of R&D excellence is important as well. This includes attracting and retaining the most talented PhDs from around the world. For any country to realize its global competitive potential, it will need to create a full ecosystem revolving around attracting and retaining the most talented researchers; encouraging links between universities and the private sector; enlarging the flow of technology transfers supported by efficient and effective intellectual property rights; and creating schemes to specifically support young innovative companies at the cutting edge of development.[9]

Sustainable funding
In most countries, the bulk of the funding for schools and universities still comes from governments, although this is beginning to change as companies and foundations have begun to contribute. There are a few examples of entrepreneurs funding centers or chairs, but this is still relatively rare outside of the US. In general, most alumni around the world do not feel strong ties to their own schools and universities, which are still seen as the realm of governments. There needs to be a stronger culture of "giving back" which requires that schools track and engage alumni. Engagement of the private sectors also should be further encouraged.

It is clear that public interventions have affected the behavior of schools, universities and educators, increasing the focus on entrepreneurship education. The field of entrepreneurship education is still relatively young and it is therefore important and necessary that this support is continued until entrepreneurship is embedded in a sustainable manner in schools and universities and supported through informal education systems. Efforts to communicate with policymakers about the need, benefits and possible actions to take to encourage and support entrepreneurship education should be increased. At the same time, too much start and stop financing should be avoided, and plans for making the programs sustainable should be considered and integrated from the start. This requires a shared vision by all stakeholders of the desired outcomes at the policy level.

1.6.3 Challenges

A number of challenges remain across entrepreneurship education for youth, higher education and social inclusion.

No "one size fits all" answer
There is no "one size fits all" solution for entrepreneurship education. The challenges and opportunities for entrepreneurship vary dramatically in different parts of the world as well as for different segments of the educational journey. It is therefore not possible to take only one approach. Given the multifaced nature of entrepreneurship, educational programs must also be multifaced. Nor is it possible to import models from other parts of the world without modification. Local context must be taken into account in devising and tailoring a set of programs and initiatives relevant for each area. In countries, regions, cities and towns around the world in which entrepreneurship education is most prevalent, we can see that often this was the result of many different approaches and actors playing various roles, whether individually or through multistakeholder partnerships.

Continuous learning
Entrepreneurial learning models, knowledge and good practice across sectors and national borders need to be better shared. There are many new models being tested around the world, both inside and outside of formal educational systems. These models need to be shared more broadly to fuel new and more effective approaches to entrepreneurship education.

Within the formal education system, more must also be done to facilitate faculty and teacher collaboration, exchanges and research across borders. While collaboration may be strong between schools within a given country, there is a large gap in cross-border activities. Currently, networks and working relationships between faculty teaching entrepreneurs are limited and there is little sharing of good practice.

Greater mobility and exchange of experience between educators is needed, not only between schools and universities but also between academia and the business world. Programs need to be developed that allow educators to spend a significant amount of time at other institutions and/or in the private sector to truly engage, learn and grow.

Academic acceptance/legitimacy
Another issue is the acceptance of entrepreneurship within academia more broadly. While entrepreneurship is still not fully accepted as an

academic discipline, many schools and universities have created niches in this area. A growing numbers of universities are offering "concentrations" or "majors" in entrepreneurship, many have academic entrepreneurship departments and a large percentage is offering entrepreneurship courses. However, entrepreneurship is still trying to find its home. Faculty champions of entrepreneurship often have to fight internal battles for support and funding of their activities. Efforts are often fragmented and driven by external actors instead of by the education system itself.[10]

Effective measurement and evaluation

Greater clarity is needed regarding the purpose and goals of entrepreneurship education. These should be based on a broadly defined set of outcomes, not only on narrow measures such as the number of start-ups created. Measures need to not only cover short-term results, but also medium- and longer-term results. It also needs to be cross-country, including as many countries and regions as possible. To date, much of the existing data is from the US and Europe, even though entrepreneurial activity could actually be higher in many other parts of the world. As each of the three main chapters cover, measurement is still one of the biggest challenges in entrepreneurship education and one we hope will be addressed as a result of the report.

Scalability

While an increasing number of entrepreneurship education programs exist today compared to a decade ago, scalability and penetration remain key challenges. Technology provides a mechanism for reaching greater economies of scale as well as providing greater access. At the same time, given the explosion of activity in this field, educators and providers struggle to take advantage of the growing body of knowledge and experience that exists. It is not easy to find the right information at the right time about other programs and initiatives which one might leverage and/or approach as partners. Again, technology can help provide solutions. Additionally, the system is not developmental across the key parts of education – from primary, through secondary to tertiary. This is an area which is beginning to receive attention but in which much more work is needed:

> Every citizen, no matter where they live or what their circumstances, has an equal right to a quality education. Based on more than a decade of working with education leaders, governments, businesses and development organizations, Microsoft firmly believes that information technology can help transform both teaching and learning, enabling higher quality education experiences for everyone. (Craig Mundie, Chief Research and Strategy Officer, Microsoft)

1.7   RECOMMENDED ACTIONS FOR KEY STAKEHOLDERS

To prepare for educating the next wave of entrepreneurs, entrepreneurial individuals and entrepreneurial organizations, actions are necessary at the international, national, regional and local levels. All sectors have a role to play. Policymakers, academic institutions, the business community and other key stakeholders need to work together to seize this opportunity to fuel the engine of the economy's future growth and to improve social well-being by preparing young people to thrive and succeed in a globally competitive and dynamic world.

Governments should encourage and support entrepreneurship education, both in the formal school systems as well as in various informal education channels. This includes supporting programs to train teachers and other educators (including business people and entrepreneurs) to teach entrepreneurship. As the report outlines, the teaching methods required to teach entrepreneurship effectively are dramatically different from traditional lecture-based teaching methods. Educational institutions at all levels, primary, secondary and tertiary, need to embrace entrepreneurship education and embed it into not only the curriculum but, perhaps more importantly, into the way they operate and teach. Most school systems around the world are government owned and/or financed. Teaching materials and methods are based on tools and techniques from the last century. The entire system needs revamping or a reboot to adjust to the needs of the society of the future.

Sticking to the status quo is dangerous. We need to challenge ourselves and our institutions to address the needs of the future, not those of the past. Educators themselves need to have more mechanisms to learn and share with each other, particularly since the field of entrepreneurship is still relatively new in many educational institutions and, unlike in other disciplines like math or science, there is not a set, agreed-upon curriculum or quality standard.

Entrepreneurship education also needs to extend more effectively beyond educational systems – many effective models are being developed in foundations, community organizations, NGOs, etc. These efforts should be supported and encouraged. The use of technology and media tools is also critical but needs to be coupled with the development of locally relevant content. The development of online educational games to engage young people in entrepreneurship is an important new and developing area.

Entrepreneurship education is not an "extra" or a "nice to have". It is not an option. It is a necessity in today's world. We need ubiquitous entrepreneurship and innovation – it should not be limited to those who actually start companies. It needs to permeate society and our way of operating.

1.7.1 Recommended Actions for Governments

It is clear that public interventions have affected the behaviour of universities and faculty, increasing the focus on entrepreneurship education. The field of entrepreneurship education is still relatively young in many parts of the world and it is therefore important and necessary that this support is continued until entrepreneurship is embedded in a sustainable manner in schools and universities. Efforts to communicate with policymakers about the need, benefits and possible actions to take to encourage and support entrepreneurship education should be increased.

Transform the educational system

- Develop ambitious national plans for entrepreneurship education at all levels: primary, secondary and higher education (example: Norway).
- Create working groups to bring together players from different ministries which are involved in entrepreneurship education (entrepreneurship often cuts across several ministries: education, economy, research and technology, etc.) to develop coordinated solutions and approaches.
- Encourage the creation of public or private agencies and/or foundations to support and foster entrepreneurship education.
- Work with leadership in educational institutions:
  - Agree on shared outcomes, targets and measures linked to funding mechanisms.
- Reassess the rules and regulations for academia:
  - Recognition and acceptance of teaching by practitioners.
  - In undergraduate education, recognize entrepreneurship as a legitimate career path.
  - Creation of appropriate rewards and recognition.

Build the entrepreneurial ecosystem

- Provide the appropriate regulatory framework for:
  - Start-ups.
  - Growth firms.
  - Employment contracts.

  – Intellectual property and transfer.
  – Risk taking (bankruptcy laws).
- Support the local physical infrastructure necessary for entrepreneurship education.
- Ensure a consistent and adequate level of funding for entrepreneurship education programs:
  – Provide tax incentives, including those to encourage donations to universities to support entrepreneurship programs.
  – Provide resources (and seek private-sector matching) to help fund entrepreneurship teaching and research.
  – Ensure that the initiatives funded are sustainable and provide the necessary funding to reach sustainability.
  – Encourage the development of local angel and venture capital funds.
- Support training programs of educators (professors, teachers, practitioners, students):
  – Using interactive pedagogies.
  – Developing new and relevant course materials.
  – Focusing on the critical "how-to" of becoming leaders in entrepreneurship education.
  – Building career development and accreditation opportunities.
- Provide support to encourage the sharing and exchange of practice:
  – Facilitate the sharing of good practice across institutions and borders, both within regions and internationally.
  – Create opportunities for professors and researchers from various countries to work together on projects.
  – Provide support for international mobility and exchanges of educators and researchers.
- Provide support for the development of entrepreneurship course materials and case studies.
- Encourage the development of social capital/ecosystem networks:
  – Support organizations providing linkages and networking events.

Strive for effective outcomes and impact
Work with academia and other stakeholders to develop appropriate measurement and evaluation of the impact of entrepreneurial institutions, not just outputs, of entrepreneurship programs:

- Support longitudinal studies and data collection.
- Develop measures which take the specific programme goals, local market needs and context into account.

Leverage technology as an enabler

- Support the ICT infrastructure necessary for entrepreneurship education:
  - IT-broadband, telecommunications.
- Support the development of technology as both a tool and delivery method for entrepreneurship education (and education in general), not only for entrepreneurship per se, but also for leadership and personal development:
  - Computers in schools and community centers.
  - Development of online training materials relevant in the local context.

1.7.2 Recommended Actions for Academic Institutions

Most initiatives are led by individual champions, whether inside or outside the academic institution, but a commitment is also needed from the highest levels of the school or university.

Transform the educational system
Engage university leaders in actions to gain their commitment to reshaping the institutional paradigm: institutional vision, policies and outcomes, structures, values and rewards.

Build the entrepreneurial ecosystem

- Encourage all faculties/disciplines to develop opportunities for students at every level to experience entrepreneurship. Integrate entrepreneurship into the curriculum and build towards a multidisciplinary learning environment:
  - Increase the number of schools offering entrepreneurship courses, programs and activities.
  - Augment the number entrepreneurship courses, programs and activities and make them available to a broader group of students.
  - Make entrepreneurship a required course.
  - Integrate entrepreneurship across other disciplines.
  - Encourage entrepreneurship across disciplines, particularly in science and technology.
  - Build projects and programs across disciplines.
- Encourage the use of interactive teaching methods:
  - Promote the application of "learning by doing" through project-based learning, internships and consulting.

- Leverage the uses of case studies for discussion-based learning.
- Develop the proper incentives, assessment, rewards and recognition to encourage educators to try these approaches.
- Involve entrepreneurs and companies in entrepreneurship courses and activities.
- Broaden and build a strong pipeline of entrepreneurship professors and teachers:
  - Hire more professors and teachers fully dedicated to entrepreneurship.
  - Recruit professors and teachers who have entrepreneurship experience.
  - Support workshops and training programs for teachers.
  - Provide training for entrepreneurs, business people and other practitioners to become effective educators.
  - Develop appropriate incentives and celebrate successes.
  - Review regulations on the participation of entrepreneurs, business people and others in teaching activities.
  - Encourage the development of specialized entrepreneurship doctoral programs.
- Encourage the sharing of best practices among teachers and across institutions and countries.
- Support the development course materials (books, cases, online games, videos, etc.), not only for entrepreneurship per se, but also for leadership and personal development.
- Engage a diverse body of students in existing offerings and provide support and facilities for allowing students to develop their own initiatives, whether through clubs, laboratories, etc.
- Engage and reach out to the business community, public sector and other players in the ecosystem.
- Encourage the engagement of alumni, entrepreneurs and other practitioners in the classroom.
- Facilitate spin-outs from technical and scientific institutions:
  - Advance core research and innovation.
  - Accelerate the application of science and technology to market through technology transfer offices and/or other mechanisms.
  - Establish stronger links between academia, business and entrepreneurs.
  - Facilitate the provision of direct training and/or support programs for entrepreneurs in the process of starting companies.
  - Provide the appropriate training for staff, particularly in the area of technology transfer.

 – Ensure the time (sabbaticals, if necessary) for faculty to engage in entrepreneurial activities.

Strive for effective outcomes and impact

- Develop a clear framework of desired outcomes of entrepreneurship education by:
    – Developing individual capabilities, attitudes, and mindsets.
    – Encouraging application of those capabilities (as evidenced through start-ups and other ventures).
    – Contributing to economy/society.
- Create effective measures and track those over the long term to understand the impact of entrepreneurship education.
- Ensure a consistent and adequate level of funding for entrepreneurship education programs:
    – Provide resources (and seek public and private sector matching) to help fund entrepreneurship teaching and research.
    – Provide the necessary funding to reach sustainability.
    – Encourage the development of local angel and venture capital funds.
- Set high-quality standards for entrepreneurship curricula and research:
    – Encourage the development of research on entrepreneurship as well as the field of entrepreneurship education.
    – Ensure research and teaching covers all of the entrepreneurial growth phases, not just the start-up phase.
    – Develop high-quality local content, case studies and course materials.
    – Facilitate the development of high-quality, locally relevant materials.
    – Create degree programs, consistent with those at an international level.
    – Promote entrepreneurship as a legitimate academic discipline.

Leverage technology as an enabler

- Support the development of technology as both a tool and delivery method for entrepreneurship education (and education in general), not only for entrepreneurship per se, but also for leadership and personal development:
    – Computers in schools and community centers.
    – Development of online training materials relevant to the local context.

1.7.3   Recommended Actions for Companies

Companies, and especially entrepreneurs, have an important role to play in developing entrepreneurship education.

Transform the educational system

- Encourage governments and academia to make entrepreneurship education a key priority for the education agenda in both formal and informal education and all age levels.
- Encourage mutually beneficial business – university collaborations.

Build the entrepreneurial ecosystem

- Support the development of entrepreneurship within schools and universities by providing resources for professorships/chairs, educators, institutes and entrepreneurship centers.
- Engage with academic institutions as well as other organizations providing entrepreneurship training by providing expertise, teaching and mentoring:
  - Encourage the involvement of employees (as speakers, mentors, role models).
  - Exchanges of academic and company staff.
- Participate actively in the ecosystem, providing and sharing social capital.
- Partner with other stakeholders in the ecosystem to launch specific initiatives to develop effective programs and processes for entrepreneurship education:
  - Forums and events.
  - Training and/or mentoring entrepreneurs and students.
  - Training faculty.
  - Competitions and awards.
  - Accelerators, incubators, labs.
  - Entrepreneurship centers/institutes.
  - Curriculum development.
  - Online educational and training tools.
  - Global exchange networks.
- Encourage programs that target underdeveloped or underserved groups such as women, minorities, disadvantaged or disabled people.
- Share tacit knowledge/capabilities with NGOs and other organizations that support entrepreneurs. This indirectly promotes entrepreneurship education by supporting the capacity of organizations

which develop entrepreneurs. In so doing, it enables such organizations to operate more effectively, thereby increasing their impact on the entrepreneurial educational process.

Strive for effective outcomes and impact

- Work with academic institutions, governments and others to develop more effective measurement tools.
- Provide funding for research on the field of entrepreneurship education and evaluation tools such as longitudinal studies as well as statistics.

Leverage technology as an enabler
Provide expertise and partner with educators to develop effective online tools and materials for entrepreneurship education.

1.7.4 Recommended Actions for Other Actors

These could be foundations, NGOs, quasi government agencies, entrepreneurs, media, etc.

- Raise awareness about entrepreneurship as well as the importance of entrepreneurship education.
- Profile entrepreneurial role models:
  - Create more public recognition vehicles for entrepreneurs through the media, awards, etc.
  - Develop and share stories and case studies profiling successful entrepreneurs.
- Engage the media to share these stories more broadly as well as to change the mindset about entrepreneurship and entrepreneurs, particularly in countries or regions in which there are negative perceptions.
- Leverage existing networks offering good practice in entrepreneurship education.
- Create mechanisms for sharing practices and research not only through conferences and meetings but also through online sites or wikis which can be updated directly by those active in the field.
- Encourage the development of innovative new tools and approaches for entrepreneurship education.
- Develop and support programs that target underdeveloped or underserved groups such as women, minorities, disadvantages or disabled people.

The above recommendations attempt to outline some of the actions which can be taken by various stakeholders. Champions are needed at all levels and in all sectors. Both bottom up and top down approaches are necessary for different elements of the process. No one actor in the ecosystem can address these challenges on its own. Multistakeholder partnerships are essential for building the commitment and addressing the broader set of issues which are necessary for creating and sustaining a more entrepreneurial society. Capacity building is therefore important for all players, not just entrepreneurship educators. In that regard, policymakers, academic leaders and even the media can benefit from entrepreneurship training.

There is no "one size fits all" answer. Context matters. The challenges and opportunities for entrepreneurship vary dramatically in different parts of the world. It is therefore critical that the local context is taken into account and that the relevant local players are engaged in the process:

> We are facing a transition, and we must take this opportunity to provide today's students and entrepreneurs with the tools and the thinking that is required for the future. Collaborative technologies can fundamentally transform both how we teach and learn.
>
> We need to harness the power of the Internet and these new technologies for creating and sharing knowledge that will prepare students with the skills to compete in the 21st century. (John T. Chambers, Chairman and CEO, Cisco)

1.8   CONCLUSIONS

Entrepreneurship and entrepreneurial skills are core components to building socially inclusive and highly participatory economies in an increasingly global and competitive world. While the report highlights and raises awareness of the importance of entrepreneurship education in spurring economic growth and achieving the Millennium Development Goals, it also urges action.

The report consolidates existing knowledge and good practices in entrepreneurship education around the world to enable the sharing and development of innovative new tools, approaches and delivery methods. It also provides recommendations to governments, academia and the private sector on the development and delivery of effective education programs for entrepreneurship. This is only the beginning – the launch of a process in which the recommendations can be discussed on the global, regional, national and local levels and implemented with the involvement of key stakeholders.

Innovation and economic growth depend on being able to produce future leaders with the skills and attitudes to be entrepreneurial in their professional lives, whether by creating their own companies or innovating in larger organizations. Entrepreneurship education is the first and arguably the most important step for embedding an innovative culture and preparing the new wave of entrepreneurs, entrepreneurial individuals and organizations.

The entrepreneurial movement is well underway. There is a high and growing level of interest in entrepreneurship from students, faculty, university administrators, employers and policymakers, as well as an increasing number of initiatives throughout the world. The moment is right for a significant evolution of entrepreneurship education. While we can't determine today the exact nature of the next wave of entrepreneurship, we do know that it will require more creative, innovative and entrepreneurial attitudes, skills and behaviors.

The report is meant to be a catalyst and call for action on entrepreneurship education. We need to learn from models around the world and focus on integrating the most relevant and high-quality practices into the context relevant for each country and region. This should be a long-term commitment, however, not one that starts and then stops a few years later. Sustainability is a key issue. That means the objectives of entrepreneurship education should be clear from the start and outcomes should be measured to ensure that the intended results are being delivered.

The findings of the full report will be shared through the WEF regional summits and other leading international fora during the course of 2009, with the goal of deepening the findings at the regional and local levels and initiating concrete actions that can advance entrepreneurship education as a critical component for addressing the global challenges of the 21st century.

NOTES AND REFERENCES

* *Unlocking Entrepreneurial Capabilities to Meet the Global Challenges of the 21st Century – A Report of the Global Education Initiative* was published under the direction of Klaus Schwab, Founder and Executive Chairman, World Economic Forum (WEF) in Switzerland, April 2009, by a team led by Ana Sepulveda and Karen E. Wilson. Karen Wilson wrote this Executive Summary. Within the Full Report, Steve Mariotti and Daniel Rabuzzi wrote Chapter I "Entrepreneurship Education for Youth"; Christine Volkmann wrote Chapter II "Entrepreneurship in Higher Education"; Shai Vyakarnam wrote Chapter III "Entrepreneurship Education for Social Inclusion"; and Karen Wilson wrote Chapter IV "Steering Board Case Studies" and Chapter V "Recommendations", and was responsible for the Full Report's organization and editing. The team had a Steering Board and Technical Advisory Committee, whose members provided valuable input and are listed in the Full Report. The Full Report is available on the World Economic Forum website at http://www.wef.org.

1. *Final Report of the Expert Group Entrepreneurship in Higher Education, especially within non-business studies*, Brussels, European Commission, March 2008.
2. The Rule of 72 is a heuristic calculation yielding the number of years for an investment with compound interest to double. Divide 72 by the interest rate and the quotient is approximately the years to double. For example, an investment yielding 9 percent per annum compound interest doubles in approximately 72 divided by 9 = 8 years.
3. Solomon, G., Susan Duffy and Ayman Tarabishy, "The State of Entrepreneurship Education in the United States: A nationwide survey and analysis", *International Journal of Entrepreneurship Education*, 1, 2002, 65–86.
4. Clark, B.R. *Creating Entrepreneurial Universities: Organizational Pathways of Transformation*, Oxford, New York: Emerald Group Publishing, 1998.
5. Gibb, A. and P. Hannon, *Towards the Entrepreneurial University?* Durham, Birmingham: National Council for Graduate Entrepreneurship, 2006.
6. Bok, D., *Universities in the Marketplace: The Commercialization of Higher Education*, Princeton, NJ: Princeton University, 2003.
7. Schramm, C.J, *Report to HM Treasury and the National Council for Graduate Entrepreneurship*, Phoenix: Kauffman Foundation, 2006.
8. C.K. Prahalad, *The Fortune at the Bottom of the Pyramid: Eradicating Poverty Through Profits*, Upper Saddle River, NJ: Pearson Prentice Hall, 2004.
9. European Private Equity & Venture Capital Association, "Private Equity and Venture Capital: An Engine for Economic Growth, Competitiveness and Sustainability", *Public Policy Priorities*, Brussels, February 2005.
10. European Commission, *Entrepreneurship Education in Europe: Fostering Entrepreneurial Mindsets Through Education and Learning*, Oslo, 2007.

2. A global perspective on education and training

Alicia Coduras Martinez, Jonathan Levie, Donna Kelley, Rognvaldur J. Sæmundsson and Thomas Schøtt*

2.1 INTRODUCTION

In the closing decades of the 20th century, entrepreneurship gained increased recognition among economists as a significant driver of improvements in societal welfare. Across the globe, governments have acknowledged the importance of their role in motivating individuals, businesses and related stakeholders to perceive and develop new opportunities that can enact positive change and create economic growth in their societies.[1] This entrepreneurial spirit is now seen as the main source of innovations in nearly all industries, leading to the birth of new enterprises and the growth and renewal of established organizations.

The impact of entrepreneurship education and training on individual attitudes, actions, and ambitions is of particular interest to policymakers, educators, and practitioners. It is generally believed that individuals who perceive they have the skills and knowledge to start a business are more likely to do so. However, as the next section demonstrates, Global Entrepreneurship Monitor (GEM) expert surveys in most countries suggest that entrepreneurship education and training, both in school and outside of school, is inadequate. Recognizing this concern among hundreds of experts across the globe, the GEM consortium chose education and training as its special topic for 2008. Of the 43 countries participating in the 2008 survey, 38 added questions about entrepreneurship education and training to their adult population surveys and 30 countries added questions to their expert surveys. This report expands on initial findings from these surveys reported in the GEM 2008 Executive Report.[2]

The importance of entrepreneurship education and training was stressed in a recent report by the Global Education Initiative of the WEF summarized in Chapter 1:

while education is one of the most important foundations for economic development, entrepreneurship is a major driver of innovation and economic growth. Entrepreneurship education plays an essential role in shaping attitudes, skills and culture – from the primary level up . . . We believe entrepreneurial skills, attitudes and behaviors can be learned, and that exposure to entrepreneurship education throughout an individual's lifelong learning path, starting from youth and continuing through adulthood into higher education – as well as reaching out to those economically or socially excluded – is imperative.[3]

Many studies have addressed the supply side of entrepreneurship education and training: for example, teacher and student evaluations of program effectiveness,[4][5] national and regional reviews of the availability and nature of programs[6][7] and assessments of the value of entrepreneurship education in general.[8] Chapter 1 describes a range of entrepreneurship programs across the world, including government, NGO and multinational initiatives, and at a range of education levels from primary schools to universities, as well as post-school initiatives. While these studies provide useful information on what education and training is on offer, they do not tell us who takes this training and what trained individuals gain from their training.

GEM is in a unique position to provide information on the frequency and impact of entrepreneurship education and training among different countries. GEM polls individuals, rather than firms, and so is well placed for exploring entrepreneurship education and training in people. Because GEM does not rely on business registrations, it can reveal insights about individuals that have engaged in both formal (registered) and informal (unregistered) entrepreneurial activity. GEM can also capture the impact of training in starting a business on entrepreneurial awareness, attitudes, intentions and activity.

In addition, while many studies have been conducted in one or a few countries, this report analyzes GEM Adult Population Survey (APS) data on training in starting a business from 38 countries spanning a range of economic development levels.[9] The data are harmonized to allow for comparisons among these countries. This is supplemented by GEM National Expert Survey (NES) data from 31 countries on the insights and opinions of entrepreneurs, policymakers, debt and equity providers, and other experts on the state of entrepreneurship education and training in their countries.[10]

The 2008 APS survey asked respondents if they had ever taken part in training in starting a business in school ("school-based training") or outside of school ("non-school-based training"). For non-school training, survey interviewers asked respondents to identify the main provider of the program. They also asked respondents if they took this training voluntarily or if it was compulsory (for example, a required part of a school or government program). This distinction enables us to identify outcomes that could not be due to self-selection. In other words, it permits us to measure more accurately the "gain from training", or increased odds of engaging in entrepreneurial behavior that is due to the training itself rather than a consequence of some prior desire to behave entrepreneurially.

Readers should be aware that the data on which this report draws have several limitations. These include the following:

- The surveyed population spans a broad age range: from 18 to 64 years. The extent of training in a country may be a function of its age profile, and population level comparisons need to consider this. The analyses of impact from training were controlled for age group.
- Cultural factors and economic development level, as well as specific government policies, can affect the nature and impact of education and training generally.
- The sources of training for each respondent are not a guide to the type or the quality of training received by individual respondents.
- The countries in our database are not necessarily representative of the economic groups from which they are drawn. Thus, while we believe this is the largest global study of the prevalence, sources and effect of training in starting a business and in expert views of the state of entrepreneurship education and training in their countries to date, there is much more work to do.

In summary, our goals for this report are the following:

- Demonstrating national differences in perception by experts of the current quality and availability of entrepreneurship education and training in their countries.
- Demonstrating differences in the prevalence and nature of entrepreneurs and non-entrepreneurs who have received training in starting a business across countries.
- Demonstrating the impact of training on entrepreneurial awareness, attitudes, intentions, and activity and
- Identifying implications for policymakers, educators, and practitioners.

First, however, we provide an overview of entrepreneurship education and training, drawn from the current literature on the subject, in the next section.

2.2 CURRENT ISSUES IN ENTREPRENEURSHIP EDUCATION AND TRAINING

2.2.1   The Nature of Entrepreneurship Education and Training

Individuals may participate in entrepreneurship education and training at various points in their lives, and this education and training may take different forms. For example, all primary school pupils in Scotland receive "enterprise education" which is not specifically about training in starting a business, but about being enterprising and entrepreneurial in a more general sense.[11] In some universities, students may receive education "about" entrepreneurship. This education is not designed to provide training in starting a business. Instead, new venture creation is the context of an academic education, not the goal. Some university students experience a mix of "about" and "how-to" in entrepreneurship classes. At the other end of the spectrum from academic education, an employer or a government agency may offer training in starting a business to employees about to lose their jobs.

In this report, we define entrepreneurship *education* in broad terms as the building of knowledge and skills "about" or "for the purpose of" entrepreneurship generally, as part of recognized education programs at primary, secondary or tertiary-level educational institutions. We define entrepreneurship *training* as the building of knowledge and skills in preparation for starting a business. Thus, the purpose of entrepreneurship training is very specific, unlike the purpose of entrepreneurship education, which can be much broader.

Complicating the picture further, individuals may receive education about/for entrepreneurship and/or training in starting businesses in primary and secondary school, during college or university studies. These courses may be part of a formal education program that grants certificates or degrees, or they may involve non-credit-bearing courses. Other informal training programs operating outside the mainstream education system include courses, seminars or other types of training offered by local business organizations, employers, or a government agency.

Some argue that the earlier people are exposed to entrepreneurship, the more likely they will become entrepreneurs in some form during their lives (see Chapter 1 above). Evidence of this can be seen in the higher prevalence of entrepreneurial activity among individuals whose parents have been self-employed or running their own businesses.[12] It could be surmised that children of entrepreneurs develop particular perceptions and skills from observing their parents and participating in family business activities. Perhaps some education and training programs can substitute for this learning.

This raises issues about which types of entrepreneurship education and training approaches work best. It may depend on the educational context: for example, whether one is learning in primary or secondary (grade) school, colleges or universities, or non-school training programs. Most authors agree, however, that experiential learning, or "learning by doing," is more effective for developing entrepreneurial skills and attitudes than traditional methods like lectures.[13] [14] Several studies carried out in innovation-driven countries, including Singapore,[15] Sweden,[16] and the UK[17] show that entrepreneurs learn best with an experiential learning approach.

Another consideration is about what to teach. A survey of entrepreneurs by Sexton[18] revealed the ten most desired topics for achieving and managing fast growth. These were primarily business concerns, such as financing growth, managing cash flow, hiring and training employees, and selling. Yet entrepreneurship education and training may need to be much broader. It can impact attitudes, help people recognize opportunities and think creatively, and enable them to build leadership skills and confidence.[19] Recognizing this, a recent European Commission Report[13] suggested that the goal of entrepreneurship education should be to promote creativity, innovation and self-employment. Entrepreneurship education and training therefore entails more than the development of particular business skills. It can influence an individual's motivation to strive for something that might otherwise seem impossible or too risky. In short, it can create positive perceptions and desire among individuals to start businesses.

A further issue is where to teach entrepreneurship. Entrepreneurship is inherently multidisciplinary in nature. While entrepreneurship education and training requires the teaching of numerous business skills, students in non-business subjects may benefit from this training. The European Commission[13] even questions whether business schools are the most appropriate place to teach entrepreneurship, given its view that the most innovative and feasible ideas are likely to come from the technical and creative disciplines. Similarly, Katz[20] in 2003 declared that growth in entrepreneurship education and training is likely to come from outside business schools.

The requirements of educating "for" entrepreneurship call into question the usefulness of traditional education practices, implying, as Chapter 1 emphasized, a need for a mindset shift from mainstream education and training routines. New teaching pedagogies and cross-disciplinary content present challenges for educators and institutions. Sorgman and Parkison[21] state that many school teachers are unprepared for these new challenges. As Chapter 1 indicates, changing existing school systems will take time.

Multidisciplinary business content and experiential approaches will need to be integrated into the basic training that teachers receive. They conclude that "training the trainers" may be as great an effort as developing the curriculum.

On the supply side, university PhD programs are not providing enough faculty to meet the demand for entrepreneurship education.[20] [13] Many tertiary institutions, where their statutes permit, rely on "adjunct faculty": business people who teach entrepreneurship part-time. Current faculty, locked into narrow disciplinary structures, may not adapt well to the requirements of entrepreneurship education.[22] Additionally, internal funding systems in multi-faculty institutions may hinder the offering of entrepreneurship education beyond the business school. Consequently, the development of effective programs for entrepreneurship likely requires more than adding new courses. Institutional-level considerations may therefore play a key role in the development of entrepreneurship education in an economy.

Educators and policymakers may need to consider how to broaden access and increase the scale and scope of entrepreneurship training, beyond university locations and other on-site programs. This may require greater use of technology. Internet-based learning, for example, may be effective in extending a program's geographic reach or if demand is high.[22] [4] Creative computer applications may attract and hold the interest of some people, influencing their attitudes towards and understanding of entrepreneurship.

While the requirements and challenges of entrepreneurship education and training are numerous, there are also many opportunities for influencing perceptions, and developing the skills and ambitions of current and potential entrepreneurs. With this report, we address fundamental questions about the differences in entrepreneurship training among different economies around the world, and estimate the impact of training in starting a business on entrepreneurial awareness, attitudes, intentions and activity. In the remainder of this chapter, we provide background on three main economic groupings of countries and review current understanding about the impact of entrepreneurship training.

2.2.2 Entrepreneurship Education and Training and Economic Development

In the GEM research, countries are classified into three groups based on their level of economic development. The GEM theoretical model shows three sets of economic framework conditions: those that constitute the basic requirements for economic activity, those that enhance efficiency, and those that promote entrepreneurship and innovation. As countries progress economically, the relative importance of these three sets of economic framework conditions to further economic development changes. This method of classifying economies has been used in the Global Competitiveness Reports for some time.[23] [24]

In "factor-driven" countries with mainly extractive type economic activity, Porter and Schwab argue that the focus of government should be on enhancing the basic requirements of economic development, such as stable government, basic infrastructure, and primary health care and education.[25] With the exception of well-managed countries that are exceptionally well endowed with natural resources, such as Saudi Arabia, most entrepreneurial activity in factor-driven countries may be necessity-driven, and government attention is best focused on providing a basic foundation for enabling this activity, rather than, for example, providing sophisticated training in opportunity entrepreneurship.

As an economy develops, and as the employment of relatively cheap labor becomes an increasingly less viable source of advantage, necessity entrepreneurship declines and governments may start to pay more attention to entrepreneurship. The most developed nations, no longer able to depend on low labor costs, must instead compete in ways that are more creative. For the governments of such countries, high-quality basic factors and efficiency enhancers are generally present at sufficient levels. The quality and quantity of entrepreneurship and innovation then becomes a source of national competitive advantage. One of the primary entrepreneurial framework conditions recognized by GEM is the nature and level of entrepreneurship education and training. According to the GEM model, then, the relative importance of entrepreneurship education and training increases as economies develop economically.

Table 2.1 shows the 38 countries participating in the education and training special topic grouped into factor-driven, efficiency-driven and innovation-driven economies. Although the sample of countries crosses many geographic regions and levels of economic development, it is not necessarily evenly representative of the world. The factor-driven countries in the sample represent only 10 percent of the factor-driven countries in the world, and half of them were classified by the 2008 Global Competitiveness Report as in transition to the efficiency-driven group. Our sample contains 40 percent of the world's efficiency-driven economies and 45 percent of the innovation-driven economies. The United States, Canada, Australia and New Zealand were absent from the sample of innovation-driven countries.

*Table 2.1   GEM economies participating in the 2008 education and
training special topic focus, grouped by level of economic
development*

Factor-driven	Efficiency-driven	Innovation-driven
Bolivia	Argentina	Belgium
Bosnia and Herzegovina (+)	Brazil	Denmark
Colombia (+)	Chile	Finland
Ecuador (+)	Croatia (+)	France
Egypt	Dominican Republic	Germany
India	Hungary (+)	Greece
	Iran	Iceland
	Jamaica	Ireland
	Latvia	Israel
	Macedonia	Italy
	Mexico	Japan
	Peru	Republic of Korea
	Romania	Slovenia
	Serbia	Spain
	South Africa	United Kingdom
	Turkey	
	Uruguay	

Note: The (+) indicates economies in transition to the next level of economic
development.

The GEM Model, shown in Figure 2.1, illustrates three sets of framework conditions that influence entrepreneurship, which in turn impacts
national economic growth. These three sets are basic requirements, efficiency enhancers, and entrepreneurship and innovation. As the GEM
Model shows, entrepreneurship education and training is represented
as a specific entrepreneurial framework condition affecting entrepreneurial attitudes, activity, and aspirations – and, as a result, economic
development.

Much has been written about entrepreneurship education and training in innovation-driven economies, starting primarily in the 1980s and
accelerating after the turn of the century as interest in entrepreneurship
increased and the contribution of new businesses to the growth of a
national economy gained recognition. Entrepreneurship education, in
fact, has its roots in what are now classified as innovation-driven countries; the first efforts to deliver entrepreneurship courses were attributed to
Shigeru Fujuii of Kobe University in Japan in 1938,[23] and Myles Mace at
Harvard Business School in 1947.[20]

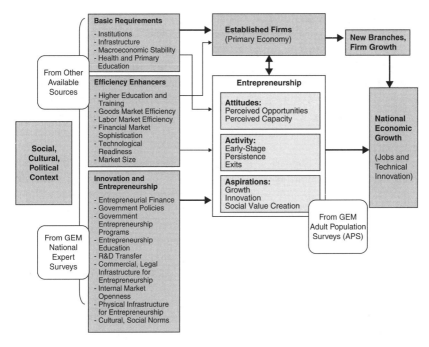

Source: 2009 GEM Global Report.

Figure 2.1 The GEM theoretical model

In the innovation-driven countries, people commonly believed – and often still do believe – that entrepreneurship is not teachable, and even that successful entrepreneurs did not need higher education. People like Bill Gates and Steve Jobs, both dropping out after a few years of college, made for interesting news stories. It became apparent, however, that these did not represent typical entrepreneurs, particularly for businesses with knowledge-based products and services. Many governments in innovation-driven economies have since declared their commitment to entrepreneurship education, identifying it as a key priority.[21][26]

In these wealthier economies, entrepreneurship education is believed to be relatively established, and attention has turned toward assessing existing programs, sharing best practices, identifying constraints, and providing recommendations. There have been numerous studies evaluating training, school and university education programs in countries such as the UK, [27][28][29] Sweden,[30] German-speaking countries,[31] Australia,[32] and Oman,[33] to name a few.

Katz in 2003 declared that entrepreneurship education has reached maturity in the United States and that future expansion lies elsewhere.[20] Indeed the field may experience its greatest growth outside the innovation-driven countries. For example, Li et al.[34] reported that entrepreneurship education has been well received in China, but is still a relatively new practice in higher institutions. Here, entrepreneurship education is an emerging concept. Yet it may have a significant role to play in transitioning entrepreneurial activity from necessity to opportunity-based in the efficiency-driven countries, and enhancing innovation and international competitiveness.

In factor-driven countries, training may be offered as part of a social or government campaign to improve skills and create jobs, as Finweek reports on a program in Namibia.[35] In these poorer countries, providing a basic education to as many people as possible is a major concern of policy makers. Entrepreneurship education and training is likely to take different forms than in the innovation-driven or efficiency-driven countries. As previous GEM reports show, in these countries entrepreneurship rates tend to be high, but mainly necessity-based and with lower growth aspirations.

2.2.3   Does Entrepreneurship Education and Training Make a Difference?

While there is extensive literature on entrepreneurship education and training, evidence demonstrating the influence of training on entrepreneurial activity is still lacking.[36] Greater understanding is needed about how programs and learning strategies help develop skills that lead to the formation of new ventures.[37] Chapter 1 argues that there is strong evidence that entrepreneurship can boost economic growth and, in turn, alleviate poverty. However, they do not identify studies specifically linking entrepreneurship education to economic growth.

Can entrepreneurship education or training impact one's entrepreneurial orientation? Many studies have indicated a link between entrepreneurship and both need for achievement and internal locus of control (a belief in one's ability to control one's destiny). Hansemark,[38] for example, found that these two traits were higher among enrollees in a one-year entrepreneurship program in Sweden, compared with those not receiving this training. While we need to acknowledge these studies, we also need to question whether entrepreneurship is a function of stable traits or learned behaviors. Past research has, for the most part, failed to identify a consistent set of personality traits associated with entrepreneurship, other than the two aforementioned traits. This is likely good news for educators, policymakers, and practitioners, given that traits are generally considered inborn and unchangeable. As such, most of the literature on the impact of entrepreneurship education and training is oriented toward the influence of education on the perception of skills, attitudes, and intent to start businesses.

A recent study for the Small Business Administration Office of Advocacy[39] found that university graduates that have taken entrepreneurship courses are more likely to select careers in entrepreneurship, develop patented inventions or innovative processes, services or products, and work in small businesses. Researchers have suggested that education and training for entrepreneurship should positively influence actions by enhancing the skills required to start and grow a venture.[39 40] For example, it can enhance one's cognitive ability for managing the complex process of opportunity recognition and assessment.[41] One way this can be done is by providing examples of the entrepreneurship process, and by using role models individuals can identify with. This can show people what is possible, and equip them with the ability to recognize, assess and shape opportunities.[42]

In contrast, Gatewood[43] sees potential negative effects. Focusing on public sector venture assistance, she suggests that while these programs can improve the abilities and problem-solving approaches of potential founders, they can discourage entrepreneurs who are refused assistance. Moreover, those receiving training may not start their businesses because they may realize they do not have the right skills or that they do not have a viable opportunity, thus preventing learning by doing.

Perhaps the above indicates that training can help ensure that those businesses actually started will be more successful. If high small and medium-sized enterprise (SME) failure rates are a consequence of a lack of training, as Ibrahim and Soufani [44] suggest, perhaps training can weed out inexperienced entrepreneurs or those with an infeasible opportunity. This, however, places the burden on sound screening and training practices in the early stages, when uncertainty is highest. Even then, opportunities screened out of programs may lead to missed opportunities because capable entrepreneurs may shape poor-quality opportunities into more viable ones. In addition, they gain experience that creates new learning and builds skills. This in turn raises a question about the exclusiveness of programs: should they be selective or encourage broad participation? It also casts doubt on the effect of training: are higher success rates among selective programs due to the pre-screening or the training itself?

While knowledge and skills can increase the success of a venture, these resources will not be put to use if the inspiration to start a business is not there to begin with. Attitudes and intention are important in boosting the chance individuals will attempt an entrepreneurial endeavor at some point in their lives.[45] Studies on the influence of education and training on attitudes have found a positive link to interest in entrepreneurship, attitudes toward entrepreneurship, and perception of the feasibility of starting a business. Examples include post-secondary education in Northern Ireland,[4] university students in England[45] and Germany,[14] and secondary school pupils enrolled in an entrepreneurship program in Australia.[46] However, other studies have found decreases in intention after entrepreneurship education programs, for example in a Dutch school[47] and a German university.[48] Other studies show that prior exposure to entrepreneurship and prior intention can change the effect of entrepreneurship training programs.[49]

These country-level studies provide tantalizing glimpses of possible relationships between entrepreneurship education and training and subsequent behavior. However, it is not at all clear from the literature whether people on average experience a gain from training in terms of their awareness of or attitudes towards entrepreneurship, their entrepreneurial intentions or indeed their entrepreneurial activity. The next section reviews the state of entrepreneurship education and training across the world, as seen by carefully selected experts in each of 31 countries.

2.3　THE STATE OF ENTREPRENEURSHIP EDUCATION AND TRAINING IN 31 COUNTRIES: EXPERT OPINIONS

2.3.1　The Level and Quality of Entrepreneurship Education and Training as Perceived by National Experts

GEM national teams conduct National Expert Surveys (NES) in their countries, polling a selected sample of individuals who are deemed expert in at least one entrepreneurial framework condition (EFC), or aspect of the environment for entrepreneurship. The principal EFCs recognized by GEM are: financial support for entrepreneurs, public policy support, bureaucracy and taxes, government programs, research and development (R&D) transfer, access to professional and commercial infrastructure, internal market dynamics and barriers, access to physical infrastructure and services and, finally cultural and social norms. Typically, four experts are identified per EFC, of which one is an entrepreneur, two are providers of that EFC, and one is an expert observer.

The results of this survey add insights on key framework conditions that can impact the entrepreneurial process in an economy. In this chapter, we summarize the expert opinions collected by 31 national teams. On average, each national team interviewed 42 experts, with a minimum of 31 and a maximum of 80 experts interviewed. Only one team interviewed less than 35 experts.

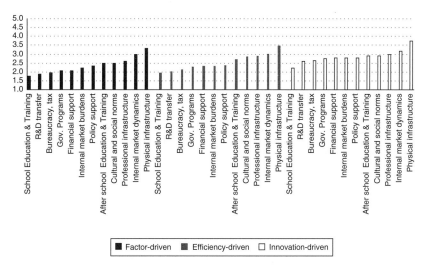

Note: Framework conditions are ordered from the lowest to the highest evaluation within each economic group. The measures range from 1 = poor to 5 = excellent. Total number of countries in sample: 31.

Source: GEM National Expert Survey 2008.

Figure 2.2 *Average ratings by national experts in three economic groups on the level of entrepreneurial framework conditions in their country*

In each country, experts were asked to state the level of their agreement or disagreement, along a 5-point scale, with a series of statements designed to capture their views on a range of entrepreneurial framework conditions. With respect to entrepreneurship education and training, they were asked to state their opinions on two issues: the adequacy of provision of formal entrepreneurship education and training provided at primary and secondary schools, and the adequacy of provision of entrepreneurship education and training offered through a variety of sources beyond primary and secondary schooling, such as colleges and universities, government and professional programs, etc.[50]

Figure 2.2 shows the average un-weighted ratings of experts by economic group on these two issues in relation to the other entrepreneurship framework conditions measured. In each economic group, entrepreneurship education in primary and secondary schools received the worst evaluation by the experts. The average economic group rating for this EFC increases with increasing level of economic development, reflecting a general improvement in EFCs as countries develop economically.

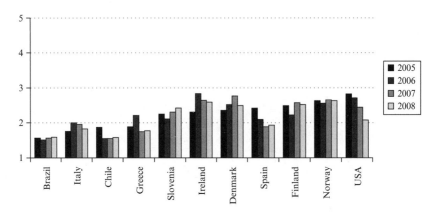

Source: GEM National Expert Survey 2005 to 2008.

*Figure 2.3   Average ratings by national experts on the state of
entrepreneurship education and training at school in a sample
of GEM nations for the years 2005 to 2008*

Entrepreneurship education and training in schools has received low ratings every year since expert surveys commenced in 2000. Figure 2.3 shows the results for the period 2005 to 2008 for a selection of countries. In most countries, the ratings are consistent from year to year, even though the pool of experts changes. Two exceptions are Spain and the United States, where expert ratings have become more negative. Clearly, this issue is of concern to experts.

Experts rate the level of entrepreneurship education and training provided beyond school more highly than school training, and it tends to rank in the middle range of all EFCs. In absolute terms, however, it only approaches a neutral rating on average in the efficiency-driven economic group. This suggests that experts in many countries feel that this EFC could be improved. Figure 2.4 shows the evolution of ratings for this EFC over the 2005 to 2008 period in a selection of countries. The ratings are consistent over time in most countries, although in Brazil the ratings appear to have improved.

2.3.2   Entrepreneurs' Need for Assistance and the Adequacy of Training Provision Outside the Formal Education System

In 2009, 30 countries included two additional items in their NES survey. The first item elicited expert opinions on whether entrepreneurs in general in their country needed external assistance in planning their businesses

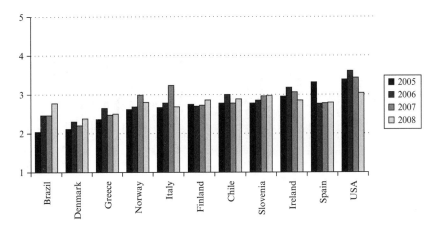

Source: GEM National Expert Surveys 2005 to 2008.

Figure 2.4   *Average national expert ratings on the state of non-school entrepreneurship education and training in a sample of GEM nations for the years 2005 to 2008*

prior to start up. The second item covered the adequacy of entrepreneurship education and training provided by public and/or private agencies independent of the formal education system.[51] Figure 2.5 shows the average ratings by experts on these items in each country. The results show a perceived need for external assistance for entrepreneurs starting businesses, with Brazil, Iran and Mexico reporting the highest levels. Only Finland received a neutral rating on this issue.

Figure 2.5 indicates that, in six economies (Germany, Finland, South Korea, Ireland, Spain, and the United States), experts believe that public and/or private agencies provide adequate entrepreneurship education and training outside the formal education system. The remaining countries report low or moderate perceptions on this factor. Only in Germany and Finland is the level of informal education and training rated higher than perceptions about the need for assistance in starting businesses. For the other countries, perceptions about the adequacy of training offered do not match the perceived need for assistance.

The unusually positive result for Finland is noteworthy. As Kyro[26] reports, Finland's government has committed to entrepreneurship education throughout its school system. A report from the Finnish Ministry of Education[52] states: "The aim of the Ministry of Education is to enhance an entrepreneurial spirit among Finns and make entrepreneurship a more attractive career choice." This may have led Finnish experts to rate their

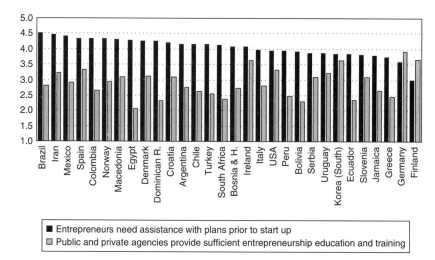

Source: GEM National Expert Survey 2008.

Figure 2.5   *Experts' average evaluations in 30 GEM countries regarding
the need of entrepreneurs for external assistance with planning
prior to start up, and the sufficiency of entrepreneurship
education and training provided by public and/or private
agencies in 30 GEM nations*

country's assistance as sufficient. It is also consistent with the APS survey
results in the next chapter, which show that Finland has the highest level
of entrepreneurship training among the 38 countries surveyed.

In addition to being asked to rate their agreement with a range of items,
experts were also asked to list positive and negative aspects of the environment for entrepreneurship and make recommendations. The frequency
with which experts mentioned an EFC provides another guide to its relative importance. In 2008, across 30 countries, 30 percent of mentions of
constraints included the state of entrepreneurship education and training.
This was the third most frequently mentioned constraint, after financial
support and government policies. It constituted over half of constraints
mentioned in Egypt and South Africa, compared with only 15 percent in
Finland, 8 percent in Argentina and none in Iran.

Surprisingly, entrepreneurship education and training was the second
most frequently cited EFC in relation to positive aspects of the environment for entrepreneurship. This suggests that while provision across most
countries may be inadequate, there are good initiatives in many countries.
On average, 25 percent of mentions of positive developments or initiatives

were in the domain of this EFC. Over half of mentions of activities that fostered entrepreneurship in the United States described positive aspects of entrepreneurship education and training in their country, compared with 2 percent in Germany, 5 percent in South Africa, 6 percent in Iran and 7 percent in Turkey.

Experts were asked to make recommendations to improve the environment for entrepreneurship in their country. Forty-nine percent of the recommendations on average across the 30 countries were about entrepreneurship education and training – more than any other EFC. The exception here was Iran, where only 5 percent of recommendations related to this EFC. By contrast, 71 percent of Turkish recommendations and 68 percent of South African recommendations were in this area.

In conclusion, it is clear that in most countries, entrepreneurship experts regard the provision of entrepreneurship education and training as inadequate. However, in all countries at least one expert mentioned examples of good practice in this area.

2.4   PREVALENCE AND SOURCES OF TRAINING IN STARTING A BUSINESS

2.4.1   Prevalence Rates of Trained Individuals in the Working Age Population

In this section, we report on the proportion of working age adults who have received training in starting a business in the adult population across the 38 participating countries. Survey respondents reported whether they had ever received training in starting a business, either during primary or secondary school, or outside school. We compare these rates across countries and economic groups, noting the proportions of voluntary and compulsory training. In addition to providing an estimate of the relative demand for training in a country, this information is valuable in estimating the effect of training on subsequent entrepreneurial behavior.

Figure 2.6 shows the average prevalence rate of working age individuals who have received training in starting a business across the 38 countries for which data are available. In total, an average of 21 percent of working age adults in these countries has received training in starting a business at some point in their lives. Of those receiving training, the majority, 61 percent, engaged in this training voluntarily (13 percent of the total working age population). Twenty percent of trained individuals had only received compulsory training (4 percent of the working age population), while 14 percent (3 percent of the working age population) had both

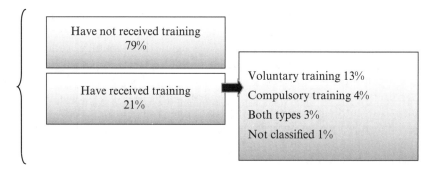

Source: GEM Adult Population Survey 2008.

Figure 2.6   *Average level of training in starting a business in the*
                adult working age population (18–64 years) across all 38
                participating countries

voluntary and compulsory training. This indicates that training in starting a business is mainly through self-selection. As mentioned above, this has important implications for the assessment of cause and effect, to which we return in section 2.5.

The country average summary of training depicted in Figure 2.6 needs cautious interpretation, for several reasons. First, factor-driven countries are under-represented in our sample. Second, country-level prevalence rates vary widely, even among countries with similar levels of economic development. Figure 2.7 presents the proportion of working age people who have received training in starting a business, by country, in increasing order of prevalence. The results show wide variation, from 6 percent in Turkey to 49 percent in Finland. Most countries, however, fall within the range of 10 percent to 30 percent. High levels of training were reported in five countries (Belgium, Slovenia, Columbia, Chile, and Finland), where more than 30 percent of the adult population have received any training. At the low end, five countries (Turkey, Egypt, Dominican Republic, Romania, and Brazil) reported training levels of less than 10 percent.

The wide variation in entrepreneurship training levels evident in Figure 2.7 indicates that country-level factors may be more important than practices or customs in different global regions. Figure 2.8 shows training levels for the three economic groups, organized by gross domestic product (GDP) level within the groups. As this figure shows, the uneven distribution pattern we see geographically is also evident in economic orderings. Within groups of countries that are at a similar stage of development (resource-driven, efficiency-driven, and innovation-driven), there is a high

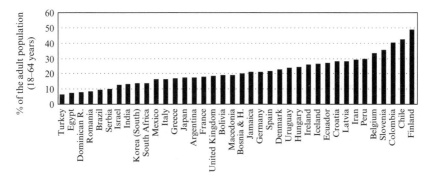

Source: GEM Adult Population Survey 2008.

Figure 2.7 *Proportion of the adult working age population (18–64 years) that has ever received training in starting a business by country, presented in increasing order of prevalence*

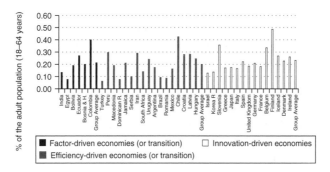

Source: Adult Population Survey 2008.

Figure 2.8 *Prevalence of start-up training in the participating countries ranked by GDP within each economic group*

level of variation, with at least one country with high training levels in each group (Columbia, Chile, and Finland).

We next examine the level of voluntary and compulsory training. Individuals engaged in voluntary training have, by definition, chosen to take it, perhaps relative to other pursuits. Compulsory training, on the other hand, represents a required activity. For example, individuals could be required to take a course to complete a degree or certificate program, or to satisfy requirements relating to registering a business or receiving assistance or funding.

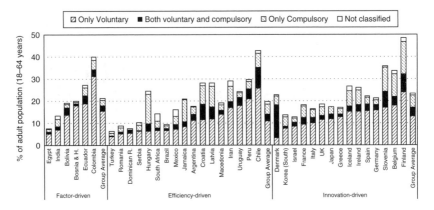

Source: GEM Adult Population Survey 2008.

*Figure 2.9   Levels of voluntary and compulsory start-up training (ordered
             by level of voluntary training within economic groups)*

Figure 2.9 shows the breakdown in compulsory versus voluntary training by economic groups. In factor-driven countries, less than one fourth of
trained individuals had received any compulsory training. In the other two
groups, between one third and one half of those who receiving training
had taken compulsory training. This is consistent with the GEM theoretical model, where improving basic requirements like infrastructure, health
and primary education take greater priority in factor-driven economies.
Factor-driven countries tend to show higher levels of early-stage entrepreneurial activity, but this is likely to be more necessity-based, and less
growth-, innovation-, and international-oriented.

   Some countries demonstrate relatively high proportions of compulsory training. In Denmark, for example, over 65 percent of those trained
received both compulsory and voluntary training, with an additional
15 percent receiving only compulsory training. So four fifths of trained
individuals in Denmark were required to take training in starting a business. In Hungary, almost 60 percent of those receiving training did so
only on a compulsory basis (with an additional 14 percent receiving both
compulsory and voluntary training). Other countries reporting a relatively
high level of compulsory training include Jamaica, Croatia and Latvia
in the efficiency-driven group, and Iceland, Ireland, and Slovenia in the
innovation-driven group.

   There seems to be no relationship between early-stage entrepreneurial
activity rates and the ratio of compulsory to voluntary training. For
example, among innovation-driven countries, Denmark and Slovenia

have low rates of early-stage entrepreneurial activity, while Ireland and Iceland have high rates. All show high ratios of compulsory to voluntary training.

In summary, more than one fifth of the working age (18–64 years) population across the 38 participating countries had received training in starting a business as of mid-2008. The country-level prevalence rate varies considerably. Most countries show a level between 10 percent and 30 percent, with a few countries having higher or lower prevalence rates. On average, there is not a significant difference in level or variability between the three economic groups. For most countries, but not all, more than half of the trained population engaged in this training voluntarily. We next examine the sources of this training.

2.4.2 Sources of Training in Starting a Business

In this section, we investigate how sources of start-up training vary across countries and economic groups. In our examination of training sources, we make a distinction between "in-school" and "non-school" training. In-school training is training provided as part of primary or secondary education. Non-school training comprises sources beyond primary and secondary schooling, such as colleges, universities, public agencies, chambers of commerce, trade unions and employers. Secondly, we distinguish between "formal" and "informal" training. Formal training is received as a part of a formal education, e.g. primary or secondary education or as a part of a tertiary-level certificate, diploma or degree program. Informal training refers to all other types of training. These might include non-credit-bearing evening courses at a university, local business organization, or a government agency. These dimensions provide different perspectives on the nature of the education training system in each country.

These distinctions are important, because they can capture the extent to which a government is providing entrepreneurship training through the formal education system and how early in a person's schooling. Additionally, they capture the relative importance of informal training sources, which may help people at a time when they are more directly engaged in starting businesses, rather than focused on their education more generally. A closer examination of informal sources can reveal whether informal training is concentrated through one or many suppliers: whether it is the responsibility of universities, private organizations, government, or other sources.

Figure 2.10 shows the prevalence of training broken down into in-school and non-school training, and organized by frequency of in-school only training within economic groups. The level of in-school training

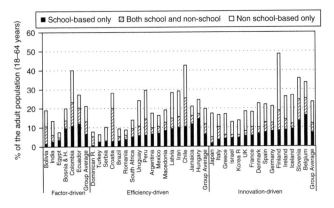

Source: GEM Adult Population Survey 2008.

Figure 2.10   *Prevalence of in-school and non-school training, ordered by frequency of in-school only training within economic groups*

in the adult population varies across countries: from 2 percent of the adult population in Turkey to around 25 percent in Belgium, Chile and Slovenia. Non-school training ranges from 4 percent in Egypt and Turkey to 40 percent in Finland. Only 30 percent of trained individuals in Japan and Serbia received in-school training, compared to around 75 percent in Ecuador, Jamaica, and Belgium.

From Figure 2.10 we can see that, on average, the proportion of non-school training to total training is similar (68–69 percent) across the three economic groups (this includes "non-school only" and "both in-school and non-school"). However, the proportion of in-school training is highest (62 percent) in the factor-driven economies and lowest (52 percent) in the innovation-driven economies (includes "in-school only" and "both in-school and non-school"). The proportion of individuals that received training from both sources in relation to total training is also highest in the factor-driven economies (31 percent) and lowest in the innovation-driven economies (21 percent). These results imply that in-school and non-school training are roughly equally important sources of training in the factor-driven economies, but the relative importance of non-school training is greater in more developed economies.

As Figure 2.11 shows, most trained individuals have had formal training. Most of these have had informal training in addition to formal training. Individuals who have had only informal training are rarer. The prevalence of individuals with formal training varies from 4 percent of the adult population in Serbia and Turkey to 40 percent in Finland.

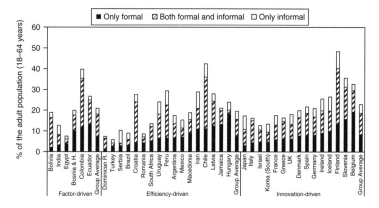

Source: GEM Adult Population Survey 2008.

Figure 2.11   *Prevalence of formal and informal start-up training by country and economic group, ordered by frequency of formal only training*

For informal training, the range is from 4 percent in Egypt, Turkey and Romania to 35 percent in Finland. The prevalence of individuals with both types ranges from 1 percent in Serbia to 27 percent in Bolivia.

The high level of overlap between formal and informal training indicates that both formal and informal systems are important sources of entrepreneurship training, and suggests that they complement each other.

Table 2.2 provides a more detailed view of formal training in the participating countries. It shows that school training as a proportion of total formal training ranges from 43 percent in Greece to 90 percent in Mexico.

Training at tertiary level as a proportion of total formal training ranges from 21 percent in Hungary to 73 percent in Finland. In most countries, training at school is more prevalent than training at the tertiary level. On average, this ratio is higher for the efficiency-driven economic group than for the other two, but there is also a wide variation within each group. Tertiary-level training is more prevalent than training at school in only four countries: Colombia, Greece, Japan, and Finland.

Table 2.3 provides a more detailed view of informal training sources in the participating countries. The most frequent source of informal training in most of the countries is self-study, with up to 88 percent (Croatia) of those receiving informal training citing this source. The next most common source of informal training across the dataset is informal university programs, followed by courses offered through business associations.

Table 2.2   Prevalence of formal training across countries and economic groups (ranked by prevalence of school training)

Country	School only (%)	Tertiary level only (%)	Both (%)	School total (%)	Tertiary level total (%)	Ratio of school / tertiary level (%)
Factor-driven						
Colombia (+)	29	41	30	59	71	0.8
Bolivia	41	35	24	65	59	1.1
India	41	27	32	73	59	1.3
Bosnia and Herzegovina. (+)	67	23	10	77	33	2.3
Egypt	65	23	13	77	35	2.2
Ecuador (+)	57	18	24	82	43	1.9
Group average	50	28	22	72	50	1.6
Efficiency-driven						
Uruguay	42	41	17	59	58	1.0
Latvia	44	39	16	61	56	1.1
Peru	38	36	25	64	62	1.0
Turkey	59	36	5	64	41	1.6
Chile	44	33	23	67	56	1.2
Argentina	61	27	13	73	39	1.9
Iran	61	25	14	75	39	1.9
Serbia	73	24	2	76	27	2.8
South Africa	52	22	26	78	48	1.6
Jamaica	66	19	15	81	34	2.4
Macedonia	67	19	14	81	33	2.5
Dominican Republic	70	17	13	83	30	2.8
Romania	60	17	23	83	40	2.1
Croatia (+)	56	17	27	83	44	1.9
Hungary (+)	79	15	6	85	21	4.1
Brazil	74	11	15	89	26	3.4
Mexico	73	10	17	90	27	3.4
Group average	60	24	16	76	40	2.2
Innovation-driven						
Greece	33	57	9	43	67	0.6
Japan	31	55	15	45	69	0.7
Finland	27	53	20	47	73	0.6
Israel	49	43	9	57	51	1.1
Denmark	55	40	5	60	45	1.3
Iceland	53	39	7	61	47	1.3

Table 2.2   (continued)

Country	School only (%)	Tertiary level only (%)	Both (%)	School total (%)	Tertiary level total (%)	Ratio of school / tertiary level (%)
United Kingdom	51	39	11	61	49	1.2
Republic of Korea	54	36	11	64	46	1.4
Spain	47	33	20	67	53	1.3
Italy	56	32	12	68	44	1.5
Ireland	55	29	16	71	45	1.6
Germany	59	27	14	73	41	1.8
Slovenia	56	22	22	78	44	1.8
France	60	22	19	78	40	1.9
Belgium	66	16	19	84	34	2.5
Group average	50	36	14	64	50	1.4

Source: GEM Adult Population Survey.

The least frequently mentioned sources are training programs provided by public agencies and those offered through employer initiatives.

Use of online programs is most frequent in Chile (62 percent of those receiving informal training) and Slovenia (51 percent). Frequency of use does not imply popularity. In Chile, online training is linked with business registration. Another notable pattern is the low frequency of government programs. Few countries show a high level of public agency training. Exceptions are South Africa at 69 percent and Iran at 50 percent of those receiving informal training.

In summary, levels of in-school versus non-school training, and formal versus informal training, vary widely across economies and levels of economic development. The high proportion of formal training reveals the importance of schools, colleges, and universities in delivering this framework condition. In most countries, more people have received formal training from schools than from tertiary-level institutions, indicating that schools have a broader reach. The degree of overlap between formal and informal training suggests that formal training on its own is not enough for many people. A demand for informal training also exists, perhaps shortly before, during, or after a venture is started. Finally, people have a variety of choices for pursuing informal training. The high frequency of self-study suggests that many individuals either cannot access or afford organized training – or perhaps doubt its efficacy.

Table 2.3 Prevalence of informal start-up training by country and economic group

GCR, group	Informal training sources						
	University, College (%)	Local business associations (%)	Public agencies (%)	Employer (%)	Self studies (%)	Other (%)	Online (%)
Factor-driven							
Bolivia	9.1 (34.6)	8.2 (24.1)	4.6 (16.6)	10.3 (27.9)	45.9 (86.5)	11.4 (26.0)	6.1 (21.0)
Bosnia and Herzegovina (+)	2.9 (28.9)	2.4 (24.1)	1.5 (15.1)	4.5 (45.3)	8.6 (86.2)	1.8 (18.2)	2.0 (20.1)
Colombia (+)	10.7 (37.9)	6.1 (21.5)	5.5 (19.6)	5.3 (18.7)	23.8 (84.5)	7.2 (25.4)	3.5 (12.3)
Ecuador (+)	4.6 (32.5)	4.3 (30.5)	2.7 (19.0)	3.5 (24.3)	10.5 (73.1)	3.8 (26.9)	2.3 (16.1)
Egypt	1.4 (37.0)	1.1 (28.0)	1.7 (43.6)	1.3 (34.0)	2.4 (62.0)	0.5 (12.0)	1.0 (27.0)
India	2.7 (26.3)	2.9 (28.8)	2.8 (27.9)	2.2 (22.1)	4.9 (48.9)	3.6 (35.8)	1.4 (13.6)
Efficiency-driven							
Argentina	5.8 (54.0)	5.7 (52.9)	2.3 (21.4)	4.2 (39.2)	9.4 (86.6)	1.7 (16.0)	2.4 (21.5)
Brazil	2.0 (31.5)	4.4 (71.2)	1.1 (17.7)	1.0 (16.1)	2.3 (35.5)	2.3 (35.5)	0.5 (6.5)
Chile	11.3 (35.8)	8.5 (26.8)	10.9 (34.4)	11.8 (37.5)	25.7 (80.8)	14.4 (45.4)	19.9 (61.5)
Croatia (+)	9.7 (25.7)	7.7 (19.1)	4.8 (12.1)	12.8 (26.3)	53.9 (87.7)	10.0 (18.8)	12.4 (22.5)
Dominican Republic	6.9 (41.6)	6.2 (29.0)	3.3 (17.4)	6.4 (33.6)	53.5 (55.5)	0.9 (8.0)	1.1 (10.1)
Hungary (+)	1.9 (28.9)	0.9 (14.1)	1.5 (22.7)	0.9 (14.1)	1.4 (21.1)	0.1 (0.8)	0.3 (3.9)
Iran	4.0 (22.1)	2.4 (13.0)	9.2 (50.3)	3.1 (17.2)	9.8 (53.7)	3.4 (18.3)	1.8 (9.3)
Jamaica	2.8 (36.0)	1.2 (15.6)	2.7 (33.7)	1.3 (16.1)	4.5 (55.9)	0.6 (7.0)	0.6 (0.5)
Latvia	5.1 (32.0)	2.3 (14.7)	3.2 (20.3)	4.2 (25.9)	12.6 (78.4)	1.5 (9.7)	6.8 (39.4)
Macedonia	3.5 (33.5)	3.1 (29.7)	1.8 (17.0)	3.3 (31.9)	8.2 (79.1)	2.4 (23.1)	2.3 (21.4)
Mexico	1.7 (18.3)	2.4 (26.5)	1.5 (16.5)	3.0 (31.5)	3.6 (38.5)	2.4 (25.2)	0.9 (8,7)

Peru	12.5 (53.2)	6.5 (27.4)	5.2 (21.4)	7.7 (33.0)	17.3 (65.6)	7.7 (33.3)	4.6 (17.5)
Romania	1.4 (32.9)	1.1 (26.8)	0.8 (18.3)	1.5 (36.2)	2.8 (65.7)	1.7 (40.0)	0.7 (15.7)
Serbia	1.4 (19.5)	1.0 (13.5)	2.4 (32.3)	1.2 (16.5)	2.8 (37.6)	0.5 (6.8)	0.8 (11.3)
South Africa	4.4 (51.1)	3.3 (38.4)	2.6 (69.1)	2.9 (35.5)	5.6 (65.2)	2.2 (25.8)	0.8 (9.4)
Turkey	1.0 (24.0)	0.6 (14.7)	0.7 (17.7)	1.5 (37.5)	2.7 (67.7)	0.7 (17.7)	0.7 (17.7)
Uruguay	9.5 (54.2)	9.4 (53.1)	3.9 (22.2)	6.6 (37.5)	12.9 (74.0)	4.3 (24.3)	3.4 (19.1)
Innovation-driven							
Belgium	4.7 (32.3)	3.0 (20.5)	4.4 (30.3)	2.0 (13.9)	7.7 (53.3)	4.0 (27.4)	1.1 (7.3)
Denmark	3.4 (22.1)	3.4 (22.1)	4.3 (27.4)	2.0 (13.5)	5.0 (33.3)	1.6 (10.9)	1.5 (9.9)
Finland	10.8 (30.6)	5.7 (16.2)	7.7 (21.6)	3.8 (10.9)	30.5 (86.4)	8.0 (22.6)	4.8 (12.8)
France	2.1 (17.2)	5.5 (45.3)	4.8 (39.3)	1.8 (15.2)	8.2 (67.2)	4.0 (33.0)	2.5 (20.3)
Germany	1.8 (13.9)	7.5 (57.2)	4.2 (32.5)	4.7 (35.7)	10.2 (78.5)	3.2 (24.2)	0.8 (6.1)
Greece	1.3 (12.1)	4.2 (38.1)	2.6 (23.7)	2.1 (19.2)	7.9 (72.4)	1.1 (9.8)	1.8 (16.7)
Iceland	4.4 (25.7)	2.6 (15.2)	2.8 (16.4)	4.5 (26.2)	14.2 (82.5)	4.2 (24.5)	7.8 (44.6)
Ireland	6.9 (40.5)	4.6 (26.7)	6.5 (38.1)	5.0 (29.3)	13.7 (80.5)	1.0 (5.8)	1.5 (8.8)
Israel	3.3 (41.0)	3.4 (41.4)	3.1 (35.9)	2.7 (33.1)	5.8 (71.7)	1.5 (17.9)	0.8 (10.3)
Italy	5.2 (22.2)	7.1 (32.3)	2.4 (7.2)	6.3 (26.8)	29.3 (80.1)	1.8 (8.6)	1.8 (15.0)
Japan	8.7 (60.7)	2.7 (18.8)	1.8 (12.6)	4.6 (31.9)	12.1 (84.4)	2.4 (16.7)	3.7 (25.6)
Korea (South)	3.9 (44.1)	2.7 (30.1)	1.4 (15.8)	1.6 (18.2)	4.4 (49.4)	1.0 (11.4)	1.4 (12.4)
Slovenia	9.2 (45.5)	6.4 (31.7)	5.2 (25.8)	6.3 (31.0)	15.5 (76.8)	3.5 (17.9)	10.8 (51.2)
Spain	8.0 (56.4)	6.2 (43.8)	5.6 (39.5)	4.8 (33.7)	10.0 (70.2)	7.2 (50.6)	5.7 (39.4)
United Kingdom	4.5 (36.6)	3.2 (26.3)	3.1 (25.5)	3.0 (24.8)	9.6 (78.3)	0.6 (5.1)	1.2 (9.5)

Note: Percentages shown are for the adult population and, in parentheses, as a percentage of those receiving any informal training.

Source: GEM Adult Population Survey 2008.

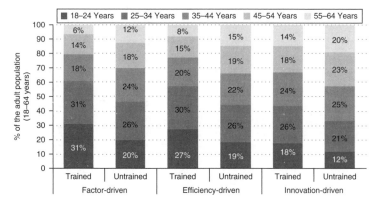

Source: GEM Adult Population Survey 2008.

Figure 2.12   Age distribution of those who have and have not received start-up training, by economic group

2.4.3   Demographics of Trained Individuals

In this section, we describe the individuals who have and have not received training in starting a business, comparing them in terms of age, gender, education and income across economic groups.

Figure 2.12 compares the age profiles of trained and untrained individuals in each of the three economic groups. Unsurprisingly, populations age as countries develop; with better health care and education, people live longer. However, there are differences between the age profiles of trained and untrained individuals in all three economic groups. Trained individuals are more likely to be found in the two younger age bands (18–24 and 25–34) and less likely to be in the three older age bands. This suggests that training in starting a business may have increased in recent decades and, in particular, provision for younger people may have increased, possibly through the formal education system.

Figure 2.13 shows that trained individuals are more likely to be men than women, and untrained individuals are more likely to be women than men in all three economic groups. This is not surprising since in many countries, women have lower entrepreneurial intentions and activity than men, and so they are less likely to seek training voluntarily. While similar proportions of men and women had taken voluntary training in some countries, only in Latvia and Hungary are women significantly more likely than men to have volunteered for training. The proportion of men and women who have taken compulsory training also varied widely by

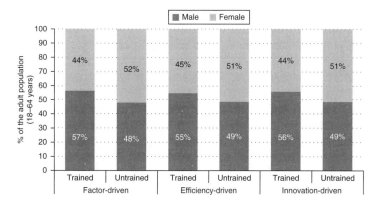

Source: GEM Adult Population Survey 2008.

Figure 2.13 Gender distribution of those who have and have not received start-up training by economic group

country. However, on average in factor-driven countries, for every ten men with compulsory training there were seven women, compared with eight in efficiency-driven countries and nine in efficiency-driven countries. Because voluntary training was more prevalent than compulsory training, the gender difference in training prevalence is mainly due to lower rates of voluntary training among women, and this did not appear to vary with increasing economic development (in all three economic groups, for every ten men who had volunteered for training, there were eight women).

Figure 2.14 shows that individuals with at least some post-secondary school education are more likely to have received training in starting a business. In most countries, this is true for voluntary and compulsory training. Such individuals have spent more time in the formal education system, so they are more likely to have had more training opportunities. However, this group tends to be more entrepreneurial anyway, and so they may have been more likely to both see a need to learn about starting a business and be more likely to see value in such training.

Figure 2.15 shows that the profile of untrained individuals is poorer than the profile of trained individuals. This association is stronger in factor-driven or efficiency-driven countries than in innovation-driven countries. In addition to the obvious reason: training may help make individuals wealthier, individuals from wealthy households may have more opportunity to engage in training – wealthier households can afford to educate their children for longer periods. Furthermore, poorer individuals may not have the time or money to devote to training.

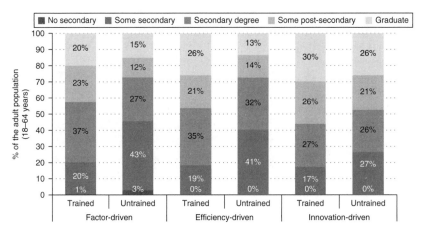

Source: GEM Adult Population Survey 2008.

*Figure 2.14   Education distribution of those who have and have not
received start-up training by economic group*

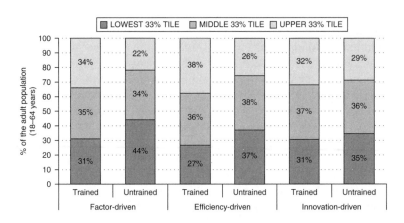

Source: GEM Adult Population Survey 2008.

*Figure 2.15   Income distribution of those who have and have not received
start-up training by economic group*

2.5 THE RELATIONSHIP BETWEEN TRAINING IN STARTING A BUSINESS AND ENTREPRENEURSHIP

2.5.1 Issues in Measuring the Effect of Training on Entrepreneurial Behavior

This section considers the relationship between training and entrepreneurial awareness, attitudes, intention and activity. Previous sections have reported on the frequency and nature of entrepreneurship education and training across economies and economic groupings. We have also revealed the sources of training, and demographic information about those trained. We now address the question posed in section 2.2.3: does entrepreneurship education and training make a difference?

Our literature review in section 2.2.3 indicates a lack of evidence demonstrating the influence of training on entrepreneurial activity.[36] There is some evidence, however, that entrepreneurship education and training may enhance skills[39 40 41] and attitudes[4 14 45 46] towards entrepreneurship. We concluded that there was a need to explore the relationships between this training and awareness, attitudes, intention and activity across multiple countries, using large, representative samples in each.

Many research studies on entrepreneurship training have had difficulty assembling adequate control groups to demonstrate effects, due to cost and data protection issues.[39] GEM conducts random samples of the entire working age population in a wide range of countries. By asking random samples of the population questions about their awareness, attitudes, intention and activity, and then, later in the interview, asking them questions about any training in starting a business they may have had, many sampling biases are avoided and natural control groups are created.

It is natural to assume that those who want to start businesses would seek out information on how to do this. They might therefore seek training as part of this search. If one were to compare these people with those who did not take training, observed differences in awareness in attitudes, intention or activity might not just be due to their training, but also their prior orientation. For example, business school students tend to self-select into this type of education and, most often, into entrepreneurship training once they are at business school. Because we asked individuals whether their training was voluntary or compulsory, or both, we can isolate those who had voluntary training, and remove them from analyses of cause and effect, eliminating self-selection bias to a considerable degree.

By noting all the training a representative sample of individuals have received in their lives so far, and analyzing a broad array of outcomes,

GEM data addresses the issues of timing that have hampered progress in research on the effect of entrepreneurship education and training. People may receive entrepreneurship education and training at various times in their lives, such as at school, university, or beyond their formal education. In addition, the effects may be deferred rather than instantaneous. For example, in the short term, graduates of entrepreneurship education may recognize the need to amass specific knowledge[53] yet decide to defer action until they understand their chosen industry better. The GEM data also accounts for differences in how individuals learn. This learning can range from traditional education to experiential immersion in the phenomenon: through a placement or internship in an actual company, for example. We surveyed individuals about the full range of possible training sources, from primary school onwards, which enables us to include all combinations of training. In addition, by measuring demographic characteristics of each individual in each sample, we can control for age group, gender, education, working status and other effects that might mask the training effect.

Finally, GEM can address limitations due to differences in context. In some countries, entrepreneurship is widespread, easily observable, and culturally acceptable. In others, few individuals start businesses; any training that exists in these countries may provide a more significant source of learning. By surveying many countries, we can spot differences in cause and effect that might be a result of context.

This combination of advantages in the GEM methodology provides a unique opportunity to make a baseline contribution to our knowledge of the impact of entrepreneurship training. In addition, it can reveal opportunities for more focused follow on research.

2.5.2   Training in Starting a Business and Involvement in Entrepreneurial Activity

The GEM APS survey assesses the proportion of working age individuals in an economy that are in the process of starting a business (nascent entrepreneurs), or are owners of new businesses (not older than 42 months old). This is the basic GEM measure of early-stage entrepreneurial activity (TEA). As Figure 2.16 illustrates, across the 38 countries, entrepreneurs are more likely to have received training in starting a business (33 percent) than the rest of the working age population (20 percent). This difference is statistically significant,[54] and suggests that current early-stage entrepreneurial activity is associated, at least to some degree, with past training in starting a business.

Table 2.4 compares the proportion of the whole working age

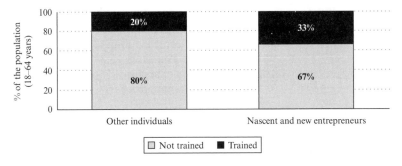

Source: GEM Adult Population Survey 2008.

Figure 2.16   *The relationship between training in starting a business and early-stage entrepreneurial activity*

population and the proportion of early-stage entrepreneurs who have received training in each nation, in three economic groups, ordered by relative frequency of training. Training prevalence varies widely across countries but the proportion of trained individuals and trained early-stage entrepreneurs is higher on average in innovation-driven countries. Around one fifth of working age individuals in factor-driven and efficiency-driven countries are trained; this rises to around one third of early-stage entrepreneurs. This compares with around one quarter of working age individuals and two fifths of early-stage entrepreneurs in innovation-driven countries.

The third column in Table 2.4, reproduced in graphical form in Figure 2.17, shows that in both factor-driven and efficiency-driven countries, as the proportion of trained individuals in a population increases, the proportion of trained entrepreneurs to trained individuals increases but at a declining rate. In other words, in countries with a low rate of training, the conversion of trained individuals to entrepreneurs appears to be higher than in countries with a high rate of training. This suggests that there may be diminishing returns to training in terms of conversion to entrepreneurial activity as training becomes widespread in these populations.

A different pattern is seen in innovation-driven countries, where the ratio increases as training becomes widespread, and then levels off, and declines only when over a fifth of the working age population have been trained. This suggests that increasing the quantity of training may generate increasing returns to entrepreneurial activity in innovation-led countries, up to a point. This pattern seems to fit the GEM model, which suggests that improving the entrepreneurship education and training EFC would be most effective in innovation-driven countries.

Table 2.4   Prevalence of training in starting a business in the working-age and early-stage entrepreneurial population

Country	Trained individuals aged 18–64 (%)	Trained nascent and new entrepreneurs (%)	Ratio of trained entrepreneurs to trained individuals
Factor-driven			
Egypt	7.6	14.0	1.8
India	13.4	23.0	1.7
Bolivia	19.1	30.8	1.6
Bosnia and Herzegovina	20.0	31.4	1.6
Ecuador	27.2	39.4	1.4
Colombia	40.1	53.5	1.3
Group average	21.2	32.0	1.5
Efficiency-driven			
Turkey	6.3	15.1	2.4
Dominican Republic	7.7	15.8	2.1
Romania	8.7	16.1	1.9
Brazil	9.4	20.4	2.2
Serbia	10.2	20.8	2.0
South Africa	13.9	22.7	1.6
Mexico	16.2	24.8	1.5
Argentina	17.5	29.0	1.7
Macedonia	19.1	36.2	1.9
Jamaica	21.0	37.4	1.8
Uruguay	24.1	40.2	1.7
Hungary	24.5	40.7	1.7
Croatia	28.1	42.3	1.5
Latvia	28.3	42.4	1.5
Iran	29.1	50.4	1.7
Peru	29.6	55.0	1.9
Chile	42.6	61.1	1.4
Group average	19.8	33.6	1.7
Innovation-driven			
Israel	12.8	17.5	1.4
Republic of Korea	13.6	21.8	1.6
Italy	16.5	28.1	1.7
Greece	17.0	30.3	1.8
Japan	17.4	31.3	1.8
France	18.1	35.0	1.9
United Kingdom	18.4	37.8	2.1
Germany	21.1	41.2	2.0
Spain	22.0	44.3	2.0

Table 2.4 (continued)

Country	Trained individuals aged 18–64 (%)	Trained nascent and new entrepreneurs (%)	Ratio of trained entrepreneurs to trained individuals
Denmark	22.6	45.0	2.0
Ireland	26.1	46.6	1.8
Iceland	26.8	51.7	1.9
Belgium	33.6	55.4	1.6
Slovenia	35.8	58.2	1.6
Finland	48.6	69.6	1.4
Group average	23.4	40.9	1.7

Source: GEM Adult Population Survey 2008.

2.5.3 Gain from Training: GEM's Core Measure of the Effect of Training in Starting a Business

The core measure of effect used in analyzing the GEM training data is "gain from training".[55] The gain from training is a numerical measure that estimates effect, while controlling for all the issues noted in section 2.5.1 that have hampered previous studies in this area. In order to address the self-selection problem, we compare the effect of having had compulsory training versus not having had any training on entrepreneurial awareness, attitudes (such as skills or opportunity perception or fear of failure), intention to start a business and early-stage entrepreneurial activity, controlling for the demographic background of an individual. Large random samples of the working age population provide natural controls.

Gain from training is a country-based measure that can be interpreted at a group or individual level. First, it can be thought of as the increase in the proportion of people in the country who have a characteristic, such as a particular attitude, because of compulsory training (but not voluntary training) in starting a business, controlling for demographic differences (age group, gender, education, working status). Thus, a gain of two would mean that if we were to take two samples of people, differing only in that one group had just compulsory training in starting a business and the other did not, we would find that twice as many people in the compulsory training group have this attitude compared to people in the other group.

Second, it can be thought of as the increase in the odds that an individual with a given set of demographic characteristics will have a particular entrepreneurial orientation if they had ever taken compulsory training

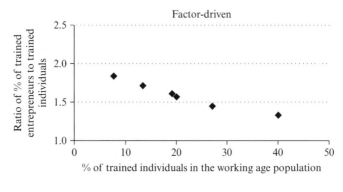

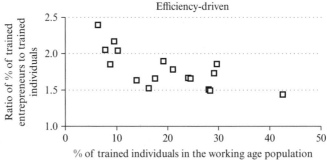

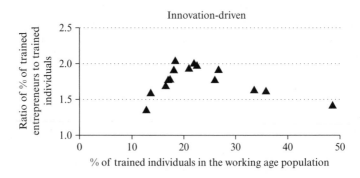

Source: GEM Adult Population Survey 2008.

Figure 2.17   Ratio of percentage of trained entrepreneurs to trained individuals in the working age population for each country, arranged by economic group and order of increasing percentage of trained individuals (but not voluntary training) versus an individual with identical demographic characteristics but with no such training. As an example, a gain of two would indicate that an individual's chances of having a particular orientation are doubled if they have taken compulsory training.

Table 2.5 reports the gain to training in TEA rates for each country for which sufficient data were available.[56] The estimates of gain are for raising awareness of new business entrepreneurs, improving three different entrepreneurial attitudes (opportunity perception, start-up skills self-perception, and fear of failure), increasing intent to start a business within the next three years, and increasing early-stage entrepreneurial activity. For each country, we report the gain from training and level of significance (none, low, moderate, high).

Because compulsory training is relatively rare in many countries, it is possible that non-significant results are due to the small size of the sample. Therefore, we provide figures that display economic group averages (Figures 2.18 and 2.19) and geographical global region (Figures 2.20 and 2.21). For each country group we report the average gain (Figures 2.18 and 2.20) and percentage of countries in which the significance level of the gain from training is at least moderate (p < .05) (Figures 2.19 and 2.21). This enables the reader to make their own judgment about the general effect of training in different parts of the world.

A number of trends are evident in this data. Among factor-driven countries, the effects of training on awareness and attitudes are muted. This is perhaps not surprising since in these countries, activity rates are typically high, with many people struggling to make a living for themselves. Thus starting a business, often born of necessity rather than opportunity, is normal and commonplace. Training appears to double intention rates but not activity rates in factor-driven countries. Again, this makes sense if one considers that the conditions for starting a business may be less than ideal in factor-driven countries. According to the GEM national expert survey, the average combined rating on the overall environment for entrepreneurship, based on a 1 to 5 point scale, was lowest for factor-driven countries (2.6), compared to 2.8 for efficiency-driven countries and 3.0 for innovation-driven countries.[57] Moving from intentions to actual starting businesses may therefore represent a greater challenge in factor-driven countries.

The efficiency-driven countries display a different overall pattern. At this level of economic development, training significantly increases awareness and skills self-perception. In these countries, TEA rates tend to be lower than in factor-driven countries, and training may increase awareness and self-perception of skills among those who have not previously considered this economic phenomenon. Figure 2.19 shows that only 40 percent

Table 2.5   *Gain to training in early-stage entrepreneurial activity (TEA) for 38 countries, by country and economic group, in order of increasing gain to training in activity*

Factor-driven countries	Gain in TEA rate from training	Efficiency-driven countries	Gain in TEA rate from training	Innovation-driven countries	Gain in TEA rate from training
Ecuador	1.0	Iran	0.8	Spain	1.1
Bolivia	1.2	Jamaica	0.8	Denmark	1.2
India	1.3	Latvia	1.2	Korea	1.3
Colombia	1.5	Peru	1.3	Republic	
Egypt	1.6	Macedonia	1.3	Slovenia	1.4
Bosnia and	2.5*	Chile	1.5	Finland	1.5
Herzegovina		Mexico	1.5*	Greece	1.8**
		Hungary	1.5**	Ireland	1.9**
		Dominican	1.6	Japan	2.1*
		Republic		Italy	2.3**
		Croatia	1.7*	Iceland	2.3***
		Uruguay	1.7**	United	2.4***
		Brazil	2.1**	Kingdom	
		Serbia	2.1**	Belgium	2.6***
		South	2.6***	Germany	2.8***
		Africa		Israel	3.0***
		Romania	3.3*	France	4.3***
		Turkey	3.3***		
Average gain	1.5	**Average gain**	1.8	**Average gain**	2.1
Countries with significant gain at 5% level (%)	0 percent	**Countries with significant gain at 5% level (%)**	38 percent	**Countries with significant gain at 5% level (%)**	60%

Note: Key to statistical significance levels: * low (p<.1); ** medium (p<.05); *** high (p<.01).

Source: GEM Adult Population Survey 2008.

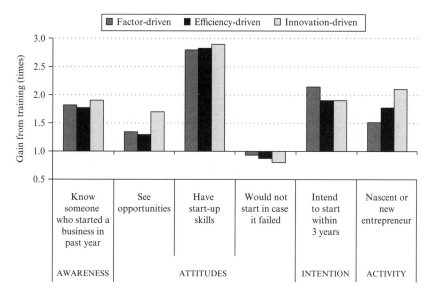

Source: GEM Adult Population Survey 2008.

Figure 2.18 *Gain to training in entrepreneurial awareness, attitudes, intention and activity for 38 countries, by economic group*

of these countries saw significant increases in intention, with a similar percentage increasing activity significantly. In both cases, the average gain was a doubling of either intention or activity rates for trained individuals.

Among innovation-driven countries, TEA rates are around half that of efficiency-driven countries, but the proportion of opportunity-to-necessity entrepreneurship is triple that of the other two groups of countries. As Figure 2.19 shows, 70 percent of these countries exhibit significant gains in awareness among trained individuals, and 40 percent show gains in opportunity perception. Skills perception was significantly higher among trained individuals in all innovation-based countries, with an average tripling in the prevalence of skills perception. Two thirds of countries registered significant increases in intention rates, and 60 percent of the countries saw significant increases in TEA rates, with an average two times gain for both.

Across all countries, training did not seem to affect fear of failure, except in Hungary, Slovenia and Greece, where fear of failure decreased by between 60 and 80 percent among those who had taken compulsory training. On average, training appears to triple the level of skills perception across the entire dataset, although small proportions of compulsory training in some poorer countries may have resulted in lack of significance

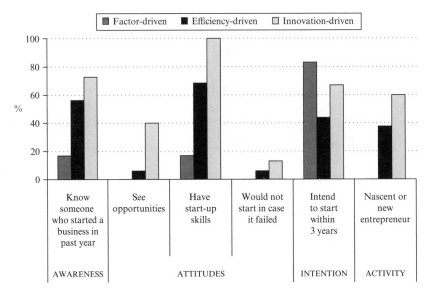

Source: GEM Adult Population Survey 2008.

*Figure 2.19   Proportion of countries in each economic group in which
             the gain from training is statistically significant, by type of
             entrepreneurial orientation*

on this measure. Start-up intention rates appear to double across all
countries on average, but gain from training in early-stage entrepreneurial
activity increases from factor-driven to efficiency-driven to innovation-
driven countries. This may be a result of increasingly favorable institutional settings for entrepreneurship in richer countries. In other words,
weaknesses in the environment for entrepreneurship or the lack of trigger-
ing conditions[58] may prevent intention from translating into action.

Figure 2.20 summarizes the average gains from training at the regional
level for four blocks of countries with natural contextual affinities. Only
six sample countries out of the 38 were not included in these blocks: Egypt,
South Africa, India, Iran, Israel and Turkey. Figure 2.21 shows the percentage of countries in each block in which the gain from training was significant, for each type of entrepreneurial behavior. The patterns in Figures
2.20 and 2.21 support the proposition that institutional weaknesses may
prevent a gain in intent leading to a gain in activity. Differences between
Eastern and Western Europe illustrate this point, where, despite significant gains in awareness and skills perception in most Eastern European
countries, a gap remains between intention and activity. There is no such

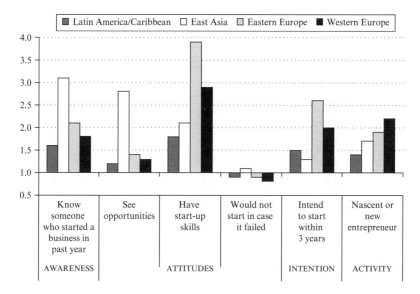

Key: Latin America/Caribbean　East Asia　Eastern Europe　Western Europe

Source: GEM Adult Population Survey 2008.

Figure 2.20　Gain to training in entrepreneurial awareness, attitudes, intention and activity for 32 countries, by global region

gap in Western Europe, however. A general measure of the environment for entrepreneurship from the NES survey shows a higher average score for Western Europe (3.0 on a scale of 1 to 5),[59] compared with 2.8 for Eastern Europe and 2.7 for Latin American and Caribbean countries. In Korea and Japan, institutional barriers, as well as cultural perceptions, may also prevent the gains in awareness and attitudes from translating into intention and action.

Finally, training in Latin America and the Caribbean appears, on average, to have little or no effect. However, this is against a backdrop of high TEA rates generally, and a less favorable institutional environment. In 2008, the average TEA rate in these countries was 18 percent, compared with 8 percent in Eastern Europe and 6 percent in Western Europe.[60]

In conclusion, the GEM 2008 data conclusively points to a gain from training which varies by context. Training is most effective in contexts with favorable institutional environments, where the training-induced positive skills perceptions and intentions can be translated into action. Training appears to be particularly effective in Western European countries with low rates of early-stage entrepreneurial activity, such as Belgium, France, Germany and the United Kingdom.

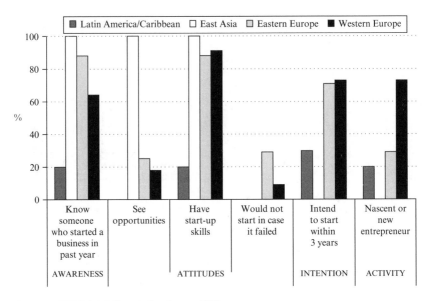

Source: GEM Adult Population Survey 2008.

Figure 2.21   Proportion of countries in each global region in which the gain from training is statistically significant, by type of entrepreneurial orientation

2.6   THE USE OF ADVISORS BY ENTREPRENEURS

2.6.1   Types of Advisors

Advice from other people is a source of learning that complements, and sometimes substitutes for, the formal and informal programs of entrepreneurship training discussed in previous chapters. In 2008, five GEM national teams cooperated to conduct a study of the types of people that entrepreneurs go to for advice. This section reveals the range of advisors entrepreneurs can call on. It shows how this can differ across countries and between entrepreneurs who have, and have not had, training in starting a business. The five surveyed countries – Brazil, Denmark, Iran, and Korea, and Latvia – represent a great diversity of cultures and continents. In this study, individuals identified as nascent entrepreneurs and business owner-managers were asked if they had received advice from any of a comprehensive set of 22 different types of advisor.[61] For analysis, we grouped these advisors into five spheres of influence:

- the private sphere of family and friends, who are likely to give support or discouragement;
- the job sphere of managers and work-colleagues, who may serve as sounding boards;
- the experience sphere of experienced entrepreneurs, business people, and people with expertise, who may convey tacit knowledge;
- the professional sphere such as bankers, lawyers, accountants, who offer codified knowledge; and
- the market sphere of competitors, collaborators, suppliers and customers who may provide knowledge about the market.

These five spheres were identified in previous studies of entrepreneurs and their networks. An entrepreneur's advisory network is the set of all the different advisors they had received advice from for their new business (for nascent entrepreneurs) or the set of all the advisors they had received advice from in the past year (for owner-managers of businesses that were up and running).

For this study, 1993 networks of advisors of start-up entrepreneurs and owner-managers were analyzed in terms of the types of advisor in each network (554 in Iran, 529 in Brazil, 192 in Latvia, 467 in Korea and 251 in Denmark). Of the entrepreneurs reporting these networks, 25 percent had received training in starting a business (42 percent of the Iranians, 14 percent of the Brazilians, 14 percent of the Koreans, and 29 percent of the Danes).

Table 2.6 shows the frequency of use of different advisor types in each of the five spheres of influence for each country. The countries are ordered according to their communal values as measured by the World Values Survey, from traditional to secular-rational.[62] This seems appropriate since our interest is in how individuals interact with other people.

Patterns are apparent in the frequency of use of different advisor types. For example, in the private sphere, friends were employed as advisors more often than family members in all five countries. Use of parents and other family was more frequent in Iran and Brazil than in Korea and Denmark, with Latvia occupying an intermediate position. This may reflect differences in the degree to which parental authority and family connections matter in these countries.[63] In the job sphere, entrepreneurs tend to have used work colleagues rather than managers as sources of advice. This is not surprising; employees who are planning to leave to start their own businesses may be reluctant to confide in their managers. In the experience sphere, over half of Danish entrepreneurs used mentors and experts, compared with less than 40 percent of Latvians and Koreans, less than a third of Iranians and Koreans, and less than a quarter of Brazilians.

Table 2.6   Percentage of advisor type networks which include a particular advisor type

		Iran	Brazil	Latvia	Korea	Denmark
Private	Spouse	31	42	37	22	44
	Parent	45	33	31	15	18
	Other family	43	47	36	25	20
	Friends	43	51	53	33	50
Job	Current work colleagues	22	24	29	23	48
	Earlier work colleagues	16	15	20	18	31
	Current manager	8	5	10	10	26
	Earlier manager	5	7	6	12	17
	Somebody abroad	3	4	17	5	23
Experience	Someone starting a business	17	11	33	13	25
	Mentor	32	22	36	37	53
	Expert	29	23	25	39	58
	Investor	7	8	18	9	16
Professional	Researcher	7	4	13	6	14
	Banker	5	6	16	6	29
	Lawyer	4	5	24	3	23
	Accountant	5	12	27	9	49
	Advisor	4	7	13	7	18
Market	Collaborator	8	8	23	14	36
	Competitor	4	3	11	9	18
	Supplier	14	20	20	18	33
	Customer	20	28	28	24	40

Source: GEM Adult Population Survey 2008.

Danes were also significantly more likely to use professional and market-based advisors than entrepreneurs from the other countries.

Table 2.7 shows that Danish entrepreneurs tended to have almost twice as many types of advisors as entrepreneurs in the three other countries, with an average of seven types of advisor, while Latvian entrepreneurs had six and Brazilian, Iranian and Korean entrepreneurs less than four.

The relative frequency of use of different advisor types and the prominence of different spheres also varies by country. The prominence of a sphere in a country was measured by calculating the relative frequency of use of advisors types in the sphere (for a network, the average number of advisor types used in the sphere as a percentage of the number of advisor types in the sphere) and dividing this by the number of advisor types, and then averaging across the networks in the country. The prominence

Table 2.7   Summary statistics on advisor types used by entrepreneurs in Iran, Brazil, Latvia, Korea and Denmark

	Iran	Brazil	Latvia	Korea	Denmark
Mean number of advisor types	3.8	3.9	5.6	3.6	6.9
Prominence of advisor types in private sphere	13.2	12.2	9.1	7.0	4.5
Prominence of advisor types in job sphere	1.9	1.7	2.3	2.6	3.6
Prominence of advisor types in experience sphere	3.5	2.3	3.3	5.3	5.1
Prominence of advisor types in professional sphere	0.4	0.8	2.1	1.0	4.1
Prominence of advisor types in market sphere	1.6	2.5	2.2	2.9	3.9
Number of advisor type networks	554	529	192	467	251

Note: Prominence of a sphere is calculated as the relative frequency of use of advisor types in the sphere (for a network, the average number of advisor types used in the sphere as a percentage of the number of advisor types in the sphere) and dividing this by the number of advisor types, and then averaging across the networks in the country.

Source: GEM Adult Population Survey 2008.

of the private sphere declines from left to right in Table 2.7. In fact, this measure correlates highly and negatively with communal values across the five countries ($r = -0.94$). The private sphere is the most prominent sphere in every country except Denmark, where it takes second place behind the experience sphere. While none of the public spheres correlate quite as strongly with communal values as the private sphere, they all correlate positively ($r = 0.69$ to 0.81). This is consistent with lower authority of the family and higher instrumentality of personal relationships in countries that have more secular-rational communal values.

2.6.2   Use of Advisors by Trained and Untrained Entrepreneurs

Table 2.8 compares the use of advisors in different spheres by entrepreneurs who have and have not had training in starting a business. It suggests that, with the exception of Iran, trained entrepreneurs have more advisor types in each sphere than untrained entrepreneurs.[64] Table 2.9 summarizes these data and confirms that there was no overall difference in the number of advisor types selected by trained and untrained entrepreneurs in Iran. In contrast, relative to untrained entrepreneurs, trained entrepreneurs in

Table 2.8 *Average number of advisor types per sphere of influence identified by entrepreneurs who have and have not had training in starting a business, by country*

		Iran	Brazil	Latvia	Korea	Denmark
Private sphere	Trained	1.6	2.1	1.8	1.3	1.7
	Untrained	1.6	1.7	1.3	0.9	1.2
Job sphere	Trained	0.5	1.1	1.1	1.0	1.7
	Untrained	0.6	0.5	0.6	0.6	1.4
Experience sphere	Trained	0.9	1.4	1.6	1.4	1.8
	Untrained	0.8	0.5	0.6	0.9	1.4
Professional sphere	Trained	0.2	0.9	1.2	0.6	1.6
	Untrained	0.3	0.2	0.6	0.3	1.2
Market sphere	Trained	0.4	1.1	1.1	1.1	1.6
	Untrained	0.5	0.5	0.5	0.6	1.1
Number of advisor type networks	Trained	234	76	100	64	73
	Untrained	319	453	92	403	178

Source: GEM Adult Population Survey 2008.

Table 2.9 *Average number of advisor types identified by entrepreneurs who have and have not had training in starting a business, by country*

		Iran	Brazil	Latvia	Korea	Denmark
Trained entrepreneurs		3.7	6.6	7.4	5.4	8.3
Untrained entrepreneurs		3.9	3.4	3.8	3.3	6.3
Number of advisor type networks	Trained	234	76	100	64	73
	Untrained	319	453	92	403	178

Source: GEM Adult Population Survey 2008.

Brazil and Latvia had double the number of advisor types, while they have two-thirds more advisor types in Korea and Denmark.

One would expect that trained entrepreneurs have a wider variety of advisor types in each sphere because of the training they received, or if they undertook training voluntarily, due to the demonstrated desire of these entrepreneurs to seek external help. This does not appear to be so in Iran, and further research is needed to understand this result.

To test if training is associated with an increased variety of advisors entrepreneurs choose to take, we compared the variety of advisor types used by untrained entrepreneurs with the variety of advisor types chosen by entrepreneurs who had only undergone compulsory training. As we showed in section 2.4.3, entrepreneurs with higher levels of education are more likely to have had training than those with lower levels of education.[65] For this reason, we controlled for level of education in a multivariate test,[66] along with gender, age, type of entrepreneur (whether nascent entrepreneur or the owner/manager of an existing business) and country. The associations between variety of advisor types and both education and training are statistically significant and substantial. This suggests that entrepreneurs who have taken training have, on average, a wider variety of advisor types when education, gender, age, stage of the business and country are controlled for.

Taken together with the results from previous sections, these results suggest that education, training and getting advice from others are three sources of learning which appear to reinforce one another. In most countries, the more education an individual receives, the more likely he or she is to have taken training. In addition, the more education and training an entrepreneur receives, the wider the variety of advisors in his or her network.

2.7   CONCLUSIONS AND IMPLICATIONS FOR POLICY

2.7.1   Conclusions

This report represents an early effort to provide a global perspective on the prevalence, sources, and effect of entrepreneurship training in national populations. The GEM research has long reported, through its National Expert Surveys, that entrepreneurship training is lacking in many countries across the world. This fueled interest in including this topic in the GEM Adult Population Survey for 2008. Additionally, although there is considerable literature on entrepreneurship education and training, much of it takes a supply-side perspective, focusing on the evaluation or review of programs offered. We believe our efforts provide useful information about who has received training, from what sources, and whether past training is associated with current entrepreneurial perspectives and actions. We summarize our key findings below:

- Entrepreneurship experts in 31 participating countries consistently evaluated entrepreneurship education and training at primary and secondary school level as the weakest of the entrepreneurship framework conditions in their countries.

- Across the 38 countries in which training in starting a business was measured, 21 percent of the adult population has received training. There is a large variation at the country level ranging in most cases from 10–30 percent, but this variation seems to be unrelated to average wealth and stage of economic development of the country.
- Voluntary training is more common than compulsory training. Two thirds of those who have received training have done so voluntarily. Only one third have received compulsory training.
- A majority of those who have received training, around 80 percent, have done so during their formal education. However, many of those receiving formal training also sought training through informal sources.
- People who have received training are most likely to be 35–54 years of age and have at least completed secondary school, and more likely to be a man than a woman. Trained individuals in innovation-driven economies are more likely to be older and to have attained a higher education level compared to the other two groups, but these differences reflect general demographic differences between these economic groups.
- Training is likely to increase awareness of entrepreneurship, increase self-efficacy, and heighten intentions. However, it has less influence on opportunity identification and fear of failure.
- Gain from training in terms of increased activity is greater in more developed economies, i.e. if basic requirements, efficiency enhancers, and other entrepreneurial framework conditions are present. In factor- and efficiency-based economies, increasing training coverage appears to generate diminishing returns, while in innovation-driven countries, it appears to generate increasing returns up to a point where around a fifth of the population have received training.
- Entrepreneurs who have received training in starting a business tap into a wider variety of advisors to help them start or run their businesses. The nature of advisors varies with the culture of a country. Entrepreneurs in more traditional countries tend to rely more on family and friends, whereas entrepreneurs in more secular-rational countries tend to choose other types of advisors.

2.7.2   Implications for Policy, Educators and Practice

Based on our conclusions, we suggest a number of implications for policy-makers, educators, and entrepreneurs:

- Policymakers in innovation-driven economies may consider entre-preneurship training to be an efficient mechanism for increasing entrepreneurial activity, especially where the existing level of trained individuals in the working age population is below around 20 percent. In factor-driven or efficiency-driven countries, however, our data does not suggest that increased investment in entrepreneur-ship training would generate similar returns. However, this may be due to identifiable bottlenecks in the provision of basic require-ments, efficiency-enhancers, or other entrepreneurial framework conditions. It may simply be the case that providing training will not have a major impact until there is adequate infrastructure, economic stability, market and technological readiness, or other conditions. Therefore, the wider economic and social context should be taken into account in developing entrepreneurship education and training policy in factor- and efficiency-driven countries.

- An alternative reason for the lack of association between training and increased activity revealed in our analysis of factor-driven and efficiency-driven economies may be poor-quality training. This has several implications for policy makers and educators. First, policy-makers or educators could determine the particular training needs of entrepreneurs in a particular economy, and then evaluate the adequacy of training programs in meeting these needs. Second, training programs could be evaluated within and across countries; this may be helpful in identifying the strengths and weaknesses of different training programs, as well as enabling people from differ-ent programs and countries to share ideas for effective training.

- Our results indicate that individuals tend to get training in starting a business as part of their formal education. This shows how impor-tant schools, colleges and universities are in providing a foundation for entrepreneurship. Given the emphasis on providing this training as early as possible (expressed in Chapter 1), and the views of GEM national experts, educators in primary and secondary school levels could be encouraged to build effective training programs into their curriculum. This may be particularly critical in countries where most of the population is less likely to pursue education beyond primary and secondary schooling. Experiential learning techniques and teaching a wide variety of students, not just those oriented toward business topics, may increase the reach and effectiveness of these programs. Program objectives should fit the country context. For example, in countries where non-school training opportunities are scarce, the objective may be to develop the skills and motivation for entrepreneurship. In countries where entrepreneurial activity is limited but non-school training is widely available, programs that enhance awareness and attitudes might be more appropriate.

- Our finding that formal and informal training overlap implies that formal training may provide a foundation, but many people may also need specific knowledge and skills, perhaps when they become interested in starting a business or have taken steps to do so. Cost effective, convenient training sources, such as self-study and web-based programs, are one way of meeting such needs and they are becoming more widely available. Entrepreneurs could consider accessing these sources – or, indeed, supplying them.

Our results show that entrepreneurship training can be a lifelong pursuit that includes a foundation built in primary and secondary schooling, and opportunities for both formal and non-formal training in the years beyond school. Entrepreneurship training at the tertiary level should not be limited to those taking business subjects. This would enable entrepreneurship to become an informed career option for everyone, that can be exercised when a combination of circumstances make this a viable alternative.

2.7.3 Suggestions for Further Research

A number of issues have surfaced in the course of our research that would be worth investigating further:

- First, our analysis suggests that entrepreneurship training may enhance self-efficacy, or start-up skills self-perception, but seems to be poor at enhancing opportunity recognition. It may be that planning-based programs are good at making people believe they know how to start a business. However, the other crucial ingredient is recognition of an attractive opportunity. Research could investigate the extent to which training programs impart skills in opportunity recognition, perhaps through experimental designs or longitudinal studies of graduates.
- Second, we know little, if anything, about "what" is taught in the entrepreneurship training programs taken by the survey respondents and "how" they are taught. Apart from a limited number of prior studies,[18] we do not know which parts of training curricula are most valued by entrepreneurs. A follow-up study could ask entrepreneurs what topics in their training provided the most valuable guidance to them in starting their businesses, and in which aspects of new business management they felt most unprepared. Related to content is delivery: what pedagogies or experiences worked best for

trainees, and did these pedagogies differ between those who did and did not become entrepreneurs? These issues could be explored using case-based research or surveys.

- Third, there is a need for further research on learning from advisors. In section 2.6, a pilot study of five countries revealed culturally bound differences in the way entrepreneurs choose advisors, but also suggested that entrepreneurs who have been trained in starting a business tap into a wider variety of advisors entrepreneurs call on for help. Much more remains to be discovered about how entrepreneurs use advisors (including the number, not just type, of advisors), and the nature and quality of advice received. Social networking methodologies may be helpful in researching this topic further.

- Fourth, further research might help explain the apparent diminishing returns to increasing rates of training in factor- and efficiency-driven countries, and increasing returns followed by diminishing returns in innovation-driven countries as coverage of training increases in a country. While this might be an artifact of our cross-sectional research design, it may also be a consequence of identifiable bottlenecks in framework conditions. These bottlenecks may be identifiable by examining patterns in GEM National Expert Survey data and other secondary sources of information on framework conditions. This research could help governments use resources more efficiently and generate more entrepreneurial activity.

- Finally, we need to conduct more analysis to find out which sources of entrepreneurship training have most effect on entrepreneurial behavior. For example, does school-based training provide a vital foundation for embedding entrepreneurial thought, or is it too early in the education cycle? Is informal training more effective than formal training? The answers to questions like these could guide policy makers and educators in understanding the training needs of the entrepreneurs they rely on to generate new wealth in their economies.

NOTES AND REFERENCES

* This report is a reprint, with appropriate changes made in references ('Chapter 1' throughout refers to this volume), of *Global Entrepreneurship Monitor Special Report: A Global Perspective on Entrepreneurship Education and Training*. Alicia Coduras Martinez is Associate Research Professor in the Department of Entrepreneurship and Family Business. Instituto de Empresa, Business School. Madrid, Spain. Jonathan Levie is Reader in the Hunter Centre for Entrepreneurship at the University of Strathclyde, Glasgow, United Kingdom. Donna Kelley is Associate Professor of Entrepreneurship

at Babson College, Rognvaldur J. Sæmundsson is Associate Professor at Reykjavik University School of Business, Iceland, and Thomas Schøtt is Associate Professor and National Team Leader, GEM Denmark, Department of Entrepreneurship and Relationship Management, University of Southern Denmark. Please direct correspondence to Donna Kelley at dkelley@babson.edu.

1. Blenker, Per, Poul Dreisler and John Kjeldsen, "A Framework for Developing Entrepreneurship Education in a University Context", *International Journal of Entrepreneurship and Small Business*, 5:1, 2008, 45–63.
2. Bosma, N., Z. Acs, E. Autio, A. Coduras, and J. Levie, *Global Entrepreneurship Monitor 2008 Executive Report*, Global Entrepreneurship Research Consortium, 2009.
3. World Economic Forum, *Educating the Next Wave of Entrepreneurs: Unlocking Entrepreneurial Capabilities to Meet the Global Challenges of the 21st Century: A Report of the Global Education Initiative*. Switzerland: World Economic Forum, 2009, 7–8. Chapter 1 above reprints the Executive Summary of the Report.
4. Hegarty, Cecilia, "It's Not an Exact Science: Teaching Entrepreneurship in Northern Ireland," *Education + Training*, 48:5, 2006, 322–335.
5. Cheung, Chi-Kim, "Entrepreneurship Education in Hong Kong's Secondary Curriculum: Possibilities and Limitations", *Education + Training*, 50:6, 2008, 500–515.
6. Levie, Jonathan, *Enterprising Education in Higher Education in England*, London: Department of Education and Employment, 1999, 40.
7. Autio, Erkko, *Entrepreneurship Teaching in the Öresund and Copenhagen Region*, Lyngby, Denmark: Technical University of Denmark, 2007.
8. Shinnar, Rachel, Mark Pruett and Bryan Toney, "Entrepreneurship Education: Attitudes Across Campus", *Journal of Education for Business*, 84:3, 2008, 151–158.
9. The GEM APS data are a random sample of the working age population in a country. See Bosma, N., Z. Acs, E. Autio, A. Coduras, J. Levie, *Global Entrepreneurship Monitor 2008, Executive Report*, Global Entrepreneurship Research Consortium, 2009.
10. The GEM NES is a selected sample of individuals who are deemed expert in at least one EFC, or aspect of the environment for entrepreneurship. GEM recognizes nine major EFCs, of which three, including entrepreneurship education and training, have two major components. In each country NES, typically at least four experts are identified per EFC, of which one is an entrepreneur, two are providers of that EFC, and one is an expert observer.
11 See www.determinedtosucceed.gov.uk.
12. Henley, Andrew, "Entrepreneurial Aspiration and Transition into Self-Employment: Evidence from British Longitudinal Data", *Entrepreneurship and Regional Development*, 19:3, 2007, 253–280.
13. European Commission, *Entrepreneurship in Higher Education, Especially Within Non-Business Studies: Final Report of the Expert Group*, Brussels, Belgium, 2008.
14. Walter, Sascha and Dirk Dohse, *The Interplay Between Entrepreneurship Education and Regional Knowledge Potential in Forming Entrepreneurial Intentions*, Kiel, Germany: Kiel Institute for the World Economy, No. 1549, 2009.
15. Tan, Siok San and Frank Ng, "A Problem-Based Learning Approach to Entrepreneurship Education", *Education + Training*, 48:6, 2006, 416–428.
16. Rasmussen, Einar and Roger Sørheim, "Action-Based Entrepreneurship Education", *Technovation*, 26:2, 2005, 185–194.
17. Raffo, Carlo, Andy Lovatt, Mark Banks and Justin O'Connor, "Teaching and Learning Entrepreneurship for Micro and Small Businesses in the Cultural Industries Sector", *Education + Training*, 42:6, 2002, 356–365.
18. For example, Sexton, Donald, Nancy Upton, Larry Wacholtz and Patricia McDougall, "Learning Needs of Growth-Oriented Entrepreneurs", *Journal of Business Venturing*, 12, 1997, 1–8.
19. Stevenson, Howard and David Gumpert, "The Heart of Entrepreneurship", *Harvard Business Review*, 63:2, 1985, 85–94.

20. Katz, Jerome, "The Chronology and Intellectual Trajectory of American Entrepreneurship Education: 1876–1999", *Journal of Business Venturing*, 18, 2003, 283–300.
21. Sorgman, Margo and Kathy Parkison, "The Future is Now: Preparing K-12 Teachers and Students for an Entrepreneurial Society", *Journal of Entrepreneurship Education*, 11, 2008, 75–86.
22. Janssen, Frank, Valerie Eeckhout and Benoit Gailly, "Interdisciplinary Approaches in Entrepreneurship Education Programs", White Paper, 2005.
23. Solomon, George, Susan Duffy and Ayman Tarabishy, "The State of Entrepreneurship Education in the United States: A Nationwide Survey and Analysis", *International Journal of Entrepreneurship Education*, 1:1, 2002, 1–22
24. Porter, Michael, Jeffrey D. Sachs and John W. McArthur, "Executive Summary: Competitiveness and Stages of Economic Development", in Porter, Michael., Jeffrey J. Sachs, Peter K. Cornelius, John W. McArthur and Klaus Schwab (eds), *The Global Competitiveness Report 2001–2002*, New York: Oxford University Press, 2002, 16–25.
25. Porter, Michael and Klaus Schwab, *The Global Competitiveness Report 2008–2009*, Geneva, Switzerland: World Economic Forum, 2008.
26. Kyro, Paula, "Entrepreneurship Education and Finnish Society", Working Papers in Economics. School of Economics and Business Administration, Tallinn University of Technology, 2006, 63–80.
27. Birley, Sue and Allan Gibb, "Teaching Small Business Management in the UK: Part 1", *Journal of European Industrial Training*, 8:4, 1984, 17–24.
28. Gibb, Allan, "Designing Effective Programmes for Encouraging the Business Start-up Process: Lessons from UK Experience", *Journal of European Industrial Training*, 11:4, 1987, 24–32.
29. Jones-Evans, Dylan, William Williams and Jonathan Deacon, "Developing Entrepreneurial Graduates: An Action-Learning Approach", *Education + Training*, 42:4/5, 2000, 282–288.
30. Klofsten, Magnus, "Training Entrepreneurship at Universities: a Swedish Case", *Journal of European Industrial Training*, 24:6, 2000, 337–344.
31. Klandt, Heinz, "Entrepreneurship Education and Research in German-Speaking Europe", *Academy of Management Learning and Education*, 3:3, 2004, 293–301.
32. Jones, Colin and Jack English, "A Contemporary Approach to Entrepreneurship Education", *Education + Training*, 46:8/9, 2004, 416–423.
33. Khan, Golum and Darwish Almoharby, "Towards Enhancing Entrepreneurship Development in Oman", *Journal of Enterprising Culture*, 15:4, 2007, 371–392.
34. Li, Jun, Yuli Zhang and Harry Matlay, "Entrepreneurship Education in China", *Education + Training*, 45:8/9, 2003, 495–505.
35. "Identifying Future Entrepreneurs: Project Tackles Issue of Unemployment by Stimulating Job Creation", *Finweek*, 20, 2007, 26–28.
36. Béchard, Jean-Pierre and Denis Grégoire. "Entrepreneurship Education Research Revisited: The Case of Higher Education", *Academy of Management Learning and Education*, 4:1, 2005, 22–43.
37. Garavan, Thomas and Barra O'Cinneide, "Entrepreneurship Education and Training Programmes: A Review and Evaluation: Part 1", *Journal of European Industrial Training*, 18:8, 1994, 3–12.
38. Hansemark, Ove, "The Effects of an Entrepreneurship Programme on Need for Achievement and Locus of Control of Reinforcement", *International Journal of Entrepreneurial Behaviour and Research*, 4:1, 1998, 28–50.
39. Summit Consulting, *Toward Effective Education of Innovative Entrepreneurs in Small Business: Initial Results from a Survey of College Students and Graduates*, Washington, DC: Small Business Administration Office of Advocacy, 2009.
40. Honig, Benson (2004), "Entrepreneurship Education: Toward a Model of Contingency-Based Business Planning", *Academy of Management Learning and Education*, 3:3, 2004, 258–273.

41. DeTienne, Dawn and Gaylen Chandler, "Opportunity Identification and its Role in the Entrepreneurial Classroom: A Pedagogical Approach and Empirical Test", *Academy of Management Learning and Education*, 3:3, 2004, 242–257.
42. Fiet, James, "The Pedagogical Side of Entrepreneurship Theory", *Journal of Business Venturing*, 16, 2000, 101–117.
43. Gatewood, Elizabeth, "The Expectancies in Public Sector Venture Assistance", *Entrepreneurship: Theory and Practice*, 17, 1993, 91–95.
44. Ibrahim, A.B. and K. Soufani, "Entrepreneurship Educaiton and Training in Canada: A Critical Assessment", *Education + Training*, 44:8/9, 2002, 421–430.
45. Souitaris, Vangelis, Stefania Zerbinati and Andreas Al-Laham, "Do Entrepreneurship Programmes Raise Entrepreneurial Intention of Science and Engineering Students? The Effect of Learning, Inspiration and Resources", *Journal of Business Venturing*, 22, 2007, 566–591.
46. Peterman, Nicole and Jessica Kennedy, "Enterprising Education: Influencing Students' Perceptions of Entrepreneurship", *Entrepreneurship: Theory and Practice*, 17, 2003, 129–144.
47. Oosterbeek, Hessel, Mirjam Van Praag and Auke Ijsselstein, "The Impact of Entrepreneurship Education on Entrepreneurship Skills and Motivation", *European Economic Review*, 2009.
48. Weber, Richard, Georg von Graevenitz and D. Harhoff, "The Effects of Entrepreneurship Education. Munich School of Management, University of Munich", Discussion Paper 2009-11, August 2009.
49. Fayolle, Alain, Benoît Gailly and Narjisse Lassas-Clerc, "Effect and Counter-effect of Entrepreneurship Education and Social Context on Students' Intentions", Estudios de Economía Aplicada, 24:2, 2006, 509–523.
50. The statements experts were asked to state their opinions on were:
    1. In my country, teaching in primary and secondary education encourages creativity, self-sufficiency, and personal initiative.
    2. In my country, teaching in primary and secondary education provides adequate instruction in market economic principles.
    3. In my country, teaching in primary and secondary education provides adequate attention to entrepreneurship and new firm creation.
    4. In my country, colleges and universities provide good and adequate preparation for starting up and growing new firms.
    5. In my country, the level of business and management education provide good and adequate preparation for starting up and growing new firms.
    6. In my country, the vocational, professional, and continuing education systems provide good and adequate preparation for starting up and growing new firms.

    In factor analysis conducted in each year since 2000, items 1, 2 and 3 have consistently loaded on to one factor with high reliability, while items 4, 5 and 6 have loaded on to a second factor with high reliability
51. The first item statement was "In my country, entrepreneurs in general need external assistance with their plans prior to start-up". The second item statement was "In my country, there are enough public and/or private centres or agencies that can provide persons with adequate education and training on entrepreneurship independently of the educational formal system".
52. Ministry of Education, Finland, *Guidelines for Entrepreneurship Education*, Publication of the Ministry of Education, Finland, 2009, 14.
53. Fiet, James and Patel Pankaj, *Prescriptive Entrepreneurship*, Cheltenham, UK and Northampton, MA, USA: Edward Elgar, 2008.
54. Chi Sq. = 1154.8, p-value = 0.000
55. Gain from training is calculated using binary logistic regression. This enables calculation of the "odds ratio" for compulsory versus no training, while controlling for other possible effects such as the demographics mentioned above. A further advantage of

using this technique is that it estimates whether the effect of training is statistically significant, or a possible artifact of random fluctuations in the data.

56. Demographic data were not available for Argentina and are therefore absent from this analysis.

57. The factor-driven countries for which expert data were available were Bolivia, Bosnia and Herzegovina, Colombia, Ecuador, Egypt and Iran. The efficiency-driven countries were Brazil, Chile, Croatia, Dominican Republic, Jamaica, Macedonia, Mexico, Peru, Serbia, South Africa, Turkey, and Uruguay. The innovation-driven countries were Finland, Germany, Greece, Denmark, Ireland, Italy, Korea, Slovenia and Spain.

58. Shapero, Albert, "The Displaced, Uncomfortable Entrepreneur", *Psychology Today*, November 1975, 83–88.

59. The countries in Western Europe for which NES data were available were Denmark, Finland, Germany, Greece, Ireland, Italy and Spain. NES data for Eastern countries were available for Bosnia and Herzegovina, Croatia, Macedonia, Serbia and Slovenia. NES data for Latin American countries were available for Bolivia, Brazil, Chile, Colombia, Dominican Republic, Ecuador, Jamaica, Mexico, Peru and Uruguay

60. All logistic regressions were checked for model fit and overall significance. A small number of regressions indicated poor model fit, suggesting important variables were missing from the model. These were: Bosnia and Herzegovina (TEA); South Africa (know entrepreneur); Turkey (intent, skills); Latvia (opportunity); Jamaica (know entrepreneur); Greece (know entrepreneur, intent, fear of failure); Spain (skills) and Japan (skills).

61. Individuals starting businesses were asked the following question: "Various people may give advice on your new business. Have you received advice from . . . your spouse or life-partner? . . . your parents? . . . other family or relatives? . . . friends? . . . current work-colleagues? . . . earlier work-colleagues? . . . a current boss? . . . an earlier boss? . . . someone in another country? . . . someone who is starting a business? . . . someone with much business experience? . . . someone with expertise on what you do? . . . a researcher or inventor? . . . a possible investor? . . . a bank? .. a lawyer? . . . an accountant? . . . a public advising services for business? . . . a firm that you collaborate with? . . . a firm that you compete with? . . . a supplier? . . . a customer? Existing owner-managers were asked "various people may give advice on your business. During the last year, have you received advice from . . . your spouse or life-partner? . . . your parents? . . . and so on, for the same 22 kinds of advisors.

62. As an example of their diversity, on the world values survey scale of community values, which varies from -2 to +2, where -2 would be a highly traditional society and +2 would be a highly secular-rational society, the latest available scores for these five countries are: -1.22 (Iran); -0.98 (Brazil); 0.72 (Latvia); 1.11 (Korea); 1.16 (Denmark).

63. World Values Survey website, http://www.worldvaluessurvey.org/.

64. Each difference between two advisor type averages for each country/sphere combination in Brazil, Latvia, Korea and Denmark was found to be statistically significant in a one-tailed t-test.

65. Denmark is an exception here, possibly because of the exceptionally high standard of education in that country.

66. A multiple regression of variety of advisor types (standardized within each country and entrepreneurial stage) was conducted, with dependent variables of training (compulsory versus no training), education (standardized within each country), and also gender (binary), age (logarithm of years), stage (binary for nascent versus established) and country (a set of binary variables).

3. Chinese entrepreneurship education

Du Guirong, Yu Jinquan and Xu Lei[*]

3.1 INTRODUCTION

This chapter will focus on five aspects of entrepreneurship research and education. First, the authors view the present situation in some universities with regard to entrepreneurship education. Second, from a review of published articles in Chinese academic journals and funded projects by the Chinese National Natural Science Foundation (NNSF), the authors analyze the changing research topics on entrepreneurship. Third, the authors describe the China National Entrepreneurship Competition for University Students and discuss its strengths and weaknesses. The authors report on university students' attitudes towards entrepreneurship and conclude with some suggestions to improve entrepreneurship within China's universities.

3.2 BACKGROUND ON ENTREPRENEURSHIP EDUCATION IN CHINA

In the West, academic and pedagogical interest in entrepreneurship dates back 40 years. The first American entrepreneurship conference was held at Purdue University in 1970, at which 42 experts analyzed the entrepreneurship success rates of representative cases of companies from the Massachusetts Institute of Technology and Silicon Valley. This involved discussing the role the university played in promoting entrepreneurship development. The first International Conference on Entrepreneurship Research was held in Toronto, Canada in 1973. Scholars elaborated on the relationship of the two-way interaction between case studies of entrepreneurship and entrepreneurship education at their campuses. The Entrepreneurship Interest Groups were established in 1974 when the Academy of Management in the United States held its annual meeting. Since then, entrepreneurship research and education have increased dramatically.[1]

In China, on the other hand, entrepreneurship as a field of academic study was started in the late 1990s, after some 20 years of fast economic growth, led in part by large numbers of highly active entrepreneurs. These entrepreneurs were rarely university graduates, however. Chinese university students are less likely to be involved in start-ups than students from other countries. China's average level of student start-ups is lower than the global average, accounting for less than 1 percent of entrepreneurs compared to 20 percent to 30 percent in most developed countries.[2] Chinese society doubts the effectiveness of student start-ups and their success rates are low.[3]

Nevertheless, in the late 1990s, entrepreneurial education emerged in universities with the support of the Chinese Ministry of Education. Student interest in entrepreneurship developed rapidly after the first Business Plan Competition was held at Tsinghua University in 1998.[4][5] The entrepreneurial spirit really first took flight in 1999 when Tsinghua held its second Business Plan Competition, this time with national participation. It was renamed the National Entrepreneurship Plan Competition for University Students, sponsored by the Ministry of Education and the Communist Youth League. Since then, local governments and universities have implemented measures to encourage students to start their own businesses. This has included allowing university students to leave school before graduation to begin a high-tech enterprise and enhance their entrepreneurial abilities. As a result, more and more university students have begun their own businesses. According to Zhang Li,[6] before 2000, over 101 enterprises were founded in Xuhui District of Shanghai by teachers and students in five universities such as Shanghai Jiao Tong University.

In 2002, the Ministry of Education identified nine colleges and universities in China as pilot institutions to start entrepreneurial education: Tsinghua University, Beihang University, Renmin University, Shanghai Jiao Tong University, Wuhan University, Xi'an Jiao Tong University, Heilongjiang University, Northwestern Polytechnical University and School of Economics of Nanjing. These universities offer three entrepreneurial education models: the combination of theory and practice by Renmin University; fund support for the seed stage by Beihang University; and innovation-oriented entrepreneurship by Shanghai Jiao Tong University.[7][8]

In general, the business environment for student entrepreneurship is more favorable now than it was in the past. However Yuan Xianhai in his comparative study of business plan competitions and start-up practice revealed the severe capital problems of students' start-ups[9] and the low success rates of student businesses. Sun Zhong Fa[10] reported that the overall rate of entrepreneurship in China reached about 30 percent, but the student entrepreneurship rate was only 2 or 3 percent.

The above discussion reveals that many problems continue to exist in China concerning student entrepreneurship.

3.3 ACADEMIC RESEARCH ON ENTREPRENEURSHIP IN CHINA

The focus of university professors in China researching entrepreneurship has evolved over the last decade. From the topics that they research and the topics that the government chooses to fund, we can gain an insight into key issues for Chinese entrepreneurship education.

3.3.1 Research Fields

The authors analyzed papers from 1990 to 2010 by searching the China Academic Journals Database. From the information in the Chinese Social Sciences Citation Index (CSSCI) journals, the authors used the following topics as search keywords: entrepreneurial business, entrepreneurial management, entrepreneurial spirit, entrepreneurial education, entrepreneurial environment, venture failure, second stage capital, entrepreneurship policy, student entrepreneurship, venture risk, and venture capital exit. The authors compared research topic frequency for the years 1990 to 2010 with that of 2008 to 2010 (see Figure 3.1). The most common topic, accounting for 37 percent of the research over the entire period, was entrepreneurial business. But studies on student entrepreneurship, entrepreneurial education and the entrepreneurial environment have greatly increased in recent years. This indicates that relative interest in Chinese entrepreneurship education is rapidly increasing, as Figure 3.1 shows, while relatively, studies on business entrepreneurship, second stage capital and venture failure are decreasing.

3.3.2 Research Funding from the National Natural Science Foundation of China

The Chinese NNSF is the primary government institution mandated to manage the National Natural Science Fund. Similar to the US National Science Foundation, its aim is to promote and finance basic and applied research in China. Recently, it has distributed about ¥3 billion per year

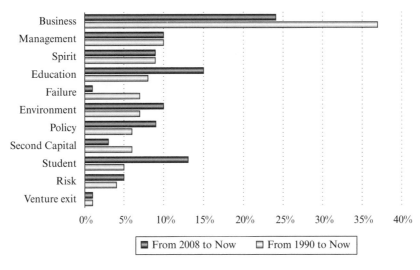

Figure 3.1   Academic research on entrepreneurship from 1990 to 2010

with about 3 percent going to management sciences, of which entrepreneurship is a part.[11]

Entrepreneurship research has drawn NNSF attention since 2000, and the number of studies has increased rapidly for six topics in entrepreneurship (see Table 3.1). These include entrepreneurial business, technology ventures, peasant-worker entrepreneurship, entrepreneurship performance, entrepreneurial talent and entrepreneurship theory. Project awards reflect not only academic quality and interest but also, more importantly, government policy interest. Clearly, government interest in entrepreneurship is increasing, which is also evident in the period of 2009–2010. The study of entrepreneurial businesses and entrepreneurship theory dominate research funding offered by the government; this shows the importance of the study of both theory and practice in the field of entrepreneurship. Table 3.1 also reveals that the government has begun to pay attention to peasant-worker start-ups.[11]

3.4   BUSINESS PLAN COMPETITIONS

Since 1999 the National Entrepreneurship Plan Competition for University Students has done much to inspire students with a passion for start-ups. The competition is popularly known as the "Little Challenge", to distinguish it from the Challenge Cup Competition of Science Achievement in

Table 3.1   Number of national natural science foundation funded projects in entrepreneurship

Time / Category	2000–2002	2003–2005	2006–2008	2009–2010	Total
Entrepreneurial businesses	1	4	6	12	23
Technology ventures	1		3	1	5
Peasant-worker entrepreneurship		1	1	2	4
Entrepreneurial performance		1	1	1	3
Entrepreneurial talent		1	1		2
Entrepreneurial theory			8	2	10
Total	2	7	20	18	47

China, which was initiated in 1989 and is known as the "Big Challenge". The Little Challenge is sponsored by the Communist Youth League Central Committee, the China Association for Science and Technology, and the Ministry of Education. The seven Little Challenges[12] held since 1999 are shown in Table 3.2.

3.4.1   Strengths of the Little Challenge

The Little Challenge, and the numerous other competitions established at participating universities to develop plans to represent each university in the Little Challenge, have had three positive effects, according to the observations of the authors.

Stimulating creativity
The reform of higher education has seen the number of students enrolled in China's universities increase by over five times in the space of a decade. This has consequently increased the difficulty with which graduating students can find employment. Creative students, capable of applying their knowledge, are more likely to find positions they desire. The Little Challenge addressed the need to train creative innovative students how to apply their knowledge and present their ideas concisely and persuasively.

Table 3.2   National entrepreneurship plan competition for university students in China

No.	Location of Little Challenge	Year	Number of universities participating	Number of plans submitted
1	Tsinghua University	1999	120	400
2	Shanghai Jiao Tong University	2000	137	455
3	Zhejiang University	2002	244	542
4	Xiamen University	2004	276	603
5	Shandong University	2006	81	110
6	Sichuan University	2008	118	168
7	Jilin University	2010	115	165

Stimulating start-up activity

The Little Challenge has established an entrepreneurship platform for students. After taking part in the Little Challenge, some excellent groups have been rewarded and their ideas adopted by some companies. This can establish a good foundation for students' future start-ups.

Stimulating applied research

The Little Challenge has led to new products and promoted collaboration between industry and universities. Research results from universities often have good potential to create business value, but most of them stay inside the schools. The Little Challenge provides an excellent platform for students to promote their research to business.

3.4.2   Weaknesses of the Little Challenge

Drawing from data on national business plan competitions for university students, the authors found that although the Little Challenge has received much attention in China, there are still some deficiencies which need improvement.

The Little Challenge's structure risks undermining its entrepreneurial spirit

Table 3.2 shows that the Little Challenge has attracted the attention of thousands of students. But has it really promoted substantial entrepreneurial activity among university students? From the 2002 Challenge, six of the 542 plans received awards; in 2004, 100 of 603 plans reached the competition's final stage[12] The reduction in submitted plans in recent years conceals the fact that the plans submitted are themselves the winners of local competitions. These numbers convey the impression that the Little Challenge has become a game for talented students. This defeats the original purpose of entrepreneurship business plan competitions – to encourage the entrepreneurial spirit of more students. The majority of universities provide training only to those teams considered to have the best opportunity to win the Little Challenge. Many more students are neglected because they lack competitive plans. Such students never find out why their plans are not as good as those of their competitors. Unfortunately, judges do not give them feedback, advice, ideas or encouragement, which candidates otherwise expect and which would benefit them.

What do these students get from this competition? Maybe, if they are lucky, they learn a little about entrepreneurship. In order to win an award, some universities recombine the teams for the competition. They only chose the best presenting students to build a team with the highest possibility of winning. A major purpose of a student entrepreneurship business plan competition should be to develop an excellent business sense and entrepreneurial skills in all students, not just for a few. But now the nature of the competition has changed to become a game of praise solely for the best students and recognition for the winning universities.

Most business plans disappear after the competition

Every year, many plans are considered to be excellent, but only a few will be put into practice. The plans end when the competition ends. There are several reasons for this. First, the plans may not be practical in real life, in the opinion of the judges. Since most students have had little business experience, there are many problems that they do not take into consideration when designing their plans. Although they may do the marketing research and analysis, their ideas exist only in their imaginations, with little evidence that they can be supported from the perspective of actual business practice or experience. The plans are still far from showing evidence that they would succeed in business. Second, in previous competitions, many teams required several million renminbi, or more, in start-up capital. This large amount of money has surprised even seasoned investors. They did not think it was reasonable to invest large amounts of money in these "pure concept" projects. Third, investors tend to pay more attention to the people than their plans. They prefer to invest in people who have previous start-up experience. This is a distinct limitation for university students as most do not have start-up experience.

In the Little Challenge, only high-tech plans can win

In the Little Challenge, winners tend to be teams with hi-tech products protected by patents. Those teams who have excellent business plans plus a patent have a better opportunity to win. But this means that many good plans are eliminated simply because they lack a patent. The hi-tech business plans with patents may hope to bring in more income but we should not neglect those plans without patents as they may have greater potential. What we need are practical plans, not just hi-tech plans. The competition goal should be to find plans with the greatest expected value. Many great and profitable new ventures do not use the latest high technology. If the competition has a bias towards hi-tech products, then other kinds of plans will be denied equal opportunities and students will get the wrong idea about what constitutes value-creating entrepreneurship.

3.5 AN EMPIRICAL STUDY OF CHINESE STUDENTS' ATTITUDE TOWARDS ENTREPRENEURSHIP

According to Sun,[10] the three major problems for university entrepreneurship students are lack of capital (31 percent), difficulty of promoting a product (25 percent) and lack of management experience (20 percent). The authors also surveyed graduate students with an interest in entrepreneurship at the Harbin Institute of Technology Shenzhen Graduate School (HITSGS). The authors sent questionnaires to 126 students who attended entrepreneurship classes at HITSGS and asked about the difficulties they thought they would face if they decided to start their own businesses. The results were as follows.

3.5.1 Most Students View Entrepreneurship as a Last Resort

Most students think that they will start their own business only if they cannot find a job. In other words, unless they are forced to, they will not start their own business. Less than 50 percent would choose to start their own businesses after graduation, if chances permit.

This demonstrates one of the differences between Chinese and foreign cultures. In Chinese culture, most people agree with the familiar saying that "a good scholar becomes an official". Moreover, many Chinese parents encourage their children to have stable jobs. In China, students are taught only how to study from elementary school through high school. Even in universities, there are no practical experiences or business skills taught in most schools, which would be very important if students wished to pursue careers related to entrepreneurship.

3.5.2   Fear of Failure is a Critical Factor Limiting Start-ups

In our study, more than 60 percent of students are afraid of failure. They wonder if their plans are practical or not. They are afraid that they will get nothing if they fail. Currently, many students come from one-child families where they have the challenge of supporting not only their own families but also their parents as they age. Start-ups involve high risk, and student start-up success rates are low. If a student's business fails, the student faces not only his own personal failure but also the impact on his family. Therefore, many students prefer stable jobs which can ensure stable incomes to support their families.

Furthermore, the cost of setting up a business is another factor they must take into consideration. If they choose to start up a business, they may have to spend three to five years, or even longer, working to develop their own companies. During this time, their peers may become more successful which may result in frustration as they lag behind. This is another reason why students may not be brave enough to take actions to start enterprises.

3.5.3   Lack of Support from Families, Partners and Investors

Entrepreneurship success is not a piece of cake. It requires support from different sources. To begin with, the student should have the support from his family if he really wants to start his own business. Entrepreneurship is not just one person's business but it involves many people. Without the support from his family, he cannot expect to reach his goal. Furthermore, students often think that it is too hard for them to find the proper partners to work with. They insist that the support of partners is very important especially when they are faced with problems. If they can work together with excellent partners, problems will become easier to solve.

Lastly, start-up capital is another problem. Among the students interviewed, some of them had an interest in start-ups. But all complain that they do not have enough capital to start their own business or they lack support from outside investors. In addition, they believe that a lack of sufficient capital is the most difficult problem facing students who wish to start their own business.

3.5.4   Lack of Social Resources

Many students revealed that without social resources – in other words, connections – it would be difficult to succeed, especially in China. They feel that with good interpersonal relationships, everything becomes easier. In China, most universities, however, lack bridges to society and the real business world. Most students know little about social reality. Without sufficient social resources to help students, there are fewer opportunities for them. Hence, they choose to start their own businesses only after they have worked for several years, if at all.

3.6 CONCLUSIONS AND SUGGESTIONS

Due to the recent economic crisis and increased numbers of graduates, it is harder for students to find good jobs now than it was in the past. This may motivate more students to start their own businesses; hence, we need to overcome the challenges faced by university students who want to start up businesses, and guide them so that they will be successful.

The NNSF in its research funding has started to pay attention to peasant-worker start-ups, entrepreneurial education and the entrepreneurial environment. This increased research effort should bring theoretical rigor to enhance the effectiveness of start-ups. Academic study on student start-ups has developed very fast in recent years, but it has yet to be supported by the NNSF. Increased attention to student start-up by the NNSF would further help to improve the practice of students start-ups in the future.

The purpose for college student business plan competitions should be to encourage more students to have an entrepreneurial spirit and passion; however, the Little Challenge has become a "fashion show" and a game played by very few students. The Little Challenge might be divided into several sections. For example, plans for hi-tech businesses should be in the hi-tech industry section, while the plans for service should be in the service section. Innovation should be encouraged in every industry, not just in hi-tech industries. If the government supports schools which have entrepreneurship education, professors and more students would have a good environment to practice their theory.

Entrepreneurship education should be developed in more universities to ensure more students a basic understanding of entrepreneurship. Many students are afraid of failure as they know little about entrepreneurship. Universities could invite successful entrepreneurs to make speeches and meet students on campuses. Their experiences and ideas would help students immensely. When students have a deeper understanding about entrepreneurship, they will have a better chance of success in the future. The authors of this chapter believe that the success rate would increase naturally if this happened.

NOTES AND REFERENCES

* Please direct correspondence to Du Guirong, Associate Professor at the Department of Economics and Management (dgr@hit.edu.cn). Yu Jinquan is a masters student at the Division of Control and Mechatronics Engineering and Xu Lei is a masters student at the Department of Economics and Management Harbin Institute of Technology Shenzhen Graduate School Shenzhen, China.

1. Xi Sheng-yang, *Theory and Practice Study on College Entrepreneurial Education in China*, Huazhong University of Science and Technology, 2007. 席升阳. 我国大学创业教育的理论与实践研究[D]. 华中科技大学, 2007.

2. Chang Jiankun and Li Shichun, "Entrepreneurship Education in the United States and its Implications", *Guangming Daily*, 28 December 2005. 常建坤,李时椿 美国创业教育及其启示[R]. 光明日报, 2005.12.28.

3. Dong Xiaohong, *Research on Management Model and Quality Evaluation of Entrepreneurial Education*, Tianjin University, 2009. 董晓红. 高校创业教育管理模式与质量评价研究[D]. 天津大学, 2009.

4. Chu Yaping and Chang Min, "Present Condition and Analysis of Ventures Started by College Students", *Ningbo Engineering College Graduate School Review*, March 2008. 储亚平, 常敏. 大学生自主创业现状探析.宁波工程学院学报, 2008 (3).

5. Wu Lingfei, *Perceived Value of Entrepreneurship and Its Impact on University Students Entrepreneurial Intention*, Tongji University, June 2008. 吴凌菲. 基于感知创业价值的大学生创业意愿形成研究[D]. 同济大学, 2008 (6).

6. Zhang Li, "Analysis and Strategy Study on College Student Start-up", *Technology and Market*, February 2008. 张 莉. 大学生创业现状分析及对策研究. 技术与市场, 2008 (2).

7. Wei Lihong and Chen Zhongwei, "Modes of Entrepreneurial Education and its Development Tendency", *Research in Teaching*, 32:2, March 2009. 魏丽红, 陈忠卫. 创业教育模式比较及创业型人才培养. 第32卷 第2期, 教学研究, 2009(3).

8. Wei Shuancheng, Cao Yang and Zhou Xiaoli. "Comparison between Sino-US Enterprising Education Modes and China's Way to Promote Enterprising Education", *Vocational Education Research*, June 2010. 魏拴成, 曹扬, 周小理. 中美创业教育模式比较与我国创业教育之发展路径. 职业教育研究, 2010 (6).

9. Yuan Xian-hai, "College Students Entrepreneurial Education", Da Zhong Ke Ji, October 2005. 袁先海.大学生创业教育现状透视[J].大众科技, 2005 (10).

10. Sun Zhong Fa, "Three Big Barriers to of College Student Start-ups", 孙忠法 直面大学生创业"三重门", http://www.qzrs.gov.cn/dyna/ds.jsp?Id=7631.

11. See NNSF website, www.nsfc.gov.cn/, 中国国家自然科学基金委员会.

12. "National Business Plan Competition for University Students", 历届挑战杯创业计划大赛, http://www1.hfut.edu.cn/organ/tuanwei/cyds/bencandy.php?fid=5&id=20 http://edu.people.com.cn/GB/79457/12824032.html.

APPENDIX

Table A3.1   Academic research on entrepreneurship from 1990 to 2010

Item	From 1990 to now (%)	From 2008 to now (%)
Venture exit	1	1
Entrepreneurial risk	4	5
Student entrepreneurship	5	13
Second capital	6	3
Entrepreneurial policy	6	9
Entrepreneurial environment	7	10
Entrepreneurial failure	7	1
Entrepreneurial education	8	15
Entrepreneurial spirit	9	9
Entrepreneurial management	10	10
Entrepreneurial business	37	24

4. Entrepreneurship education for engineering and science students: a comparison between China and the US

Huo Lingyu, Liu Lijun and Wang Ying[*]

4.1 INTRODUCTION

Technology entrepreneurship is the machine that drove the world into the new economy, where individuals are said to churn out breakthrough innovations in their own backyards, seamlessly collaborate with colleagues located on the other side of the globe, and make speedy market introductions without the slow and clumsy decision processes typical of old world corporations.

The traditional Chinese education system was not designed to teach or motivate students to become entrepreneurs in the new economy. Chinese society did not encourage an entrepreneurial attitude because social aspirations were oriented towards working in large corporations. In the last ten years, this tradition has been challenged as changes occurred in the university education system. General entrepreneurship education appeared first at colleges and universities in China. Following that, students and faculty in engineering and science have begun to realize the importance of market-oriented research and development, in which their technical ideas can be parlayed into profitable products and services. This is especially true in the high-tech start-up era of Netscape, Yahoo, Amazon.com, Alibaba, Baidu, Tencent – technology-based companies that became virtual overnight success stories in the US and China. More and more universities are discovering the importance of synergy between science, engineering and entrepreneurship degree programs and their regional business communities.

The three basic questions concerning entrepreneurship education for engineering and science students are: What is it? Why it is important? And, how can it be carried out effectively?

Figure 4.1 shows the positioning of entrepreneurship education to

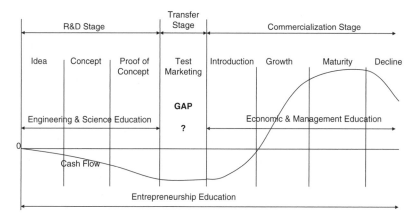

Figure 4.1   Stages of education to complement technology-based firm creation

complement the creation of a new firm by engineering and science students. Although business and engineering are tightly coupled in corporate culture, this is not usually true in academic institutions. As Schultz et al. observe, a paradigm shift is required for most engineering and science students and faculties to migrate from a technical orientation to a customer-driven perspective in which the market for an innovative product or service is emphasized.[1] Education about entrepreneurial leadership and innovation is now considered by some to be a superset of general management, not a subset. Teaching the methods and philosophy of entrepreneurial thinking has become important to academic leaders in a variety of disciplines at most universities around the globe.[2] Entrepreneurship education should focus on the transfer stage in Figure 4.1. The ultimate object of entrepreneurship education is obviously to bridge the gap between research and development (R&D) and commercialization.

This chapter describes and analyzes entrepreneurship education for engineering and science students in China compared with the US. Our study is based primarily on the work of Standish-Kuon and Rice.[3] Like them, we use a multiple-case, qualitative, and descriptive methodology. We are interested in determining the location, course type and resources of entrepreneurship education for engineering and science students to provide background for improving programs. There is no doubt that entrepreneurship education should be pursued for engineering and science students at every level. However, in that pursuit, educators need to face issues of academic legitimacy, the education system, teacher training and resource integration.

4.2 LITERATURE REVIEW

Within the US, entrepreneurship education at the university level has been evolving since the 1970s when Vesper first noted it.[4] The US literature in the last decade has increased in quantity and quality, reflecting the trend toward entrepreneurship education for non-business students.[5] [6] Luryi et al. point out that, as of 2007, more than 400 engineering schools in the US offered some entrepreneurship and business courses. Many engineering programs have recently added courses and material on engineering entrepreneurship.[2] [7] For example, Shultz et al. describe how engineering professors at the University of North Dakota, in consultation with business school faculty and engineering students interested in entrepreneurship, have converged on a four-course, 12-credit sequence that incorporates essential entrepreneurship topics into a graduate minor/cognate.[1]

Teaching, and to a lesser degree, research on new venture creation are the most common drivers of technological entrepreneurship initiatives at these universities. In the study upon which our research is largely based, Standish-Kuon and Rice report on how traditional science and engineering students in the US are being taught entrepreneurship at six American universities. Programs differ with respect to location within the university, organizational structure and approach to attracting students. The most critical factors leading to success are internal champions and interest on the part of alumni and current students. A common barrier to success is the lack of elective credits in the engineering curriculum.[3] There is considerable evidence that entrepreneurship programs add value to students, the degree programs in which they are enrolled, and the institutions that host them.[8] We can have the most dramatic educational impact on new high-growth company formation tomorrow by teaching technology students today.[9]

This field is truly part of a global phenomenon.[10] Mancenido discusses the rationale, methodology, and the results of an engineering elective course called Technology Entrepreneurship, which was designed with two objectives: to educate and to inspire Filipino engineering students.[11] Papayannakis et al. examine the introduction of entrepreneurship education in engineering curricula through a case study of the National Technical University in Greece, arguing that entrepreneurship education is critical for engineers in the knowledge-based economy.[12] Scarlat presents a Romanian experience on developing new curricula for engineering education in the area of management and entrepreneurship.[13] And finally, Carayannis et al. analyze the findings of a survey-driven study of entrepreneurship students at the undergraduate, graduate, and continuing education levels in France and the US, finding some cynicism in France concerning the environment for entrepreneurial ventures.[14]

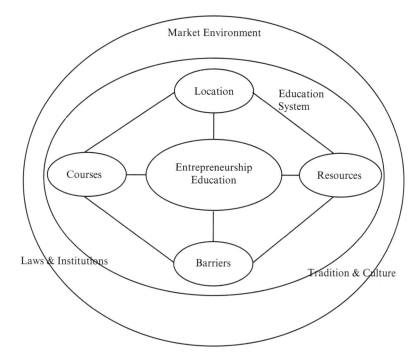

Figure 4.2   Conceptual research model

Figure 4.2 shows a conceptual research model suggested by the literature. Its main components include: (1) three main external factors that influence entrepreneurship education for engineering and science students: the market environment, laws and institutions and tradition and culture; and (2) four main factors in the university education system that influence the entrepreneurship education for engineering and science students: location within the university, course type, resources that could be used and barriers encountered. Our research uses this conceptual research model to compare US with Chinese entrepreneurial education.

Before 1998 Chinese universities did not have entrepreneurship education. In that year, China's first National Entrepreneurship Plan Competition for University Students was hosted by Tsinghua University. In April 2002, nine universities were appointed to carry out the Pilot Entrepreneurship Education Program by the Department of Higher Education of the Ministry of Education of the People's Republic of China in Beijing. Entrepreneurship education started in undergraduate management and MBA programs.[15] Now, student participation in business plan competitions and part-time work placements are increasingly common.

Li, Zhang and Matlay review the small business sector in China[16] and Millman, Matlay and Liu provide an overview of entrepreneurship education in the wider context of the Chinese educational system in transition. They describe how the Chinese government is now considering entrepreneurship as a partial solution for youth unemployment.[17] In addition, the Ministry of Education has launched the Entrepreneurship Education Pilot Program while the International Labor Organization has launched the Know About Your Business or KAB program.[18]

Clearly, entrepreneurship for engineering and science students is a new trend in the world but there has been little relevant research done in China. Descriptive, comparative methods of research looking at the characteristics of entrepreneurship for engineering and science students can increase insights into how it can be improved.

4.3   DATA AND METHODS

4.3.1   Sampling

We compare equal numbers of Chinese and US universities, with each being among the leading universities in its respective country. We selected Chinese universities that have courses, programs, centers or academic units focused on teaching entrepreneurship for engineering and science students either at the undergraduate or graduate levels or through an incubator, science and technology park or innovation units for graduates. Using these criteria, we formed an initial list of 26 Chinese universities. We were able to obtain sufficient information from the following 12 Chinese universities: Tsinghua University (Tsinghua), Beijing University of Aeronautics and Astronautics (BUAA), University of Science and Technology Beijing (USTB), Xi'an Jiaotong University (XJTU), Beijing Institute of Technology (BIT), Tianjin University (TJU), Shanghai Jiao Tong University (SJTU), University of Shanghai for Science & Technology (USST), Nanjing University of Finance and Economics (NUFE), Northeastern University (NEU), Central South University (CSU), and Northwestern Polytechnic University (NWPU).

For comparison with the Chinese universities, we needed to select 12 American universities. We included the six universities analyzed by Standish-Kuon and Rice[3] and added to them universities that have courses, programs, centers or academic units focused on teaching entrepreneurship for engineering and science students, either at the undergraduate or graduate levels. If a university had an incubator or science and technology park, and abundant information on its website about entrepreneurship education, we gave it priority. The 12 American universities are: Stanford University (Stanford), Massachusetts Institute of Technology (MIT), University of Maryland (Maryland), Johns Hopkins University (Johns Hopkins), University of California, Berkeley (UCB), University of California, Los Angeles (UCLA), Purdue University (Purdue), Rensselaer Polytechnic Institute (Rensselaer), Carnegie Mellon University (CMU), University of Colorado (Colorado), Syracuse University (Syracuse) and University of Iowa (Iowa).

4.3.2 Survey Method

We collected data on entrepreneurship programs at these universities concerning the location within the university (i.e. engineering school, non-engineering school, university, multi-school, and so on), course type (i.e. executive training course, undergraduate elective course, graduate elective course, certificate/minor course, and so on), resources (lab for entrepreneurship, incubator/science and technology park, venture capital or business angels, ongoing business relations), and obstacles to developing entrepreneurship education and factors that promote it.

For the Chinese universities, data were collected through:

● Preliminary research to identify those academic units that had teaching programs or research in entrepreneurship and to establish a personal contact.
● In-depth interviews with key people, ideally the directors of each of the university units.
● Internal documents and published research papers.
● A detailed questionnaire that was mailed and emailed to the key contact people.

The questionnaire was sent to 26 universities in China and 12 universities responded. The response rate was 46 percent. For the 12 US schools, the primary data source was their university websites.

4.4 RESULTS

Our study confirmed that course offerings, resource integration and business plan competitions characterize emerging entrepreneurship education, and there is a move towards more non-traditional modes of interactive and participative delivery. Entrepreneurship and research in entrepreneurship are gaining increased prominence. Entrepreneurship education for engineering and science students, however, is at its early development stage, is not rigorous and is only slowly gaining momentum.

4.4.1   Location Within the University

As summarized in Figure 4.3, entrepreneurship programs are based in multiple locations at universities in both the US and China, with a greater variety of locations in the US. Entrepreneurship programs are located at the university level in only three Chinese universities while they are at the university level in five US universities. In the US and China, all of the universities reported having entrepreneurship programs located outside the engineering school. Only one Chinese university reported having entrepreneurship programs located in the engineering school, while in the US, six reported having programs located in engineering schools.

4.4.2   Course Type

Figure 4.4 shows the course type and credit, and business plan competition frequencies. As with location, we found that US universities have a wider variety of course types than Chinese universities. Five Chinese universities have executive training while seven US universities do. All of the US universities have entrepreneurship undergraduate and postgraduate electives and two-thirds have certificates, while only two-thirds of Chinese universities have undergraduate electives; half have postgraduate electives, and only one has a certificate program. The popularity of business plan competitions is roughly the same, with nine in China and ten in the US. Clearly, there are many courses in the curriculum and outreach in US

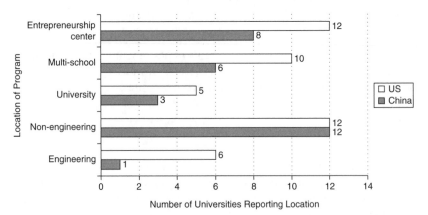

Figure 4.3   Location comparison

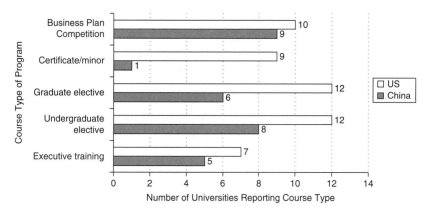

Figure 4.4   Course type comparison

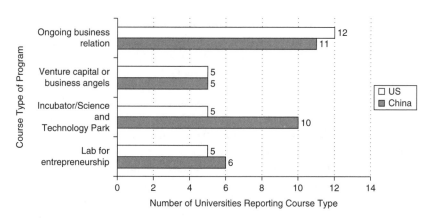

Figure 4.5   Resource comparison

while in China we tend to find limited courses but an equal emphasis on business plan competitions.

4.4.3   Resources

Figure 4.5 shows resource comparisons, including labs for entrepreneurship, incubators, venture capital or business angels and ongoing business relationships, all of which can be used by engineering and science students pursuing entrepreneurship. Half of the Chinese universities report that they have an entrepreneurship lab while five US universities report that they have labs. Ten Chinese universities have an incubator or science and technology park, while only five American universities do. In both China and the US, five universities report providing access to venture capital or business angels. All of the US and almost all (i.e. 11) Chinese universities report having good, ongoing business relationships with the entrepreneurial business community.

Data on location within the university, course type and resources are shown in Table 4.1.

4.4.4 Barriers

In addition to the quantitative information we gathered above, we asked our Chinese survey respondents about barriers to entrepreneurship for science and engineering students. We found four barriers to be the most frequently cited.

Traditional university culture and teaching is devoted to the development of professionals who offer their own labor rather than entrepreneurs who demand others' labor. As such, the university system has focused on developing "good and efficient employees" instead of prominent independent business people. Traditionally, there was no development of entrepreneurs.

Authorities in the formal, established educational system resist the initiation of new and interdisciplinary entrepreneurship programs. Traditionally, the educational system is structured by academic discipline. It is not a practical nor interdisciplinary system. The ongoing process of trying to persuade engineering professors to cooperate across departments and faculties is a difficult one.

There is a lack of funds and few specialized professors qualified to teach entrepreneurship at the university level. The same phenomenon can be found in the American university system where new departments and programs in entrepreneurship have opened in recent years, generating a demand for specialized professors that cannot be met by the existing supply.[3] But in China, the problem is more acute.

Curricula are rigid, with little room for electives. The lack of space or time for elective credits is an obstacle to introducing entrepreneurship to engineering and science students in the US as well,[3] but Chinese university programs tend to be even more rigid.

4.5 REFLECTIONS AND SUGGESTIONS

The above analysis highlights many differences between China and the US. We believe that best practices in the US should be used for Chinese

Table 4.1 Survey results

Country	University	Location					Course Type					Resource			
		Engineering school	Non-engineering school	University level	Multi-school	Entrepreneurship center	Executive training	Undergraduate elective	Graduate elective	Certificate / minor. course	Business competition	Lab for entrepreneurship education	Incubator / science and technology park	Venture capital or business angels	On-going business relations
China	Tsinghua		✓	✓	✓	✓	✓	✓	✓		✓	✓	✓	✓	✓
	BUAA		✓	✓		✓	✓		✓		✓	✓	✓		✓
	USTB		✓	✓	✓	✓					✓		✓	✓	✓
	XJTU		✓		✓	✓			✓	✓			✓		✓
	BIT		✓						✓			✓	✓		✓
	TJU		✓		✓				✓		✓		✓		
	SJTU		✓			✓	✓	✓			✓		✓		✓
	USST		✓		✓	✓	✓	✓			✓	✓		✓	✓
	NUFE		✓					✓				✓			✓
	NEU	✓	✓					✓			✓				✓
	CSU		✓			✓	✓	✓			✓		✓	✓	✓
	NWPU		✓		✓	✓		✓	✓		✓	✓	✓	✓	✓

Table 4.1 (continued)

Country	University	Engineering school	Non-engineering school	University level	Multi-school	Entrepreneurship center	Executive training	Undergraduate elective	Graduate elective	Certificate / minor. course	Business competition	Lab for entrepreneurship education	Incubator / science and technology park	Venture capital or business angels	On-going business relations
USA	Stanford	✓	✓		✓	✓	✓	✓	✓	✓	✓	✓	✓	✓	✓
	MIT		✓	✓	✓	✓	✓	✓	✓	✓	✓	✓		✓	✓
	Maryland	✓	✓		✓	✓	✓	✓	✓	✓	✓	✓		✓	✓
	Johns Hopkins	✓	✓			✓	✓	✓	✓	✓	✓		✓		✓
	UCB	✓	✓	✓	✓	✓		✓	✓	✓		✓	✓	✓	✓
	UCLA		✓	✓	✓	✓	✓	✓	✓	✓	✓	✓	✓		✓
	Purdue		✓	✓	✓	✓		✓	✓	✓				✓	✓
	Rensselaer		✓	✓	✓	✓		✓	✓	✓					✓
	CMU		✓		✓	✓	✓	✓	✓	✓	✓		✓		✓
	Colorado	✓	✓			✓	✓	✓	✓	✓	✓				✓
	Syracuse		✓			✓		✓	✓	✓	✓				✓
	Iowa	✓	✓		✓			✓	✓						✓

reference. Practicing by trial and error may be myopic, incomplete and inefficient; however, a long-term, complete solution can be found through a comparison of Chinese and US strengths and weaknesses. Chinese entrepreneurship education for engineering and science students has a long way to go. We offer the following suggestions relating to the efforts of Chinese universities.

4.5.1 Culture and Institution-Building

There must be an underlying cultural climate that recognizes and rewards innovation and creative thinking and includes entrepreneurship education in the missions of universities. There is also a need to confirm the academic legitimacy of entrepreneurship education for the engineering and science students. Institutional characteristics determine whether entrepreneurship is a top priority for the relevant faculty and the university in general. Championing entrepreneurship by high-level leaders is a key factor in this aspect.

4.5.2 Entrepreneurship Centers and Engineering Professors

Entrepreneurship centers should be set up and engineering professors should be encouraged to take part in entrepreneurship education. The entrepreneurship center plays an important role in entrepreneurship education in the US. With more and more engineering schools conducting entrepreneurship education, combining engineering and management to improve entrepreneurship education and practice is an important strategy in both the US and China.

4.5.3 Systematic Education

Introducing entrepreneurship education to engineering and science students is a fundamental change. The change will be more difficult if the development of entrepreneurial capacity is focused only in one course or a business plan competition instead of distributing the knowledge throughout all the courses of the curriculum. Certificates, minors, flexible curricula, teacher training and outreach are key factors in creating systematic education practices to meet the challenge of this change.

4.5.4 Resource Integration

The fourth key area is to integrate resource use. Labs for innovation and entrepreneurship, incubators, science and technology parks, and relationships with the business community, including venture capitalists, are all important. The leading Chinese universities we studied have more of these resources than their American counterparts. Almost every university we studied makes use of an advisory board composed of entrepreneurs and business leaders. These serve as bridges between the university and the business community. But these resources may be underutilized. One university mentioned during our survey that its science and technology park did not offer any support for its entrepreneurship education initiatives.

There are many barriers for us to overcome. We advocate communicating positively, drawing ideas from people through information sharing, publishing success stories, rewarding entrepreneurial activity and carrying out more research to report experiences around entrepreneurship education.

ACKNOWLEDGMENTS

This work is supported in part by the Humanities and Social Sciences Fund (07JA880011) of the Ministry of Education of the People's Republic of China (MEPRC), by the "Eleventh Fives Educational Plan" Fund (ADA07067) of MEPRC Beijing Municipal Commission of Education and by the Graduate Educational Innovation Program (P-0801) of MEPRC and Funding Project for Academic Human Resources Development in Institutions of Higher Learning Under the Jurisdiction of Beijing Municipality (PHR200906210) respectively. The authors gratefully acknowledge administrators and faculty at the participating universities for their time, interest and insights, particularly: Luo Jianbei at Tsinghua, Zhanlin and Lijun at BUAA and Thomas H. Byers at Stanford and Hugh Thomas at The Chinese University of Hong Kong. The study would not have been possible without their enthusiastic support.

NOTES AND REFERENCES

*   The corresponding author, Huo Lingyu, is studying for a PHD degree at the School of Management and Economics and Center for Innovation and Entrepreneurship Education Beijing Institute of Technology and is a lecturer at the School of Information, Beijing Wuzi University (sboerp@163.com). Co-authors Liu Lijun and Wang Ying are professor and lecturer respectively at Center for Innovation and Entrepreneurship Education Beijing Institute of Technology.

1.   Schultz, R.R., A.F. Johnson, W.L. Dougan, J.R. Wambsganss, C.-H.Won, B.G. Giesinger, P.P. Osburnsen and T.J. Timpane, "An Entrepreneurship Minor/Cognate for Engineering Graduate Degrees", *32nd ASEE/IEEE Frontiers in Education Conference*, 6–9 November 2002, Boston, MA, F1H-1–F1H-6.

2. Nichols, S.P. and N.E. Armstrong, "Engineering Entrepreneurship: Does Entrepreneurship Have a Role in Engineering Education?" *Antennas and Propagation Magazine, IEEE*, 45:1, February 2003, 134–138.
3. Standish-Kuon, T., and M.P. Rice, "Introducing Engineering and Science Students to Entrepreneurship: Models and Influencial Factors at Six American Universities", *Journal of Engineering Education*, January 2002, 33–39.
4. Vesper, K., "Entrepreneurship Education 1974", Society for Entrepreneurship and Application, Milwaukee, USA, 1974.
5. Hunger J.D., J.H. Davis, J.B. Gilmore, R. Wilburn Clouse, "Who Are Our Students? Entrepreneurship Education for Non Business Students: A New Trend", *USASBE Conferences Proceedings*, San Antonio, Texas, 16–19 February 2000.
6. Kuratko, D.F., "Emergence of Entrepreneurship Education: Development, Trend, and Challenges", *Entrepreneurship Theory and Practice*, 2005:9, 577–597.
7. Luryi, S., W. Tang, N. Lifshitz, G. Wolf, S. Doboli, J.A. Betz, P. Maritato, and Y. Shamash, "Entrepreneurship in Engineering Education", 37th *ASEE/IEEE Frontiers in Education Conference*, 10–13 October 2007, Milwaukee, 10–15.
8. Ohland, M.W., S.A. Frillman, G.l. Zhang, and T.K. Miller III, "NC State's Engineering Entrepreneurs Program in the Context of US Entrepreneurship Programs", *The NCIIA 8th Annual Meeting*, 18–20 March 2004, 155–161.
9. Byers, Tom, "Teaching Entrepreneurship to Engineering and Science Students", Experienced Educators at Stanford University's Stanford Technology Ventures Program (STVP), http://stvp.stanford.edu.2003.
10. Byers, Tom, "Entrepreneurship Education's Role in Promoting Entrepreneurship and Innovation", Stanford Technology Ventures Program, 1 November 2008.
11. Mancenido, M.V., "Technology Entrepreneurship in Engineering Education: Harnessing the Technology Entrepreneurs in Filipino Engineering Students", 2009.
12. Papayannakis, L., I. Kastelli, D. Damigos, G. Mavrotas, "Enterperneurship Education in Greece: Experience and Challenges for a Technical University", Paper prepared for DIME-LIEE/NTUA Athens Conference, 2008.
13. Scarlat, C., "Developing New Curricula for Engineers' Entrepreneurial Education: A Romanian Experience", *World Transactions on Engineering and Technology Education*, 6:2, 2007, 275–278.
14. Carayannis, Elias G., Dan Evans and Mike Hanson, "A Cross-Cultural Learning Strategy for Entrepreneurship Education: Outline of Key Concepts and Lessons Learned from a Comparative Study of Entrepreneurship Students in France and the US", *Technovation*, 23, 2003, 757–771.
15. Xiaoguang Li, Shubin Jiao and Jingyue Xu, "Research on Comparison of China-US from Perspectives of Entrepreneurial Environment", *Wireless Communications, Networking and Mobile Computing*, WiCOM '08, 4th International Conference 2008, 1–9.
16. Li, J., Y.L. Zhang and H., Matlay "Entrepreneurship Education in China", *Education and Training*, 45:8/9, 2003, 495–505.
17. Millman, Cindy, Harry Matlay and Fan Liu, "Entrepreneurship Education in China: A Case Study Approach", *Journal of Small Business and Enterprise Development*, 15:4, 2008, 802–815.
18. Millman, Cindy, Harry Matlay and Fan Liu, "Entrepreneurship Education in China: A Case of Vocational Training and KAB Programme", http://www.ib66.net.cn/bbs/view/id-591. 2008.

5. Combining separate modules on a cross-platform: entrepreneurship education for science and engineering

Wang Ying*

5.1 INTRODUCTION

In January 1999, the State Council of the Chinese government in its Action Plan for Education Revitalization in the 21st Century called for "strengthening the entrepreneurship education of faculty and students and encouraging them to establish their own high-tech enterprises".[1] Since then, entrepreneurship education has attracted extensive attention. Because science and engineering are more relevant to industrial production, it is especially important to guide their students in the practice of entrepreneurship. This chapter discusses entrepreneurship education among students in China's universities for science and engineering.

5.2 THE HISTORY OF ENTREPRENEURSHIP EDUCATION'S DEVELOPMENT IN CHINA'S UNIVERSITIES FOR SCIENCE AND ENGINEERING

Entrepreneurship education in China has emerged comparatively recently and its emergence has coincided with rapid college expansion, which has increased the supply of new graduates. Consequently, reduced opportunities for graduates in existing companies have endowed the development of entrepreneurship education with even greater significance. Chinese universities since 1999 have experienced a craze for entrepreneurship, to implement the State Council's directive, confirming the importance of entrepreneurship education in China.

In 1998, Tsinghua University initiated China's first entrepreneurship plan competition. The following year, the Ministry of Education together with the Central Committee of the Communist Youth League developed the competition into the biennial China National Entrepreneurship Plan Competition for University Students, better known as the 'Little Challenge'. The Little Challenge plays an important role in popularizing knowledge about entrepreneurship and advocating for entrepreneurship. Since then, quite a few colleges have launched similar competitions regarding entrepreneurship education and opened related courses on it.[2] In January 2000, the Ministry of Education issued a directive to allow college students and the graduates (including doctoral students) to suspend their schooling but preserve their status as students to establish high-tech enterprises.[3]

In 2002, as increasing numbers of graduates experienced difficulties in finding employment, the Ministry of Education increased its attention toward entrepreneurship education. In April of the same year, the Ministry of Education held a symposium in Beijing to discuss pilot work for entrepreneurship education among colleges and universities. It also pointed out that cultivating high-quality talent with the spirit of creativity, innovation and entrepreneurship is an important task of current higher education. Nine universities, including Tsinghua University and Beijing University of Aeronautics and Astronautics, were designated by the Ministry of Education as the pilot units for entrepreneurship education.[4] They took the lead in systematically carrying out entrepreneurship education programs.

In August 2005, the Central Committee of the Communist Youth League, in collaboration with the International Labor Organization, launched the Know About Business (KAB) program with Tsinghua University, Beijing University of Aeronautics and Astronautics and Zhejiang University opening KAB courses. In April 2009, the Education Association of Innovation and Entrepreneurship was established, further confirming the importance of entrepreneurship education in enhancing university students' entrepreneurial ability.

Our brief survey of the last ten years shows that China's universities for science and engineering have made substantial progress. According to the Entrepreneurship Centre of the Beijing Institute of Technology (BIT), 58 percent of universities with science and engineering programs hold entrepreneurship business plan competitions, 67 percent open elective courses on entrepreneurship to undergraduates and 42 percent open such courses to graduates. At the same time, entrepreneurship education is increasingly emphasizing complementarities between general arts, professional studies and entrepreneurship.[5]

5.3   EXISTING PROBLEMS OF ENTREPRENEURSHIP EDUCATION IN CHINA'S UNIVERSITIES FOR SCIENCE AND ENGINEERING

Although entrepreneurship education has attained some achievements in China's universities for science and engineering, there are still disparities compared with developed countries.

5.3.1   Content Is Shallow

There are no uniform teaching materials, comparatively mature teaching methods and management mechanisms.[6] Writing simple business plans and low-level entrepreneurship activities constitute the main content of current entrepreneurship education in China. With the exception of a few key universities for science and engineering that have opened full entrepreneurship programs, most of China's post-secondary institutions take entrepreneurship education no further than training for business plan competitions and career counseling. Although the importance is great, the effect is small.

5.3.2   Qualified Teachers Are Rare

Most engineering teachers have never taught entrepreneurship, so there is a lack of qualified teachers. At present, most of the teachers giving lectures about entrepreneurship belong to the academic faculty. Many of them lack experience in practical entrepreneurship. Some of them do not even have working experience in enterprises. In view of this, many colleges or universities employ entrepreneurs to give lectures as guest teachers so as to strengthen the practicality of the entrepreneurship education. Although students welcome such arrangements, difficulties in coordination, maintaining course integrity and funding, as well as the entrepreneurs' lack of teaching experience, mean that the results leave a lot to be desired.

5.3.3   Curriculums Are Not Established

Entrepreneurship courses have not won extensive recognition. Most entrepreneurship courses are electives, without structure, and are classified as "general education courses". Important courses such as developing an entrepreneurial attitude, building entrepreneurship knowledge, entrepreneurial psychology and fostering of entrepreneurship abilities have not entered the curriculum. As a major, entrepreneurship education is only opened in a few universities for science and engineering, and their effectiveness has yet to be determined. Degrees, diplomas and certificates in innovation and entrepreneurship have not been widely established.

Universities offering science and engineering programs generally lack the current international standardized course system, KAB. In fact, most of their courses relate to "career planning" or "employment guidance", without any independent or systematic entrepreneurship courses. This is due, on the one hand, to the difficulty of adding class time devoted to entrepreneurship and, on the other hand, to the fact that entrepreneurship education, properly implemented, requires systematic reform, pervading across every aspect of teaching and nurturing students. Simply starting a few courses cannot solve the entrepreneurship issue. Efforts must touch upon curriculum reform, program structure and teaching modes. At present, few universities have made a breakthrough in this respect.

5.3.4 Practical Entrepreneurship Education Is Insufficient

Entrepreneurship is very practical. However, in China, most entrepreneurship education is primarily theoretical: practice is secondary. The reason is twofold. Students are insufficiently trained to be innovative and entrepreneurial, lacking experience in grasping market trends, capturing business opportunities, utilizing relationships and sourcing funds to support their projects. Within the university, leaders often attach little importance to entrepreneurship education, often regarding it as extracurricular education. Complementary links have not been formed between entrepreneurship education and the programs' technical cores. In addition, the universities lack mechanisms to encourage students to start up enterprises. Once a student leaves the campus to start a career, he is not guaranteed to have the opportunity to go back to study. Consequently, entrepreneurship education practice has not been made a key part of higher education.

To address the above problems, this chapter describes a design for opening entrepreneurship education in universities for science and engineering. Drawing from existing entrepreneurship education achievements, this method emphasizes that entrepreneurship education should be carried out as a combination of curriculum development and entrepreneurship practice. Additionally, it should be developed through the synthesis and cooperation of different disciplines or fields.

5.4   COMBINING SEPARATE MODULES ON A CROSS-PLATFORM

To pursue entrepreneurship education in universities, priority should be given to establishing the curriculum, because the curriculum is the core foundation of higher education. In order to provide entrepreneurship education exhibiting sufficient depth, concepts and corresponding content need to be merged into the whole curriculum system. Furthermore, attention must be paid to entrepreneurship practice, due to the strong applied nature of entrepreneurship education.[7]

5.4.1   Design Ideas of Entrepreneurship Education Mode

Nowadays, the entrepreneurship curriculum, as well as entrepreneurship practice, is developing rapidly. Among the principles that entrepreneurship education should uphold are to increase students' professional caliber, reduce class hours, strengthen entrepreneurship teaching, include courses on entrepreneurship skills and design, use entrepreneurship simulations and incorporate actual practice. Entrepreneurship teaching should insist on practicality, which extends the value of entrepreneurship education courses, and it should use specific tools to cultivate students' entrepreneurship awareness and abilities.

Referring to teaching methods, the level of student participation should be increased. Method, knowledge, activity and practice should be merged together. For instance, in the process of teaching some engineering courses, teachers can promote heuristics and study-style teaching, They can reinforce student activities and intensify the cultivation and practice of students' capabilities for solving practical problems. Courses like management science and humanities can use discussion or case teaching while others can be delivered using simulation methods – for example, a stock market or law court. Students can better grasp fundamental theories through discussion and case analysis, discovering how to apply those theories, and improving their ability to analyze and solve problems.

Hence, this chapter proposes an entrepreneurship education model which consists of curriculum as well as entrepreneurship practice and develops a cross-platform model integrating modules from different disciplines.

5.4.2   Module Design

There are two main activities needed to combine separate modules on a cross-platform: curriculum setting and practice. The following sections describe these in detail.

Curriculum design

The successful implementation of entrepreneurship education requires integration with the core courses of the appropriate academic discipline or program and the system by which each program trains its students. Specifically, universities can introduce entrepreneurship into the curriculum as follows.

For students in the second semester of their first year and the first semester of their second year, introduce basic entrepreneurship education courses: for instance, entrepreneurship basics, entrepreneurship philosophy, and entrepreneurship culture. These courses should be broad and multidisciplinary, with liberal arts complementing science, and the cultivation of generalists with solid knowledge foundations for entrepreneurship. These can be taught in general courses to inspire the passion of students toward entrepreneurship, and to choose some students who have the awareness and potential for entrepreneurship to do further study in their second year.

Students in their second year of entrepreneurship education should take specialized courses such as "studies of technological innovation", "venture capital", "technological innovation management", "the foundation of new enterprises", "small business management" and "entrepreneurship principles". This forms a comprehensive entrepreneurship education curriculum.[8]

Students in their third year should take an open entrepreneurship practice course which is combined with specialized knowledge from their majors and disciplines. By carrying out a targeted and operational-oriented plan, students will hone their ability to solve specific problems through project study connected with operating enterprises. Such projects combine study with practice, enhancing the environment for entrepreneurship education.

The above courses start from a management perspective, later bringing in subject matter related to specific science or engineering specialties such as computer science. Current teaching methods have been carried out in many colleges. But they have only reached a small number of recipients. Entrepreneurship education should be oriented to all students, allowing them to know if and how they should pursue an entrepreneurial career.

The first-year general knowledge courses should place more attention on basic knowledge, while the senior courses should place more importance on case studies and practice. Students should practice in society what they have learned in the university. A balance between these two kinds of courses – theory and practice – is critical for a consistent entrepreneurship education. The third level involves a pre-graduation presentation or thesis defense of innovation projects and related entrepreneurship assignments.[9]

As such, entrepreneurship education is integrated with students' majors. Entrepreneurs in different fields can be invited to interact with students face to face, helping students to assess whether they are suitable to be entrepreneurs, and for those who are, guiding them in developing their talents and launching their careers.

The entrepreneurship education curriculum should eventually be shifted from being more knowledge-based to being more professionally oriented, encompassing multidisciplinary teaching and strengthening students' innovative abilities.

Practice

Practice is an extension and reinforcement of classroom learning, as well as the foundation for entrepreneurship education. Universities of science and engineering should increase the proportion of entrepreneurship practice in their curriculum, collaborating with students' actual innovation plans and enterprising efforts, to advance their practical abilities. Based on this emphasis on practice, we design the entrepreneurship practice module as follows (see Figure 5.1).

Through practical teaching that cultivates basic entrepreneurship ability, provides interdisciplinary entrepreneurship education and offers innovative entrepreneurship experimentation, internships, and practice-based graduation projects, universities can foster the students' basic entrepreneurship abilities. A support system can meet the needs of entrepreneurship education practice, including a university-wide basic teaching platform, a department or program specialized in developing and coordinating the teaching of entrepreneurship practice, an innovation lab, etc. With this structure, students will benefit from a complete program of entrepreneurship practice and skill training, and they will be able to determine whether they are suitable for entrepreneurship.

Students' interest in entrepreneurship can be further fostered by encouraging them to use their free time to participate in practical entrepreneurship projects in their universities or to take part in faculty research. If conditions permit, students should independently start up companies under the guidance of faculty.

Through the Students Innovation Entrepreneurship Training Plan under the National Student's Innovative Pilot Scheme (SIETP) in China,[10] universities and colleges can enhance their innovation and entrepreneurship programs for undergraduates and postgraduates. The SIETP program grew out of the Undergraduate Teaching Quality and Teaching Reform Project in Higher Education issued by China's Ministry of Education in 2007. Under a professor's instructions, a student may apply for funding to complete an innovative project, apply for an entrepreneurship program in

Figure 5.1   The practice system of entrepreneurship education

a university or other entity in the nation, publish an article in a journal or magazine, make a patent application, or even build up her own enterprise.

From 2007 to 2010, there were 15 000 students who received financial support offered by the Ministry of Education and the Ministry of Finance to do innovative experimental programs. Each program that has been approved can get ￥10 000 from the Ministry of Education. There are 60 universities in the first batch receiving financial support.

A team from BIT, for example, received internal support for designing an anti-terrorism, anti-riot robot. The team then received SIETP funding and won first place in the SIETP "My Favorite Top-Ten Projects" exhibition held by the Ministry of Education in 2008. The project cost ￥50 000–￥60 000, but produced a device that sells for more than ￥1 million in foreign markets.

Another example of entrepreneurship education competitions is the

Teaching Quality and Educational Reform Project of Beijing Higher School, initiated in 2007.[11] Each university selects excellent students to take part in competitions within their subject: mathematics modeling, physics experiments, chemistry experiments, electro-design, advertising art, and logistics design. In addition to receiving an award in their subject areas, winning contestants can also get financial support from the central and various local governments seed venture investment funds and entrepreneurship funds to partly finance their start-up costs.

Through actions such as campus multi-mode training, cooperation between universities and enterprises, university scientific and technology parks, and international cooperation (short-term training and academic visits), there are many different channels and opportunities to foster innovative and entrepreneurial talent. It is also important to encourage engineering departments and institutes to integrate their laboratory and innovation centers, parks, incubators and other resources to deepen entrepreneurship education.

What conditions are favorable to students starting up enterprises? In those technologies that need less equipment and capital investment and a shorter time from research and development to production, the feasibility and success ratio of student start-ups is higher. That is why students majoring in computer science and engineering have the highest rates of entrepreneurship in BIT. Within just the Zhong Guan Cun (the primary high technology suburb of Bejing, located near most of the city's universities) and surrounding areas, since the late 1990s there have been more than 150 BIT students who have started their own enterprises, engaging in network security technology products development, computer programming and related fields.

In contrast, students majoring in vehicles and aerospace, where BIT boasts national leadership, cannot easily start enterprises because of the huge investment required to purchase expensive equipment. Although students may have patents and do entrepreneurship projects in these fields, most of them still continue to do academic research. Only a few such students transmit their research findings to factories, building up good commercial relationships on which they might base future start-up activity.

Innovation, entrepreneurship education and implementation compose a three-part system to foster talent. The parts intersect and support each other. Together, they constitute a complete structure for students' entrepreneurship practice.

5.4.3 The Cross-Platform

Curriculum and practice modules make use of existing recourses to implement entrepreneurship education. The cross-platform, so far, is only virtual. It has yet to be fully designed but it is the future of entrepreneurship education. It is a critical component that must be planned for the long term. Entrepreneurship education, based on the processes of innovation and commercialization, is integrative and multidisciplinary, including physical sciences, engineering technology and the social sciences. The location of the cross-platform emphasizes cultivating talents from diverse fields and disciplines.

Constructing the cross-platform involves cultivating type "工" talents with a wide knowledge, deep expertise and profound basis. In the past, the type "T" talents have been extolled in the university: the horizontal stroke stands for the wide scope of knowledge while the vertical stroke represents the depth of professional knowledge. Together they form a "T" shape – both deep and wide. Entrepreneurship needs "工" talents.[12] The type "工" not only has the talents of a "T" type (wide scope plus deep professional knowledge); she also has rich practical experience.

The archetypal "工" talent would be a scientific and technological entrepreneur. She would have "T" breath of knowledge and a deep understanding of her specialty's technological, organizational and market innovations. In addition, she would have a solid basis of commercial experience. These "工" talents can be cultivated on a platform crossing the fields of science and engineering, economy and management, and pedagogy. Implementing entrepreneurship education among the science and engineering students helps satisfy society's need for diversified talents and conforms to the strategy for science and engineering universities of giving priority to science and technology while emphasizing harmonious development among different disciplines.

At present, at BIT, the effort to foster type "工" talents is focused on recruiting third-year and fourth-year students who are equipped with the foundations of entrepreneurship into experimental classes. We recommend students to intern in companies, especially those engaged in their early growth stages. Students need to take part in real entrepreneurial activities themselves, to improve their entrepreneurial knowledge and skills. Some students are placed in companies founded by alumni, where they can learn the whole process of start-up and company operation. Students can also cultivate their talents by taking part in social enterprise start-up contests. Although the economic returns of social enterprises are far lower, as profit-making is not the top priority, pressure is lower and the start-up success rate is higher.

Among those who exemplify type "工" talents are the chairmen of Horizon Research Consultancy Group and Mycos Company, who have successful entrepreneurship experience, and whose jobs are related to entrepreneurship and research employment. They deliver lectures at BIT and encourage students to join the social entrepreneurship contests organized by their companies. Through such *pro bono* work with the students, their companies can obtain product and service informations while our students combine theoretical knowledge with applied experiences. At the same time, the lectures by the entrepreneurs also promote social entrepreneurship among the students.

Constructing the cross-platform requires involvement of "first-level disciplines" from different fields. At present, in China, entrepreneurship education is not a formal first-level discipline and, in fact, is not even a second-level discipline.[13] Entrepreneurship has not been systematically brought into the national teaching arrangement. However, quite a few people in universities are exploring this issue.[14]

Following the American experience, we can establish multidisciplinary fields which cross two to three disciplines, such as management, education and engineering. The interdisciplinary field can be treated as a first-level discipline. For instance, in an interdisciplinary field made up of management, education and engineering, we can establish specialties such as technology innovation and management, technological entrepreneurship education, and technological entrepreneurship. We can also award students interdisciplinary PhDs, doctorates of engineering, masters degrees and bachelor's degrees. Regardless of the discipline, the priority is to gradually establish entrepreneurship education as a major in China's universities for science and technology.[15]

Constructing the cross-platform involves establishing certification systems for entrepreneurship education. The priorities for Chinese universities of science and engineering cultivating innovative and entrepreneurial talent are to enhance the quality of entrepreneurship education, to strengthen the connection between entrepreneurship education and industry, and to promote the internationalization of entrepreneurship education.

Currently in engineering, the international protocol system for engineering education certification and engineering professional certification has been based on the Washington Accord.[16] Entrepreneurship education in engineering has two choices. It can join the Washington Accord through a new Chinese Entrepreneurship Education Institute, with other engineering institutes, to be recognized as a certified institution that would jointly certify related majors. Or it can establish national, or even global, entrepreneurship education institutes to independently conduct certification. Such certification would be a boost for college students who receive entrepreneurship education, helping them enter the market and pursue entrepreneurship.

5.5   CONCLUSION

Combining separate modules on a cross-platform constitutes a system of entrepreneurship education. The modules are independent from each other but also connect with each other. However, because the Chinese education system is closed, with each department maintaining a strong silo culture lacking contact with industry, combining separate modules on a cross-platform can only succeed in reforming the existing training system of university students with the determined joint efforts of government education authorities, universities and society. Universities must implement incentive policies covering equipment, teaching, research, degree enrollment and continuing education.

All departments and schools, the office of teaching affairs, and the graduate school need to establish the status of entrepreneurship education in the curriculum and in enhancing practice. For entrepreneurship education to develop effectively, it must be integrated into the curriculum, yet it is currently scattered in different departments of the university. To solve this problem, several steps need to be taken. The first step is to introduce electives in entrepreneurship. The second step is to make entrepreneurship courses compulsory for management and engineering students. The final step is to set up entrepreneurial practice courses as compulsory offerings in the curriculum. The aim of these courses is to cultivate entrepreneurial skills and encourage students to start enterprises.

The office of teaching affairs, the postgraduate students' office, and all departments should encourage students to develop their personalities and interests by allowing students to pursue cross-disciplinary studies, to choose from among a larger number of elective courses, and to increase freedom in their studies. In this way, each student can find his own entrepreneurial direction. Students who complete professional entrepreneurship education courses and meet the standard for degree programs should be awarded degrees in entrepreneurship.

University funding and personnel management should be reformed to encourage faculty from education and management disciplines to take part in entrepreneurship education research, and gradually to become professional entrepreneurship teachers. Some professors in the schools of science and engineering that have expertise in areas related to entrepreneurship education, such as schools of computer science and technology, schools of life science, and schools of mechanical engineering, should also be employed to do part-time work – teaching and supervising students' internships and practice. Professional entrepreneurs and managers who come from enterprises or companies should also be employed as part-time teachers. Eventually the model of entrepreneurship education will be similar to the Stanford model, with a core team plus affiliated faculty members from other faculties, plus adjuncts from outside the university.[17]

Through different channels, including the Institute of Science and Technology, the Youth League Committee, the School of Management and Economics, and the School of Education, we can increase investment in entrepreneurship education and provide more opportunities for students to connect with resources in society by building bridges between student entrepreneurial teams and companies. Universities should put the development of entrepreneurship education into the third phase of the "985" Program,[18] to get more investment and strengthen the status of entrepreneurship education.

Universities should set policies on independent enrollment and admit students through a comprehensive evaluation. Evaluation criteria should be widened beyond the current exam-based criteria to include a wide range of talent evaluation criteria. These can be adjusted to meet the needs of continuing professional education career programs and entrepreneurship training courses to evaluate applicants' comprehensive qualities and abilities.

Combining separate modules on a cross-platform can be helpful in integrating the resources of schools and departments, making the development of entrepreneurship education more extensive and available, and improving the quality of training. It can tap the entrepreneurial potential of students and teachers, cultivating excellent science and technology entrepreneurial talent.

NOTES AND REFERENCES

*   Associate Professor, Institute of Education, Beijing Institute of Technology. bitwy@ bit.edu.cn. This article is part of the outcomes of Humanities and Social Sciences Fund (07JA880011) of the Ministry of Education of the People's Republic of China (MEPRC) and the "Eleventh Fives Educational Plan" Fund (ADA07067) of the Beijing Municipal Commission of Education.
1.   State Council of the Peoples Republic of China Directive to the Ministry of Education, *Implement the Action Plan of Education Revitalization in the 21st Century*, January 1999. 中国国务院批转教育部 "面向21世纪教育振兴行动计划.
2.   Ding, Sanqing, "China Needs the Real Entrepreneurship Education – Based on the Analysis of the National Competition for Entrepreneurship Plan 'Challenge Cup'", *Science and Technology Management Research*, March 2007, Guangdong 87–94. 中国需要真正的创业教育——基于"挑战杯"全国大学生创业计划竞赛的分析.
3.   "A Number of Opinions in Ministry of Education on the implementation of the CPC Central Committee and State Council 'On the Decision of Strengthening Technological Innovation, Developing High Technology and Achieving Industrialization', http:// www.moe.edu.cn/edoas/website18/74/info5874.htm. January 2000. 教育部关于贯彻落实中共中央、国务院《关于加强技术创新，发展高科技，实现产业化的决定》的若干意见.

4. "Basic Situation on Promoting Innovation and Entrepreneurship Education in the Colleges and Universities", http://www.moe.edu.cn/edoas/website18/81/info1271944684837581.htm. 推进高等学校创新创业教育有关情况.

5. The statistics are based on a survey of the universities and colleges in China. Liu Lijun and Huo Lingyu, "The Status Quo and Development Trend of Entrepreneurship Education among Students Majored in Science and Engineering in China and USA", Beijing: The Innovation & Entrepreneurship Education Center of Beijing Institute of Technology, 2008, 76–82. 中美大学理工科大学生创业教育的现状及发展趋势.

6. Liu, Wei, "The History, Current Situation and Suggestions of College Students' Entrepreneurship Education", *Journal of South China University of Technology, Guangdong*, December 2006, 7–8. 大学生创业教育的历史、现状与建议.

7. Zha, Ying, "The exploration of College Students' Entrepreneurship Education Mode: the Combination of Block and Layer", *Law and Economy*, Guangxi, January 2009, 108. 块、层结合"的大学生创业教育模式探索.

8. The Stanford Technology Ventures Program offers such an integrated structure. http://stvp.stanford.edu/teaching/courses.html.

9. This requirement builds on a traditional ideological and political education currently required and BIT and elsewhere (the "moral defense" or 道德答辩).

10. *Practical University Student Innovation Plans*, http://innovation.hust.edu.cn/innovation/index.jsp. 大学生创新性实验计划.

11. "Teaching Quality and Educational Reform Project of Beijing Higher School", 北京高等学校教学质量与教学改革工程, http://xxfb.bjedu.gov.cn/image_public/UserFiles/File/235.doc. Venture Investment Foundation, 风险投资的种子基金项目, Entrepreneurship Foundation, 政府创业基金, http://www.gov.cn/gzdt/2010-05/06/content_1600716.htm.

12. See for example Seelig, Tina, *What I Wish I Knew When I Was 20: A Crash Course on Making Your Place in the World*, New York: HarperOne, 2009.

13. There are as of 2007–2009 more than 1000 first-level disciplines designated by the Ministry of Education in China, 81 of which are ranked.

14. Guo, Wanniu and Rong Yang, "Research on the Policies for College Students' Entrepreneurship Education", *Jiangsu Higher Education*, January 2009, 120–121. 大学生创业教育对策研究.

15. Standish-Kuon, T. and M.P. Rice, "Introducing Engineering and Science Students to Entrepreneurship: Models and Influential Factors at Six American Universities". *Journal of Engineering Education*, 2002:1, 33–39.

16. International Engineering Alliance, www.washingtonaccord.org.

17. http://stvp.stanford.edu/about/faculty-staff.html.

18. Project 985 is a project started by President Jiang Zemin on the 100th anniversary of Peking University in May 1998 to improve Chinese higher education.

6. Developing intellectual entrepreneurship education programs for engineering and science students in Chinese Mainland universities

Liu Lijun and Guan Sisi[*]

6.1 INTRODUCTION

Scholars are increasingly studying the effectiveness of entrepreneurship education.[1] Within entrepreneurship education, intellectual entrepreneurship education (IEE) is an emerging, global trend in research universities. We lack feasible and effective methods to implement IEE, however, especially in Mainland China, where professional faculties of research universities have little idea about how to integrate scientific and technology entrepreneurship with knowledge creation and learning.

We first need to be clear that there are major differences, as well as synergies, between IEE and traditional professional education. This requires a program design that is both feasible and effective in bringing IEE to research universities. This chapter describes such a program, the Three-Stage Open Process Intellectual Entrepreneurship Program (TOPIEP). Of course, implementing TOPIEP in research universities for engineering students involves overcoming some obstacles.

6.2 DIFFERENCES BETWEEN IEE AND TRADITIONAL PROFESSIONAL EDUCATION

In stating that IEE should be feasible, we mean that IEE can be implemented either without breaking down the original educational system's equilibrium or by setting up a new equilibrium which is a Pareto-improvement (i.e., an improvement where no unit is made worse off) over the university's current equilibrium. Thus, feasibility means that there

Table 6.1   Main differences between IEE and traditional professional education

Characteristic	Traditional professional education	Intellectual entrepreneurship education (IEE)
Teaching	Discipline-based in an academic context	Innovation process, problem-solving and application-oriented
Quality measurement	Academic quality	Multiple measures
Assessors	Academic peer review	Participants in the non-academic economy
Structure and location	Systematic within each discipline	Systematic but cross-disciplinary
Content	Homogeneous	Heterogeneous
Dynamic	Hierarchic and stable	Hierarchic and variable
Instructor network	Academic researchers and instructors	Citizen-scholars, professors of practice, researchers and instructors

are no obstacles which cannot be overcome in implementing IEE. Yet it is necessary to understand the main differences and synergies between traditional professional education and IEE in research universities. These differences are summarized in Table 6.1.

The shift from traditional profession education to IEE is part of a larger shift in innovation systems and networks and a progression toward what Smits calls the porous society.[2] IEE is not only a part of the modern university. It is also a part of the Triple Helix.[3] innovation system, using a combination of intellectual and entrepreneurial capital.[4] The transition to IEE is not a rejection of professional education. IEE is complementary rather than antagonistic to professional education.

There is considerable evidence that entrepreneurship programs add value to students, the degree programs in which they are enrolled, and the institutions that host them.[5] Professional education develops technical abilities in scientists and engineers; IEE develops the capabilities to be intellectual entrepreneurs. It is necessary to integrate students' capabilities from these two education systems. According to Plummer,[6] in today's society, the students who understand not only the science and technology of their solutions, but also the people, issues, and systems they hope to affect, become innovative leaders – entrepreneurs who have interdisciplinary talent. The more we foster this kind of talent, the better our knowledge-based society will be. Traditional professional education is not well positioned to develop students' entrepreneurial capabilities, which include communication skills, leadership, teamwork, perseverance and the ability to identify business opportunities, because, as Ferguson said, "schools break knowledge and experience into subjects, relentlessly turning wholes into parts, flowers into petals, history into events, without ever restoring continuity".[7]

Cherwitz and Sullivan say that four values rest at the heart of IEE: vision and discovery, ownership and accountability, integrative thinking and action, and collaboration and teamwork.[8] According to curriculum theory in higher education, these capabilities are transferable abilities or core abilities, which are mutually reinforcing to enhance the capability of students from different disciplines. IEE-based professional education can encourage students to become leaders through innovative curricula and interdisciplinary programs.

6.3   EFFECTIVE IEE

The most effective way to implement IEE is to bring actual, ongoing innovations into the program. IEE depends on the development of professional knowledge while students are being educated as entrepreneurs. It is a process of problem-based learning,[9] integrating knowledge creation, innovation and entrepreneurship. It is quite easy for a research university to imbed knowledge creation and technology innovation into student professional or academic education and research projects. It is much more difficult to implement IEE. Entrepreneurship education is about developing inspirational attitudes, behaviors and capacities as leaders. The construction of effective approaches for entrepreneurship education requires the construction of an effective entrepreneurship curriculum.

Leading scholars believe that entrepreneurship can be taught and that entrepreneurship is not an innate talent.[10] Yet the vast majority of engineering and science students will not become entrepreneurs. Thus, in spite of the focus on invention and entrepreneurship, the main goal of general IEE is to produce engineers with a better understanding of the business world.[11] To provide this understanding, applied theories, information and skills should be taught in a systematic manner.

We propose one systematic approach, TOPIEP, which is specially tailored for postgraduate students in engineering and science. Because IEE programs should be structured and progressive, we propose that TOPIEP be composed of three progressive levels: a Fundamental Stage for all students (including undergraduates); an Intensive Stage for those students who plan to do engineering and scientific invention, innovation and implementation; and an Advanced Stage for a highly select group of engineering and science students who plan to be entrepreneurs. For all levels, professional education forms the base. The three levels of TOPIEP are delivered in a sequence of three stages and their content differs as follows:

- Fundamental Stage. Entrepreneurial awareness, attributes including attitude and spirit, basic entrepreneurial knowledge – all conducted in a "clash room" (see below) for all students. Credits are awarded, in the normal way, when students successfully complete the courses.
- Intensive Stage. Enhancement of Fundamental Stage concepts plus training in entrepreneurial skills in innovation centers and labs for some of students. Credits are awarded, in the normal way, when students successfully complete the courses and theses. Students receive a certificate for practical work.
- Advanced Stage. In addition to the enhancement of the Fundamental and Intensive Stage concepts, the Advanced Stage includes entrepreneurial practice in the incubator or university park for a few, highly select engineering and science students. Completion of the Advanced Stage is recognized by awarding a certificate and a minor designation.

The Fundamental, Intensive and Advanced Stages constitute a hierarchical structure of TOPIEP. Because the Intensive Stage and the Advanced Stage are highly applied, students learn about the characteristics of Chinese entrepreneurial companies in a global environment, effectively fostering their abilities to become technological entrepreneurs. TOPIEP is delivered in various venues: "clash room", innovation center or laboratory, and incubator or university park. Many research universities around the world have these venues but research universities in China have not yet integrated these resources for IEE.

Although TOPIEP can be applied at both the undergraduate and the postgraduate level, its Intensive and Advanced Stages are more effective for postgraduate students in engineering and science than for undergraduates, because postgraduates have more opportunity to participate in research projects. Whereas the Fundamental Stage is instruction-based, the Intensive and Advanced Stages require an intensive commitment to research and actual enterprise roll-out, respectively. Such activities are less easily tailored to undergraduate programs.

6.3.1 TOPIEP Structure

Entrepreneurship practice is the ultimate test criteria of IEE: the better the IEE, the more successful will be the alumni entrepreneurs. One

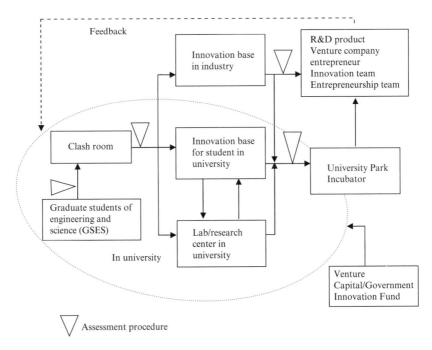

*Figure 6.1   Third-stage open process intellectual entrepreneurship
        program (TOPEIIP)*

of the main criteria of the Princeton Review Annual ranking of Top
Colleges for Entrepreneurship in the United States (as reported in
the *Entrepreneur* magazine and website) is the percentage of students
who successfully start up new businesses.[12] TOPIEP offers select students a complete process of learning, training and practice for IEE
in a Chinese research university. Some US universities, such as the
E-Team program at the University of Nevada, Reno[13] and the Venture
Accelerator Program at Maryland University,[14] offer similar programs.
But even in the US, most universities do not yet have both incubators and university science parks. In contrast, most Chinese research
universities do have both, providing a potential innovation base for
graduating students.

Figure 6.1 is a schematic diagram of TOPIEP. TOPIEP is an open
process, problem-based learning program in contrast to traditional subject
and lecture-based programs. It is also augmented with structured practice.
TOPIEP is open in four respects: in student selection, teacher selection,
process and assessment. It integrates product, process and project,[13] combining subject-based learning with experience-based teaching or training

because it broadly encompasses the set of entrepreneurial activities that students need, including team interaction.

TOPIEP is only for those students who have the potential and interest to be intellectual entrepreneurs. Additionally, although the Fundamental Stage of TOPIEP is open to students in non-technical disciplines, the Intensive and Advanced Stages are open to students only from engineering and science who seek to be innovative and creative within the constraints of technical and business feasibility. Its final target is to train educated intellectual entrepreneurs who not only have major degrees in engineering or science, but also will be awarded a minor in entrepreneurial engineering after passing through TOPIEP.

6.3.2   The Role of the Clash Room in the Fundamental Stage

Figure 6.1 shows a "clash room" in the Fundamental Stage of TOPIEP. Those students who pass through the first assessment procedure (fundamental assessment) can go into this clash room. Traditional classrooms are lecture-style. But the TOPIEP discussion classroom is a Timmons-style clash room.[15] The difference between the clash room and the lecture-style classroom is that there can be no dais in the discussion clash room, and the furniture can be moved freely.

A clash room is run as an interdisciplinary seminar. The courses are co-taught with a balance of students and instructors from different faculties: ideally with approximately one-half from engineering and sciences, one-quarter from business, and one-quarter from liberal arts and social science. The learning depends on active participation of the students and brainstorming guided by both faculty and professional mentors. Because students come from different engineering, science, business and arts/social science majors, they will have more opportunities to discuss the relationship between technology and the market in a holistic approach than they would have in a mono-disciplinary course.

Joint projects are usually based on technology from engineering and science. Business, arts and social science are helpful in fostering an innovative team. Thus, the teams sparkle with innovative ideas and can work together to design new and useful products and services. Meanwhile, the students are trained in entrepreneurial awareness, attitude and spirit, basic entrepreneurship knowledge, and entrepreneurial skills and capabilities. Market-oriented project concepts can be generated by faculty, enterprises, previous teams, and current students. At the end of this stage, a written proposal, which must include both engineering/technical and business feasibility, should be carried out by the student or student team.

6.3.3 The Role of the Innovation Base in the Intensive Stage

In order to implement innovative education programs, to promote graduate education, to integrate technology and the market, and to achieve cooperation between industry and the university, many research universities in Mainland China have established innovation centers, either by themselves or in partnership with enterprises, as authorized since 2005 by the Ministry of Education of the People's Republic of China (MEPRC).[16] Innovation centers are either on-campus graduate innovation centers and research laboratories (including research centers) or off-campus enterprise innovation bases. Most innovation centers, while being research and postgraduate oriented, can also be used by undergraduates. Innovation centers and/or laboratories play a key role in the second stage of TOPIEP.

A minority of the engineering and science students who pass and achieve higher marks in the Fundamental Stage (following full course attendance and successful submission of the engineering/technical and business feasibility assignment) can go into the second Intensive Stage. While the Fundamental Stage involves students from non-engineering and science departments, the Intensive Stage involves only engineering and/or science students, whose task it is to develop a prototype or sample of the product.

When the project researched by a student is part of the thesis supervisor's research, the students should be encouraged to do the research in the laboratory of the engineering or science department where the thesis supervisor works. When students choose projects generated by themselves or from industry, they will have to pass the technical feasibility and market feasibility assessment procedure set up by the TOPIEP program administrators to determine whether the project may enter the on- or off-campus innovation centers and to assign the students appropriate faculty supervisors.

The Intensive Stage of TOPIEP involves engineering and technical projects, carried out in innovation centers. Students do not attend lectures, but are coached by their supervisors on everything that needs to be done to identify a successful idea, make a prototype and develop its legal and business aspects.[17] The intellectual property strategy should be constructed by the students in this stage.

Completion of the project in the innovation center can be divided into two parts. One part is the thesis requirement for the student's master's or doctorate degree within the student's major. The second part is a business plan, which is necessary in order for them to apply for an innovation or entrepreneurship certificate. From the innovation center, there are four possible kinds of output: a research report or thesis, a prototype, a patent and/or a business plan.

6.3.4   The Role of Incubators in Science and Technology Parks in the Advanced Stage

Successful completion of the Intensive Stage at the innovation base is marked by completing the masters or doctoral thesis/prototype/patent and successful business plan. A highly select number of students who obtain funding (through their own resources, the university, angel investors or venture capital) and wish to start up their enterprise can go into an incubator in a science and technology park. The actual launch of a commercial enterprise is the Advanced Stage of TOPIEP.

Since 2001, the Ministry of Science and Technology and the Ministry of Education of the People's Republic of China have together authorized 62 national science and technology parks which are connected to more than 100 universities. The core functions of the parks are to incubate high-tech enterprises.[18] Most universities with university parks have their own incubators. University parks and incubators provide student enterprises with space, shared resources and mentoring, allowing them to roll out innovative, high-technology enterprises.

University parks are located beside university campuses, allowing research faculty members to continue to mentor their student entrepreneurs, develop new technology and promote the construction of advanced applications of research in accordance with market demand.[19] Incubators are generally located in the park. After successfully graduating from incubation, the new technical venture can continue to be housed in the university park or local high-tech park.

Successful incubation fulfills the university's mandate to transfer its research results into society. The park's incubator offers convenient and efficient service, including investment, finance, legal services, company registration, taxation services, intellectual property rights transfer and consulting services. Those entrepreneurial students with enterprises securing needed funding (e.g. private, venture or government capital), and which have run successfully for more than one year, successfully pass the Advanced Stage and are awarded a minor degree and certificate attesting to their successful completion of TOPIEP.

6.4   POTENTIAL PROBLEMS IN IMPLEMENTING TOPIEP AND SUGGESTED SOLUTIONS

TOPIEP is a work in progress at the Beijing Institute of Technology, where we are in the process of designing the structure of IEE for engineering and science students. We have implemented the Fundamental Stage of

TOPIEP for over 500 undergraduate and 200 postgraduate students since 2006. There are four problems to be aware of and dealt with to implement TOPIEP completely.

First, whether or not entrepreneurship has a position in engineering education is currently a topic of debate. The managers and academic decision-makers of many Chinese universities do not yet understand that IEE and traditional professional programs are reciprocal and complementary rather than antagonistic. The solution to this problem is a paradigm shift, allowing engineering students and faculty to migrate from an almost complete technical orientation to a more customer-driven perspective in which the market for an innovative product or service is emphasized, rather than simply getting a research project to the proof-of-concept stage.[20] The university should change its performance measures from strictly academic criteria to multi-valued innovative criteria. In addition, they should encourage faculty to have their own high-tech companies using intellectual property developed from their research.

Second, the resources needed for student and faculty entrepreneurs, and which also need to be integrated for effective IEE, are currently scattered in the different entities affiliated with the university, such as academic departments, innovation centers, laboratories, incubators and technology parks. Third, we lack mechanisms and resources for selecting, training, rewarding and retaining qualified teachers and mentors, which is required for IEE sustainability. How to structure these mechanisms should be explored in future research.

Last, but not least, we need to determine assessment methods in which we can judge the success of students in the three phases of TOPIEP. These methods can be based on research analyzing project feasibility,[21] incubator programs[14] and business plan competitions,[22] so our task here is not to develop a new method, but rather to combine the existing techniques into a new portfolio most appropriate to TOPIEP.

6.5   CONCLUSION

Although there are many differences between IEE and traditional professional education, these two modes of educating engineering and science students are reciprocal, complementary and synergistic, rather than antagonistic. IEE is feasible in China, meaning that it can be implemented in stages, without destroying the current educational system's equilibrium by incremental improvements and reforms.

The Fundamental Stage of TOPIEP has been successfully implemented and forms the basis for the next two stages in the hierarchical structure of IEE. Student assessment criteria can be sourced from the literature, subject to analysis and improvement. But most fundamentally, in order to implement TOPIEP in its entirety in China, university decision-makers and faculty should increase their appreciation and understanding about entrepreneurship education, actively engaging in the reform of higher education. They need to coordinate existing resources within the university and explore differing methods for selecting, training and rewarding qualified teachers and instructors. There should be a change in their performance criteria from sole dependence on academics to a knowledge-transfer, value-creation approach. TOPIEP can be both a feasible and effective way to implement IEE with Chinese characteristics and with global impact.

NOTES AND REFERENCES

*   The corresponding author is Liu Lijun, Faculty Director, Center for Innovation and Entrepreneurship Education, Beijing Institute of Technology (lijunliu2000@263.net). Guan Sisi is a graduate student at the Center for Innovation and Entrepreneurship Education, BIT. This work was supported in part by the National Philosophy and Social Sciences Fund (11AGL003), by the Humanities and Social Sciences Fund (07JA880011) of the Ministry of Education of the People's Republic of China (MEPRC) and by the Graduate Educational Innovation Program (P-0801) of MEPRC.

1.   Zhang Yuli and Li Zheng, "Development of Entrepreneurship Education Practice and Studying in Universities of the world", *Entrepreneurship Research and Education International Conference*, 943–952, 10–11 April 2006, Tianjin. 张玉利，李政"国内外大学创业教育实践与理论研究进展"《创业研究与教育国际研讨会会议论文，PART B》943-952, 2006年4月10-11日，天津, http://www.stdaily.com/gb/education/2002-09/11/content_14565.htm.

2.   Smits, Ruud, "Innovation Studies in the 21st Century: Questions from a User's Perspective", *Technological Forecasting and Social Change*, 69:9, December 2002, 861–883.

3.   Etzkowitz, Henry and Loet Leydesdorff, "The Triple Helix of University–Industry–Government Relations: A Laboratory for Knowledge-Based Economic Development", *EASST Review*, 14:1, 1995, 14–19.

4.   Dorf, Richard C. and Thomas Byers, *Technology Ventures – From Idea to Enterprise*, New York: McGraw-Hill Higher Education, 2008.

5.   Ohland, Matthew W., Sherry A. Frillman, Guili Zhang and Thomas K. Miller, "NC State's Engineering Entrepreneurs Program in the Context of US Entrepreneurship Programs", March 2004, Paper presented at the NCIIA 8th Annual Meeting, San Jose, CA.155-163, www.nciia.net

6.   Plummer, James, "Educating Engineers for the 21st Century[EB/OL]", 20 December 2009, http://soe.stanford.edu/about/changeforeducation.html.

7.   Ferguson, Marilyn, *The Aquarian Conspiracy: Personal and Social Transformation in the 1980s*, New York: St Martin's Press, 1980.

8.   Cherwitz, Richard A. and Charlotte A. Sullivan, "Intellectual entrepreneurship – A Vision for Graduate Education", *Change*, November/December, 2002, 23–27. Retrieved 13 August 2008, from https://webspace.utexas.edu/cherwit z/www/articles/change.pdf.

9.   Savin-Baden, M., *Problem-based Learning in High Education: Untold Stories*, Philadelphia, PA: Open University Press, 2000.

10. Hamermesh, Richard G., Paul W. Marshall, Michael J. Roberts and Howard H. Stevenson, "Entrepreneurship: It Can be Taught – Lessons from the Classroom", *Harvard Business School Working Knowledge*, 2002. Available at http://hbswk.hbs.edu/item/2905.html.

11. Wang, Eric L. and John A. Kleepe, "Teaching Invention, Innovation, and Entrepreneurship in Engineering", *Journal of Engineering Education*, October 2001, 565–570.

12. "Princeton Review Annual Ranking of Top Colleges for Entrepreneurship", *Entrepreneur Magazine*, http://www.entrepreneur.com/topcolleges.

13. Wang, Eric L. and John A. Kleepe, "Teaching Invention, Innovation, and Entrepreneurship in Engineering", *Journal of Engineering Education*, 10, 2001, 565–570.

14. Thornton, Karen, Sarah Djamshidi and David Barbe, "Venture Accelerator Programs: Accelerating Fledgling Technology Start-ups at University of Maryland", University of Maryland, College Park, NCIIA 8th Annual Meeting, 18–20 March 2004, 39–40.

15. Timmons, Jeffry, "The Entrepreneurship Revolution: Reflections on Forty Years as Participant and Observer", Y.L. Zhang (Chair), *Entrepreneurship Research and Education International Conference*, Tianjin, 10 April 2006

16. "Several Opinions on Implementation of Graduate Innovation Program, Strengthening Innovative Capability, Promotion Fostering Quality", Ministry of Education of the People's Republic of China, http://www.moe.edu.cn/publicfiles/business/htmlfiles/moe/moe_191/list.html. June 2005. 《教育部关于实施研究生教育创新计划，加强研究生创新能力培养，进一步提高培养质量的若干意见》（教研[2005] 1号）. http://www.moe.edu.cn/publicfiles/business/htmlfiles/moe/moe_191/list.html, 2005年6月.

17. Weilerstein, P., F. Ruiz, and M. Gorman, "The NCIIA: Turning Students into Inventors and Entrepreneurs, Antennas and Propagation Magazine", IEEE, 45:6, December 2003, 130–134. Retrieved 25 August 2008 from http://ieeexplore.ieee.org/xpl/freeabs_all.jsp?arnumber=1282188.

18. He, Jinqiu and Yan Zhang, "The Orientation of the Science and Technology Park University Functions", *Chinese University Technology Transfer*, 8 August 2005, 27–30. 何晋秋、章琰，"大学科技园的功能定位"《中国高校科技与产业化》，2005年第8期.

19. Li Jian, "Handling Correction the Four Main Relationships During the Construction of a University Park", 1 February 2004. 李健正确处理大学科技园建设中的四个关系, http://gdkj.lut.cn/kjdt/0404027.htm.

20. Lumsdaine, E., "A Multidisciplinary Approach to Teaching Invention and Entrepreneuring", *American Society for Engineering Education (ASEE) Annual Conference and Exposition Proceedings* (on CD-ROM), June 2001, 24–27.

21. For example, see Hall, J. and C.W. Hofer, "Venture Capitalist's Decision Criteria in New Venture Evaluation", *Journal of Business Venturing*, 1, 1993, 25–42; and Fried, V.H. and R.D. Hisrich, "Towards a Model of Venture Capital Investment Decision Making", *Financial* Management, 3, 1994, 28–37; and Bacher, Jagedeed Singh."Decision Making Criteria Used by Canadian Equity Investors to Evaluate Early Stage Technology Based Companies", Thesis, Waterloo, Ontario, 1999.

22. Luryi, Serge, Wendy Tang et al., "Entrepreneurship in Engineering Education", *37th ASEE/IEEE Frontiers in Education Conference*, Milwaukee, October 2007, 10–14; and "Judging List of University Entrepreneurship Competition Jiang Su Province", 2008, http://zjc.xzit.edu.cn/jy/news/edit/UploadFile/20071210105533216.DOC, 江苏省大学创业设计大赛评分表[EB/OL].

7. Entrepreneurship education in Japan

Takeru Ohe*

7.1 THE BREAKDOWN OF HOME-BASED ENTREPRENEURSHIP EDUCATION

Japan is a country made up of well-established family businesses. According to the Teikoku DataBank,[1] there are over 19000 companies more than 100 years old in Japan. Ninety-nine percent of these are classified as family businesses. This is 1.6 percent of the total 1.2 million companies in this country. The oldest company in the world, in fact, is located in Japan. Kongo-gumi, which specializes in building shrines and temples, was established in the year 578, more than 1400 years ago.[2] In order to survive over many years, often in severe economic and political environments, these businesses have upheld the entrepreneurial traditions of their family credos.

Most of these long-lasting companies have kept these family credos in either written form or unwritten form, passed down to the current generation. The credos emphasize one or more of five basic values: thankfulness, working diligence, innovation, thriftiness, and contribution to society. These five values have been broadly practiced in Japanese society in general. Family members are reminded of these values on a daily basis in their homes. In traditional homes, the living quarters are usually located on the second floor of their stores, or in their plants, or in the same neighborhood. Children grow up observing or helping with the work of their parents or employees on a day-to-day basis. The family credos are clearly expressed daily by their parents or grandparents, or even by managers of the family businesses. Home-based entrepreneurship education through the family business has kept Japan very entrepreneurial, and successful in creating many new companies in the past.

The importance of home-based entrepreneurship education in Japan[3] is reflected in Table 7.1. It shows the percentage of entrepreneurs who have encountered one or more of five different experiences that may have influenced their decisions to become an entrepreneur.

As Table 7.1 shows, 68.6 percent of entrepreneurs surveyed had

Table 7.1   Entrepreneurial experience

Total number of surveyed entrepreneurs = 44 (Male: 39, Female : 5)	The percentage of the entrepreneurs who have encountered some of experiences below	The percentage of the entrepreneurs who might have been influenced in their decision to become entrepreneur by these experiences
The percentage of entrepreneurs who have encountered at least one of the following five experiences under 18 years old	68.6	40.9
1. Family's words and actions	54.3	31.8
2. Entrepreneur's words and actions (who are not your family)	31.8	11.4
3. Classes on entrepreneurship and career development	4.5	0.0
4. Bazaars and open air markets	40.9	2.3
5. Movies, television programs and books about entrepreneurs and ventures	25.0	4.5

encountered at least one of the five entrepreneurial experiences in the survey while under the age of 18; 40.9 percent of the entrepreneurs said the experiences influenced them in their decisions to become entrepreneurs; 54.3 percent have encountered the experiences through their family's words and actions; and 31.8 percent said their encounters through the family's words and actions have influenced their decision to become an entrepreneur. It is interesting to note that of those encountering entrepreneurship through other, non-familial experiences, relatively few attribute those experiences as influencing their decision to become entrepreneurs. Since formal school-based entrepreneurship education started ten years ago, only 4.5 percent of entrepreneurs have taken entrepreneurship classes or career guidance classes, but none of them were influenced by these classes in their decisions to become entrepreneurs. This survey shows that family influences were essential to their decision to become entrepreneurs. Traditional home-based entrepreneur education therefore plays a significant role in influencing entrepreneurship in Japan.

On the other hand, Table 7.2 shows that career guidance in school had strong influence on the decision to be a company employee, instead of an entrepreneur. The questionnaire addresses the reasons why company

Table 7.2   Influence on career decision

Company employees	Categories	Total (n = 56)	
	Choices	Upon graduation (%)	At present (%)
1	I do(did) not consider other alternatives other than being an employed worker	66.1	26.8
2	The school career guidance has led me to become an employed worker	32.1	1.8
3	My parents expect(ed) me to be an employee in a company	25.0	10.7
4	I am happy being a company employee	19.6	21.4

employees chose such positions upon graduation from college or university, and why they are still working as company employees. Table 7.2 shows that 66.1 percent of the employees had not considered other alternatives than being an employee upon graduation. However, after working several years as a company employee, only 26.8 percent of the employees chose to remain as employees. Company employees were also influenced by school guidance counselors (32.1 percent) and parents (25.0 percent) to be employees upon graduation. From this result, it is clear that employees did not consider an entrepreneurship career path upon graduating from college or university.

Table 7.3 shows that the influence of parents on their children's career decisions upon graduation differs for children with company-employed parents and children with self-employed parents. Upon graduation, the majority of company employees had considered this career path upon graduation, regardless of whether their parents were employees or self-employed. But while 34.5 percent of those with employee parents received encouragement to become a company employee, only 11.8 percent of employees with self-employed parents did. Nonetheless, while 64.7 percent of company employees with self-employed parents considered becoming company employees upon graduation, only 17.6 percent currently consider remaining company employees.

During the high economic growth period before Japan's bubble burst in 1991, various cities launched development projects throughout Japan. Many manufacturing plants, including very small ones, were forced out of the cities into industrial parks located outside the cities. Many stores were forced to relocate from areas where major road networks were being built. In many instances, this resulted in the separation of living quarters from family stores

Table 7.3   Influence by parents on company employee's career decision

Choices		Parent was company employee (n = 29)		Parent was self-employed (n = 17)	
		Upon graduation (percent)	At present (percent)	Upon graduation (percent)	At present (percent)
1	I do (did) not consider alternatives other than being an employed worker	72.4	34.5	64.7	17.6
2	The school career guidance has led me to become an employed worker	31.0	3.4	35.3	0.0
3	My parents expect(ed) me to be employed in a company	34.5	10.3	11.8	11.8
4	I am happy being a company employee	24.1	17.2	11.8	23.5

and plants, diminishing the traditional home-based entrepreneurship education system. This reduced the chance for great learning opportunity, where children could observe their parents working on a daily basis.

Another reason for the breakdown of traditional home-based entrepreneurship education is due to the introduction of vending machines in family stores. Japan has the highest number of vending machines per capita in the world, with about one machine for every 23 people.[4] Nowadays, even surviving small, family-run stores have introduced vending machines to replace face-to-face selling. Thus, children lost the opportunity to learn through face-to-face selling. A third reason for the breakdown is that the children of family businesses were sent to cram schools after their regular school hours. Furthermore, they spent most of their free time playing games by themselves, watching television or reading comic books after returning from cram schools.

It is not easy to directly relate the breakdown of home-based entrepreneurship education to the current low entrepreneurship activities in Japan. However, as the GEM shows, Japan exhibits one of the lowest entrepreneurship activity rates among the 54 GEM countries participating in 2009.[5] Among the wealthy, innovation-driven economies, Japan ranks the lowest in early stage entrepreneurial activity (TEA) (Table 7.4).

Table 7.4   Entrepreneurial activities in Japan: Prevalence (%) of entrepreneurial activity and business owner-managers across GEM countries

(GEM Global 2009 Adult Population Survey (APS) For International Comparisons, sample based on 18–64 Age Group)	Average among Innovation-Driven Economies	Japan	Korea	USA
1 Nascent Entrepreneurship Rate Percentage	3.4	1.9	2.7	4.9
2 New Business Ownership Rate Percentage	3.1	1.3	4.4	3.2
3 Early-Stage Entrepreneurship Activity (TEA) Percentage	6.5	3.2	7.1	8.1

7.2   LATE START OF SCHOOL-BASED ENTREPRENEURSHIP EDUCATION

Besides the breakdown of home-based entrepreneurship education, the lack of entrepreneurship education, particularly school-based entrepreneurship education, may contribute to the current low entrepreneurship rates. Compared to the United States,[6] Japan did not consider entrepreneurship education seriously until the bubble burst in 1991, as shown in Table 7.5.

Table 7.5 shows some key events in the evolution of entrepreneurship education in Japan in the 1990s. It is very clear from Table 7.5 that Japanese entrepreneurship education began around 20 years after that in the United States. The academic community of entrepreneurship also was formed late. The Japan Academic Society for Ventures and Entrepreneurships was established in November 1997, with the first ever conference on entrepreneurship and ventures being held in Japan at the same time. However, that is still 16 years behind the first Babson College Entrepreneurship Research Conference in 1981.

Furthermore, the passage of the Japanese version of the Bayh–Dole Act[7] in 1999 was also almost 20 years behind the United States. Upon passage of Japanese version, the "University Venture 1000" plan was inaugurated by the Ministry of Economy, Trade and Industry (METI) in 2001. From 2002 onwards, technology license offices and incubation facilities were established in major Japanese universities with funds from METI. By the end of 2004 a total of 1099 ventures were established.

Table 7.5   Chronology of entrepreneurship education in Japan

	USA	Japan
1968	First undergraduate entrepreneurship concentration, Babson College	
1971	First MBA entrepreneurship concentration, University of Southern California	
1974	Entrepreneurship Interest Group of the Academy of Management formed under the direction of Karl Vesper	
1980	Bayh–Dole Act	
1981	First Babson Entrepreneurship Research Conference and first publication of Frontiers of Entrepreneurship Research	
1984	First single campus business plan competitions at Babson College and University of Texas-Austin (Moot Corp, now called venture Labs Investment Competition)	
1991		Economic bubble burst
1992		Entrepreneurship Interest Group (known as Waseda Entrepreneurship Research Unit) formed under the direction of Prof. Shuichi Matsuda
1995		First undergraduate entrepreneurship course taught, Hosei University
1996		First Venture Kids camp by Takeru Ohe
1997		The Japan Academic Society for Ventures and Entrepreneurships formed
1998		First MBA entrepreneurship concentration, Waseda University Business School
1998		First single campus business plan competition at Waseda University
1999		Japanese Version of Bayh–Dole Act

Table 7.5 (continued)

	USA	Japan
2000		First company specializing in entrepreneurship education for kids (Self-wing)
2001		University Venture 1000 Plan by METI
2002		First university-based Technology Licensing Office (TLO) and Incubation Center, Waseda University

The report by the National Commission on Educational Reform made 17 proposals to change the Japanese education system in 1996. It emphasized cultivation of "the zest for living" through creativity, experiential learning, and interdisciplinary learning. Following the recommendations, Japanese grade schools, junior high schools and senior high schools started the "Period for Integrated Study" in 2002.[8] During this period, some schools implemented various entrepreneurship education programs. Due to the lack of preparation and experience of the teachers, however, most of the schools were not successful in implementing experiential learning programs. As a result, only a few programs were based on experience-based learning, such as the V-kids Program originating at Waseda University in 1996. Unfortunately, the emphasis on the "Period for Integrated Study" has been diverted, as entrepreneurship education faced implementation difficulties within the school system.

7.3 CURRENT ENTREPRENEURSHIP EDUCATION

7.3.1 Entrepreneurship Education for Young People

In 1996, I organized one of the first entrepreneurship camps for teenagers in Toyama Prefecture.[9] Since 2000, METI has provided financial support for various programs on entrepreneurship education for young people. The Junior Achievement Program has created various initiatives, such as the Trading Game, which emphasizes teaching about the world economy and society. Others include the Quest Education Program, Dream Map Project, Check Market Project, Internship Program, and the Angel Game.

A total of 69 000 school kids have participated in the Junior Achievement Program over the five-year period.

The Junior Chamber of Commerce and the Chamber of Commerce were also active in supporting experience-based entrepreneurship education. Aizu-Wakamatsu city, Totsutori prefecture, and Sagamihara city have all received Japan Venture Awards for their active participation in entrepreneurship education. These awards are sponsored by the Organization for SME and Regional Innovation in Japan. Various non-governmental organizations (NGOs), such as the Center of Entrepreneurship Development in Kyoto and "My Vision", in Tokyo have been active in teaching entrepreneurship education. Also, private companies such as Learning Brain K.K. in Fukushima prefecture have been active in helping local schools implement experience-based entrepreneurship education.

The Ministry of Education introduced the Period for Integrated Study in 2000. This aimed to provide students with opportunities to learn and discover their own personalities and to think about their future plans. School subjects like "Human Beings and Industrial Society" have become requirements. Additionally, various entrepreneurship courses were implemented in schools. However, due to complaints from parents, who accused these programs of causing the recent decline in academic achievement, complaints from teachers about their heavy workload, and a lack of teaching skills to implement this properly, the Ministry of Education stopped this program in 2010. This poses challenges for the development of school-based entrepreneurship education within the current school systems.

In addition, in 2006 the Financial Services Agency started an entrepreneurship education program to promote knowledge about financing and the stock market. In 2003, the Minister of Health, Labor and Welfare opened My Job House in Kyoto for the purpose of giving job experience and career advice to young people. However, due to its inconvenient location, a small number of visitors and high maintenance costs, the center was forced to close down in 2010 after spending substantial funds.

On the other hand, commercial high schools have been very active in promoting experience-based entrepreneurship courses. Misawa Commercial High School in Aomori prefecture, Hiroshima Commercial High School in Hiroshima prefecture, and Mizuho Commercial High School in Yamanashi prefecture have implemented programs where students have used local materials to develop their own products, such as cakes and canned foods, written their own business plans and successfully marketed these products.

One successful example is Kiz City Japan K.K., which operates Kidzania educational entertainment facilities in Tokyo and Osaka. These

Table 7.6 Entrepreneurship courses offered in Japanese universities

University	Type	Number of courses		Non-classroom activities		
		Under-graduate	Graduate	Seminar/symposium	Business plan contest	Incubation center
Tohoku	National	6	10	○	○	○
Miyagi	Private	8	14			
Jousai Kokusai	Private	3	17	○		
Keio	Private	13	12	○	○	○
Waseda	Private	6	10	○	○	○
Ritsumeikan	Private	14	8	○	○	○
Kouchi Kouka	Private	2	15	○		

are very popular among K-6. The concept was developed in Mexico and has been expanded to more than ten cities around the world.

7.3.2 Higher Entrepreneurship Education in College and Business School

A survey conducted in 2008 by Daiwa Institute of Research found that out of the 734 colleges and universities in Japan, 247 offer a total of 1078 courses related to entrepreneurship.[10] This represents a 77 percent increase in schools offering entrepreneurship courses since 2001, and a 166 percent increase in entrepreneurship courses offered since 2001. Fifty-five percent of the schools offering entrepreneurship courses also offer entrepreneurship concentrations as both majors and minors. Thirty-eight of the colleges and universities hold business plan contests for students, and 33 have incubation facilities.

In spite of the above, 40 percent of the colleges and universities offer just a single entrepreneurship course within their curriculum. Those offering multiple entrepreneurship courses tend to be private colleges and universities. Table 7.6 lists the colleges and universities which offer more than 15 courses in entrepreneurship.

Based on the Daiwa Institute study, around 65 percent of entrepreneurship courses are taught by faculty members of the schools and the remaining 25 percent are taught by non-faculty members, such as entrepreneurs and consultants. These courses are basically taught in a one-way lecture style with occasional question-and-answer sessions. These tend to fail in arousing any student participation. Only 30 percent of entrepreneurship courses utilize student project presentations or group discussion.

As the majority of the colleges and universities offer only a single course in entrepreneurship, the course content tends to be heavily one-sided. The content focuses mainly on theory of entrepreneurship and venture management. However, where multiple entrepreneurship courses are offered, subjects and activities may include: case studies on entrepreneurship and venture management; business plans; lecture series by entrepreneurs; entrepreneurial marketing; and entrepreneurial finance.

7.4   V-KIDS PROGRAM

7.4.1   Background

The V-Kids Program[11] is based on a pseudo-business experience – to provide young people with experiences similar to those derived from home-based entrepreneurship education. The program is unique in giving elementary and junior high school students the chance to experience the actual full business cycle. This program has been conducted with assistance from local shopping centers, chambers of commerce and business leaders. Materials used include textbooks, worksheets, audio visual materials, and a teachers' manual developed by Selfwing Corporation.

The basic model of this program was developed during a short summer camp located in a national park in Toyama prefecture in 1996. Since 1998, Waseda University's laboratory has held Waseda Venture Kids Camp at Mother Farm near Tokyo. Upon its establishment in 2000, Selfwing Corporation further developed the program into the V-Kids Program. The current program accepts students between nine and 18 years old. Since its start, more than 10 000 children have taken part in this program in Japan. It has also been tested in Korea, Thailand and Malaysia as part of an expansion program. The program received the Commissioner Award of the Small and Medium Enterprise Agency for the Entrepreneurship Education Category at the Japan Venture Awards 2008 Forum.

7.4.2   Methodology of the Program

In this quasi-business program, students start their company by operating their business through to the closing of their books, experiencing a full actual business cycle. Activities include conducting market research, writing business plans, negotiating loans from a quasi-bank, producing gift items, selling to general customers, closing the books, and making donations from the profits made.

In order to ensure sustainability of the program in the schools, three basic rules are followed:

- Rule 1: No food business is allowed since it requires various complicated legal health code procedures.
- Rule 2: Each business must purchase raw materials at appropriate prices and allocate realistic manufacturing costs.
- Rule 3: The total business budget is limited to a $100 (10 000 yen) in sales for junior high schools.

The practical steps of the program are illustrated in Table 7. 7

7.4.3 Objectives of V-Kids

The objective of the V-Kids program is to help students cultivate the necessary skills they need to be self-employed and entrepreneurial. The means by which this is accomplished is through a hands-on entrepreneurship experience.

Solving problems by themselves
Under this program, teachers and trainers do not play "teacher" roles. They support the students but do not give them answers. Whenever students ask questions, the trainers prompt and guide them to solve the problems themselves. Students who devise a better way and find appropriate answers by themselves will be deemed the best contributors to their teams.

Cooperating and building teamwork
Students form teams of four to five members. They are assigned unique roles, such as President, Accounting Manager, Sales Manager and Quality Control Manager. They must fulfill the responsibilities of their roles, and cooperate with one another to maximize the team's profits. Through the program, students learn how to form opinions, share resources with their team and negotiate with one another.

Thinking with a business mind
Students are already consumers of various products and services, and can therefore understand a customer perspective. However, through this program, they are trained to take a provider's point of view. They need to apply a business mind and time-management skills to all activities. For example, during the product planning phase, rather than identifying what products they want to sell, students consider what products potential customers may want to buy. Through various exercises, they start to

Table 7.7   V-Kid Program

Steps	Subject	Program description	Aim of learning
1	Introduction	• Explanation of activities	• Arouse the interest of students
2	Starating the company	• Decision on the company name and member's role • Understand the importance of role, consider self strong point and division of roles	• Realize one's own strong points and other's strong points
3	Market research	• Acquisition of the market information on targeted customers and competing products	• Study the view point of products' provider
4	Planning the product	• Planning of products	• Plan the product to suit customer taste
5	Making the business plan	• Making the business plan (products and purchasing, number of products, price, profit, and so on)	• Understand the purpose and know-how of business plan • Learn the logical thinking
6	Collecting funds	• Presentation the business plan and requesting funds	• Learn to explain the feasibility of plan logically • Understand the importance of business plan and the responsibility of business
7	Purchasing	• Purchase the necessary materials	• Purchase the materials as planned • Have cost-consciousness
8	Making the products	• Making the products as planned on time	• Consider about quality of products • Learn time management • Make division of roles and work effectively
9	Preparing the advertisement	• Making the posters and flyers	• Consider how to display the products • Understand the purpose of advertisement and its effective method

Table 7.7   (continued)

Steps	Subject	Program description	Aim of learning
10	Preparing for sales	• Decision on the sales price	• Learn about service for customers • Study business manners • Re-realize sales, costs and profits
11	Sales activity	• Selling the products	• Learn to sell the products for customers • Acquire the challenging spirit toward success
12	Closing account	• Closing account and repaying the debt	• Reconsider sales, costs and profits
13	Summary	• Summarizing activity	• Make summary of activity of program for understanding

understand business systems and learn to take an objective point of view. The program goes beyond a virtual simulation. It provides the students with real hands-on experience for planning and operating their own businesses.

7.4.4   Basic Concepts of the Program

This program applies four fundamental concepts:

Local alliances
Students form relationships with local business people, who benefit from the students' fresh ideas and energy.

Integration of basic school subjects
Students are required to apply concepts and skills learned in school, such as language, calculus, science, social studies and arts. For example, they use math skills to calculate profits, and they use their presentation skills to explain their business ideas and plans.

Corporate compliance
Crimes have not only been committed by well-known companies in Japan, but there are also increasing numbers of Internet-related scams by college and even high school students. It is very important to inculcate ethics and compliance with legal business practices into the program.

Project-based learning
Students learn to work in teams to develop their own ideas, manufacture products based on these ideas, and market/sell the products. They understand the role of business in their society through real-life experience. It is not easy to teach creative thinking and actions in an uncertain context through traditional methods. Teachers do not simply transmit knowledge to the students; they encourage them to think independently and be creative, not only in the classroom but also through fieldwork.

7.5   WASEDA UNIVERSITY'S INCUBATION CENTER

7.5.1   The Incubation Center at Waseda

Waseda University was founded in 1882 by Mr Shigeharu Okuma. It is the third-largest university in Japan with 52 000 students. The main campus is located in the center of Tokyo. The university has traditionally produced some well-known entrepreneurs, such as Mr Masaru Ibuka, co-founder of Sony, Mr Tadashi Yanai, CEO of Fast Retailing Co., Ltd, and also Mr Lee Kun-Hee, Chairman of the Samsung Group. Statistics show that Waseda University has the largest number of student ventures of any Japanese university.[12] Table 7.8 shows those that were established between 1994 and 2008 at Waseda and other top Japanese universities. Many more ventures have been established at Waseda since then.

Waseda University set up its incubation center in 2002. It is one of the earliest such centers associated with a university in Japan. Professor Hideo Namiki from Waseda's Faculty of Education and Integrated Arts and Sciences was the first director of the center. In 2007, I took over the director's position and introduced the concept of a Teaching Incubation Center, which is explained in the next section.

Table 7.8   Number of ventures from university

Rank	University	Prof. ventures	Student ventures	Others	Total Venture
1	Tokyo University	104	26	17	147
2	Waseda University	40	48	19	107
3	Osaka University	74	8	0	82
4	Kyoto University	35	26	18	79
5	Tukuba University	30	24	22	76

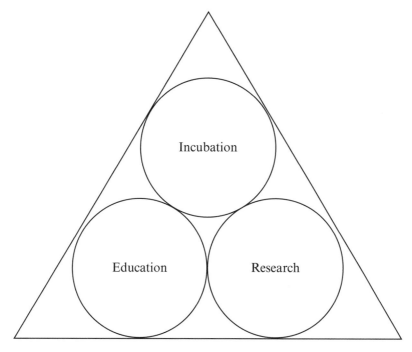

Figure 7.1   Teaching incubation center

In 2008, the Waseda Incubation Center shifted to a new location. The center now occupies the first floor of a 30-story residential tower located next to the Waseda University main campus. The center has three sections: a section with 11 private rooms, an open section with eight cubicles and six work spaces, and an administrative office with two meeting rooms. The center provides rooms of various sizes to meet the growing needs of the business ventures. A venture can stay for a maximum of three years provided it has a good track record of growth. In order to have a private office space, the venture needs to present a business plan, with recommendations from professors to the admissions committee.

7.5.2   Teaching Incubation Center

The concept of the Teaching Incubation Center is analogous to the idea of a teaching hospital. Similar to a teaching hospital, the Teaching Incubation Center has three strategic roles: incubation, education and research. As illustrated in Figure 7.1, these three roles integrate to form Waseda University's Entrepreneurship Ecosystem.

The incubation role

The Center expanded the types of ventures it accepts for incubation to include five categories: "professor ventures", "student ventures", "new corporate ventures", "affiliated university ventures", and "international ventures". This greater variety of ventures increases opportunities for synergies and expands the ventures' network, particularly by incubating more international ventures.

In order to identify potential technologies that could form the basis of new businesses, the incubation manager and a student facilitator visit research laboratories in the university about six times a year. Successful ideas that can be converted into potential business plans are invited into the Incubation Center for assistance and support.

The members of the incubation community consist of individuals who plan to start their business, individuals who have just started businesses, and firms that have graduated from the Incubation Center. Outside corporations interested in becoming members must be introduced by a faculty member of Waseda University and undergo a screening process. The center offers a reasonably priced monthly membership fee of $100 (10 000 yen) per corporation. Occupancy is based on the Plug and Play concept:[13] the idea that it is not necessary for a start-up to occupy a private room until it shows a relatively clear and reliable potential. This is reasonable since a venture's success rate is low.

In order to support management of these ventures, the center provides five consultants consisting of one CPA, one business analyst, two small and medium-sized enterprise (SME) management consultants, and one business recovery expert. Lawyers and patent agents are also available when needed. Members can receive advice from these consultants, as well as attend specialized seminars in the Incubation Center. Regular seminar topics include temporary employment, incorporation procedures, and fund raising.

To encourage interaction among ventures occupying the Incubation Center, community members, and students interested in ventures and entrepreneurship, networking events are held approximately once a month. Besides the monthly networking events, there are also special interest group events for female students and for foreign students.

An example of a successful professor venture is a company named Trade Science Corporation, led by Mr Koichi Kato. Mr Kato started the "KABU ROBO" project in April 2006 while he was a visiting researcher at the Research Institute of Information Technology and Management of Waseda University. KABU ROBO is a computerized portfolio management program. The corporation was eventually bought by MONEX K.K. for about 1 billion yen, equivalent to US$10 million, in November 2008.

The education role

To fulfill the education role, the center provides an environment for learning that cannot be gained through classroom lectures. The Incubation Center is directly involved in the "Basic Course in Venture Entrepreneur Incubation", which is supported by donations from Daiwa Securities Group. Approximately 100 undergraduate students attend the course annually, submitting business ideas as their final assignment. Daiwa Securities Group also provides internship opportunities for outstanding students. Students submitting excellent business ideas can also become community members of the Incubation Center.

In addition, I teach a course entitled "Shillman High-tech Venture Management". This is a practical course that includes venture founders as guest speakers and presentations of successful business plans. Based on the idea that entrepreneurship starts from action, the Incubation Center emphasizes practice rather than theories, and thus supports practical courses. As such, the center intends to cultivate entrepreneurship and produce entrepreneurs through entrepreneurship education. Besides these two courses, there are about 16 other courses within the entrepreneurship curriculum.

Students interested in consulting and entrepreneurship are recruited as facilitators for corporations in residence at the Incubation Center. They perform activities such as brainstorming new business concepts. Every November, the Incubation Center takes part in Global Entrepreneurship Week, sponsored by the Kauffman Foundation.

An example of a successful student venture is the case of Mr Taichi Murakami, who graduated from Waseda's School of Political Science and Economics in March 2009. He attended the Basic Course in Venture Entrepreneur Incubation in the spring semester as a freshman, and submitted a term project for Job Sense, a part-time employment website. This received the highest award in the class. The following year, he established Livesense Co., Ltd. based on this project. He expanded the services offered, including adding a full-time employment site. After he graduated from Waseda University, he moved out of the Incubation Center to occupy a larger office space so he could expand the business. Currently, the company is preparing for an initial public offering (IPO) within the next one to two years. The entrepreneur aims to become the youngest president to get a company listed in Japan.

The research role

For the research role, the center provides various research themes on business management for master's theses, doctoral theses, and journal articles, such as *Entrepreneurship Ecosystem: A Study of Waseda University*

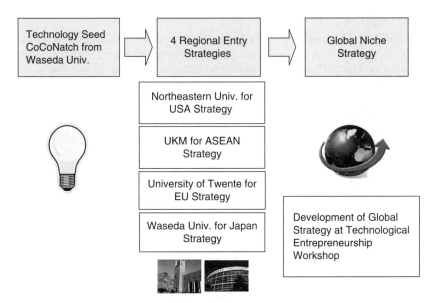

Figure 7.2   Development of global strategy at technological entrepreneurship workshop

Incubation Center,[14] *the COBLAS program for Entrepreneurship Education in ASEAN universities*[15] etc. Two continuous research themes have been pursued from 2008 till 2010.[16] One examines the roles of the incubation center and the university in helping university ventures with their global strategy. Another research theme centers on the formation of new alliances between the university and corporations.

With regards to technology development in Japan, it is said that most technologies may become obsolete in the next five years due to overreliance on the Japanese domestic market, and the diminishing share of this domestic market among small Japanese ventures.[17] To address this situation, it is necessary to deploy global niche strategies. Thus, incubation centers in the affiliated universities around the world are creating business plans for potential university spin-off venture markets in respective countries, and trying to establish global strategies through these plans (see Figure 7.2).

One example of the above is a collaborative effort between students and professors at Waseda University, Northeastern University in Boston, the National University of Malaysia (UKM), and the University of Twente in the Netherlands to develop a global niche strategy in four regions for a venture named CoCoNatch at the Technological Entrepreneurship Workshop, which will be held on 7 and 8 March 2011.

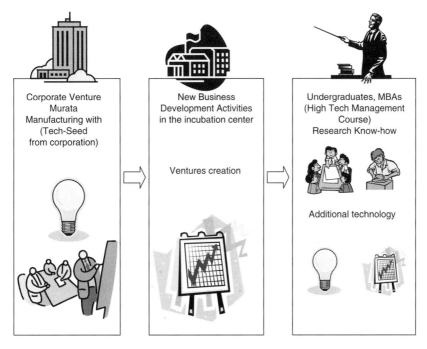

Corporate Venture Murata Manufacturing with (Tech-Seed from corporation)	New Business Development Activities in the incubation center	Undergraduates, MBAs (High Tech Management Course) Research Know-how

Figure 7.3   Business development type industrial–academic alliance

Figure 7.3 shows the business development type industrial–academic alliance between industry and academia. Because this focuses on business development, rather than technology development, conference rooms and Internet access become more important factors than research facilities. The Incubation Center offers the following services: a technological search service via incubation centers of Waseda Univerisity and affiliated universities as well as local governments, an introduction of technologies from Waseda University and its affiliated universities to corporations in Japan and overseas, and idea generation by students to help corporations develop themes for the future needs.

7.6   CONCLUSIONS

The current lack of entrepreneurship spirit in Japan can be traced to the breakdown of home-based entrepreneurship education by family businesses and the lack of entrepreneurship education for youth due to a late start and inadequate development of school-based entrepreneurship education. Success in the industrial age has also made Japan complacent and less prepared for the information age and for providing entrepreneurship education to youth.

The issues can be addressed by integrating enhanced entrepreneurship education programs into the mainstream education system. Two exemplary programs in entrepreneurship education are the V-Kids program, which received the Commissioner Award of the Small and Medium Enterprise Agency in 2008, and the Teaching Incubation Center Program at Waseda University, which has produced the largest number of student ventures of any university in Japan.

The learning models and methodologies created by such best practices can be used as benchmarks for others to follow, as well as to raise the overall level of entrepreneurial spirit in entrepreneurship education.

NOTES AND REFERENCES

* Takeru Ohe is Professor in the Graduate School of Commerce, Waseda University (tohe.ohe@waseda.jp).
1. Teikoku DataBank, *Key Factors for Millennium Companies*, Tokyo: Asahi Sinsho, 2009. 百年続く企業の条件　老舗は変化を恐れない.
2. O'Hara, W. T., *Centuries of Success: Lessons from the World's most Enduring Family Businesses*, Avon, MA: Adams Media Corp., 2004.
3. Ishiguro, J., "Analysis on the Impact of Japanese Entrepreneurship Education and Entrepreneurial Experiences for the Development of Entrepreneurs – Through Employed Workers' Survey", *IntEnt Conference* 2010, the Netherlands, 5–8 July 2010.
4. Japan Vending Machine Manufactures Association, http://www.jvma.or.jp/.
5. Bosma, N. and J. Levie, *Global Entrepreneurship Monitor 2009 Global Report*, Babson Park, MA: Gobal Entrepreneurship Research Consortium, 2009.
6. Katz, Jerome, "The Chronology and Intellectual Trajectory of American Entrepreneurship Education: 1876–1999", *Journal of Business Venturing*, 18, 2003, 283–300.
7. The Bayh–Dole Act gave US universities, small businesses and non-profits intellectual property control of their inventions and other intellectual property resulting from research funded by the federal government. It was adopted into legislation in 1980.
8. Program for Educational Reform (Ministry of Education). Available at http://wwwwp.mext.go.jp/eky2000/.
9. Ohe, T. and C. Sugiyama, *Change Kids with Entrepreneurship Education*, Tokyo: Nihon Keizai Shinbun, 1999. 起業家教育で子供が変わる.
10. "Entrepreneurship Education in Universities and Graduate Schools in Japan", 2010, available at http://www.meti.go.jp/meti_lib/report/2009fy01/0017381.pdf. 平成20年度大学・大学院における起業家教育実態調査　報告書.
11. Hirai, Y., "Short Term Effects And Impact of Waseda Venture-Kids Program as an Entrepreneurship Program for Japanese Elementary School Students", *IntEnt Conference* 2010, 5–8 July, the Netherlands.
12. "Basic Study on University Ventures in Japan", 2009, http://www.meti.go.jp/policy/. 平成20年度産業技術調査「大学発ベンチャーに関する基礎調査」実施報告.
13. "Plug and Play Tech Center", available at http://www.plugandplaytechcenter.com.
14. Ikeda, I., Entrepreneurship Ecosystem: A Study of Waseda University Incubation

Center (Japanese title: アントレプレナーシップ・エコシステムの構築に関する研究　早稲田大学インキュベーションセンターの事例から), MBA Degree Thesis, Graduate School of Commerce, Waseda University, 2010.

15. Chin, G.H., COBLAS program for Entrepreneurship Education in ASEAN Universities, MBA Degree Thesis, Graduate School of Commerce, Waseda University, 2010.

16. Report "Technological Entrepreneurship Workshop March 17–18, 2009, Waseda University, Tokyo", Report "Technological Entrepreneurship Workshop, March 9–10, 2010, Waseda University, Tokyo".

17. Agarwal, R. and Echambadi, M.S.R. "The conditioning effect of time on firm survival: An industry life cycle approach", *Academy of Management Journal* 45:5, 2002, 971–94.

8. Consulting-based entrepreneurship education: regional cases

Takeru Ohe and Siohong Tih[*]

8.1 INTRODUCTION

While entrepreneurship education often aims toward enhancing trainees' entrepreneurial intentions and small and medium-sized enterprise (SME) incubation, entrepreneurship education is yet to be fully explored and conceptualized. Conventional entrepreneurship education emphasizing theoretical understanding and classroom settings is a widely used approach in many countries. This chapter explores a more practical approach called "consulting-based entrepreneurship education" (CEE), where students develop experiential learning through consulting projects with local entrepreneurs.

This approach was relatively new to the institutes in which they were introduced, and may be new to others seeking these types of learning experiences for their students. In addition, resource allocation for educational program improvements is often limited, with priority given to those showing evidence of effectiveness and significant impact on education outcomes. As such, this chapter reviews a CEE program conducted across three Asian cultures: Malaysia, Indonesia, and Vietnam. In addition, outcome measures of student satisfaction and performance are assessed.

8.2 LITERATURE ON ENTREPRENEURSHIP EDUCATION

Entrepreneurship education and training is important for economic development, particularly in improving the quality and quantity of future entrepreneurs.[1 2 3] There has been considerable interest in entrepreneurship education and training in recent years,[3 4 5] evidenced by the growth in the number and type of program offerings, particularly at universities and educational establishments worldwide.[6 7 8] Many universities in countries such as the USA,[9 10] Canada,[11] Australia,[9] UK,[4 12] Sweden[5 13] and Malaysia,[14] have recognized the value of entrepreneurship education, and as such have been offering entrepreneurship courses and education programs.

Though the offering of university entrepreneurship education curriculum is much appreciated, there is nonetheless a question about the effectiveness of such programs: in particular, their ability to produce successful entrepreneurs. Traditional business schools tend to overemphasize quantitative and general business management concepts at the expense of the more creative skills needed for successful entrepreneurship. Hence, there is a call for restructuring entrepreneurship education programs to give more emphasis to imagination, creativity, and risk taking.[15]

In administering and evaluating the subject CEE programs in Malaysia, Indonesia and Vietnam, a team of university lecturers was assembled from these countries, as well as from Japan, where the program originated. The team members' personal experience, and interviews with administrative staff from universities throughout these three countries, revealed that most of the universities in Malaysia, Indonesia and Vietnam already offered internships, practice-based projects and entrepreneurship courses.

For example, in Malaysia, the first bachelor's program in entrepreneurship was offered by Universiti Utara Malaysia (UUM). Malaysian public universities such as UUM, Universiti Malaysia Sabah, Universiti Pendidikan Sultan Idris, Universiti Teknologi Malaysia and Universiti Kebangsaan Malaysia (UKM) also offer entrepreneurship courses and programs.

In addition, private universities in Malaysia – for example, Multimedia University and Universiti Tenaga Nasional – offer bachelor degrees in business administration, with majors in entrepreneurship. In most universities in Malaysia, masters programs in business administration offer entrepreneurship as either a core course or an elective. Course assignments include practical projects related to entrepreneurship. Students often take internship programs during their final year of study to gain business experiences. Some universities offer non-credit entrepreneurship training programs for students interested in entrepreneurship. For example, UUM offers the Program Latihan Usahawan Siswaniaga (PLUS). PLUS is a special program tailored for university students already running businesses at various locations inside the university campus. PLUS activities are designed to cultivate entrepreneurship skills and values in the students.

In Indonesia, the University of Gadjah Mada (UGM) has been offering an entrepreneurship course in their Economics Department. In this course, students learn how to develop business plans. The university also offers a rural internship program for final year students. These can involve consulting projects with SMEs and the launch of new businesses. Other universities in Indonesia, such as the University of Hasanuddin and the University of Brawijaya also offer one or two courses related

Table 8.1   Comparison of programs

	CEE	Internships	Practical Projects
Length	3–6 months (active consulting period 2–3 months plus follow-up).	3–6 months (depending on the faculty and university).	Company visits/ interviews.
Task	Consulting-based, students act as trainee consultants.	Students act as employees and are assigned particular tasks.	Students interview the companies' management or staff to get to know company practices.
Understanding of the company	Students perform an overall SWOT analysis and advise the companies on how to enhance their performance.	Students learn about the department and activities in which they are assigned.	Students perform analyses based on project requirements, for example, a marketing project will focus on market research or analysis.
Student involvement	Full involvement in planning and performing the activities suggested for the SMEs.	Involvement in specific activities.	No direct involvement; students only conduct interviews and analyses, and write reports to fulfil the requirement of the assignment.
Remarks	Immersion in a complete learning experience. Providing challenge and feedback through results achieve subsequent to the CEE program.	Learning dependent on the tasks provided. Risk that unimportant or less relevant responsibilities lead to minimal learning.	Depending on the project, outcomes may be limited to class project reports or presentations.

to entrepreneurship in their economics or business departments. At the University of Brawijaya, the entrepreneurship course is open to all university students across the different departments.

As Table 8.1 suggests, internship and practical projects can help students better understand entrepreneurship, but they can fall short in providing students with the opportunity to experience entrepreneurship in its natural setting and to understand the range of activities associated with running a business. In addition, the value of the learning is highly dependent on the nature of the projects or the tasks performed. Individual practical projects or internships might provide insufficient broad-based skills and understanding about entrepreneurship. This experience may require a combination of training programs and seminars related to entrepreneurship at the university level.

8.3 HISTORICAL BACKGROUND OF CONSULTING-BASED ENTREPRENEURSHIP EDUCATION

The CEE program was developed by a group of professors from Japan, Thailand, Cambodia, Malaysia, Laos and Indonesia. The project was led by Professor Takeru Ohe from Waseda University, Japan. The program was initiated in an entrepreneurship course in the business school at Waseda University in the spring of 2003, when the class engaged in a consulting project with a local company, Hamano Manufacturing. The program was then further developed based on a series of experimental entrepreneurship education programs conducted in Thailand, Cambodia, Malaysia, Laos and Indonesia from 2003 to 2007.[16] The academic team started by identifying topics, content and activities, and testing this structure in each of the countries. The resultant program contained 60 percent standardized content across the countries, and 40 percent localized content according to the country context.

The CEE model illustrates the interrelationship among academics (university education), the local SMEs and students as consulting apprentices. The model emphasizes the key role played by the university as both the centre of excellence for entrepreneurship knowledge and a platform for human resource development for local businesses. The linkages between these three parties are important in helping the students understand the necessary skills required, both for working in small firms and in encouraging them to start their own enterprises in the future. This education model provides graduates with crucial experience based on real business activities. Concurrently, the local SMEs involved in the program benefit from consultancy-like assistance provided by the students and experts from university.

The trial programs in the Association of South East Asian Nations (ASEAN) countries has proven fruitful. A similar concept has also been implemented in the United Kingdom (UK) through the Profit through

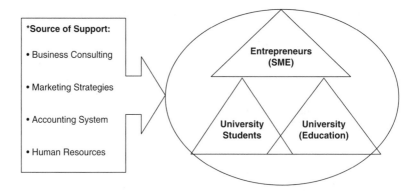

Note: Experienced lecturers and business practitioners train the students in such aspects as how to perform business analysis, develop marketing strategies and operate accounting systems. Funding sources for SMEs from local banks and government agencies were introduced during the program and students assisted the SMEs in preparing applications for this financial support. Students also developed e-commerce websites for the SMEs.

Figure 8.1   Consulting-based entrepreneurship education model

Knowledge Scheme Programme in Scotland[12] and the establishment of enterprise units in universities across the UK.[17] In those two programs, both hands-on training and entrepreneurship education improved the quality of graduates in terms of their business knowledge and readiness. This chapter reports on three of the entrepreneurship education programs that were conducted in Malaysia (2006), Indonesia (2007) and Vietnam (2008), based on the CEE model.

Each of the three universities established partnerships with local SMEs. Between 17 and 24 students participated in the programs in each nation. Professors from Japan, Cambodia, Malaysia, Indonesia and Vietnam acted as facilitators. They assigned students to selected local SMEs based on their need for assistance in developing their business. Through the programs, the students and universities provided support in such areas as marketing strategies, accounting systems, human resource management and e-commerce, as illustrated in Figure 8.1.

8.4   CEE PROGRAM IN MALAYSIA, INDONESIA AND VIETNAM

The CEE programs in Malaysia, Indonesia and Vietnam were sponsored by three different institutions. The education program cost in Malaysia was fully sponsored by the Research Institute of Economy, Trade and

Industry in Japan; and it was co-implemented by the Asia Science and Education for Economic Development Institute (AsiaSEED) and the Faculty of Economics and Business, Universiti Kebangsaan Malaysia (National University of Malaysia).

The program cost in Indonesia was fully sponsored by the Japan Bank for International Cooperation; and it was co-implemented by Waseda University in Japan, Asia SEED, the University of Brawijaya in Indonesia, and facilitated by professors from the National University of Malaysia and the National University of Management in Cambodia.

The program cost in Vietnam was fully sponsored by the Association for Overseas Technical Scholarship in Japan with co-implementation by the Foreign Trade University in Vietnam, and facilitated by professors from Waseda University, the National University of Management in Cambodia, and the National University of Malaysia (refer to Table 8.2).

In each of the countries in which the CEE program was introduced, 17 to 24 students were chosen from a group of undergraduate and/or graduate students interested in entrepreneurship education. Initially, the universities' students were informed about this program through an introductory seminar. Interested students submitted an application form and were interviewed before being selected.[18]

The organizers visited several local SMEs within reach of the participating universities to invite them to participate in the programs. The interested SMEs were then further contacted about the requirements of their participation. During the program, they would have to provide information and support, as well as attend meetings with professors and students to decide on specific activities and business strategies that the program designed for them, and allow us to assess outcomes. The participating SMEs were involved in a variety of different businesses, such as food processing, handicrafts, ceramic products, pastries, traditional herbal medicine and manufacturing of plastic bottles.

The 17 to 24 students were divided into groups, each of which would conduct full consulting-based studies for the assigned SMEs, develop business plans and perform a few marketing activities for them. A team of professors and lecturers from the programs' organizing universities were responsible for serving as facilitators and trainers to provide necessary ongoing supervision and consultation. The programs emphasized practical activities.

The teaching content of the CEE program included strengths, weaknesses, opportunities and threats (SWOT) analyses, brainstorming, critical assumption planning, attribute mapping, business plans, elevator speeches, competitor analyses, milestone planning, and examinations of product life cycles, learning cycles and consumption chains. The program

Table 8.2   Program details

Objective of sponsors	• To eliminate poverty, to decrease the unemployment rate, and to reduce regional disparity through the Educational Program for Entrepreneurship Facilitator. • To develop a pilot educational program and teaching materials to meet the needs of the actual situation in developing countries, such as ASEAN, with the goal of providing useful information, support, and close collaboration between and within Japan and ASEAN.		
	Malaysia 2005/06	Indonesia 2006/07	Vietnam 2007/08
Sponsors	The Research Institute of Economy, Trade, and Industry (RIETI), Japan	The Japan Bank for International Cooperation (JBIC)	The Association for Overseas Technical Scholarship (AOTS), Japan
Program team	20 students 7 local faculty members 5 international researchers	17 students 8 local faculty members 8 international researchers Suburban/rural locations	24 students 10 local faculty members 5 international researchers
Cost of program	RM 44 780 (RM 1 = USD 3) ~US$15 000	5 million–8 million Yen ~US$60 000	2007 1 830 000 Yen (Yen 1 = USD 85.7) ~US$21 000 2008 1 million Yen ~ US$12 000
Program objectives	• To apply the method of experimental management to Malaysian local business, and determine the most suitable method for the application of experimental management for the Malaysia situation • To use IT for e-commerce, data base development and business simulation • To enhance collaboration between industry and academia, with a local university as the center of excellence	• To develop educational program and teaching materials ,which are designed based on the actual situation in Indonesia • To develop an integrated program, a combination of field work and practical training • To support local universities in playing an important role in regional development • To promote effective collaboration among industry, government, and universities	• To give training to the teachers who will conduct the CEE program in their universities • To support the local universities' role in regional development • To apply the method of CEE in Vietnam, in order to identify modification requirements for ASEAN countries

involved several stages. At the beginning, students attended lectures on business concepts and how to prepare a business plan. This was to provide the necessary knowledge and skills in the business fields and to help them understand regional development with regard to SMEs and the local business environment.

Following each lecture, students applied the business concepts learned to the SMEs, carrying out the business activities in real business environments. They visited the SMEs and interviewed the owners and staff to gather first-hand information. Subsequently, they accessed market information via field surveys, which included interviews with potential customers about the products produced by the SMEs. Moreover, the students had to develop a business plan to help the SMEs plan future business development. An example of a CEE program schedule conducted in Malaysia is shown in Table 8.3.

8.5   PROGRAM ASSESSMENTS

The participating SMEs generally highlighted that the program has enhanced their business knowledge and performance, though not necessarily in terms of sales performance. For a few SMEs, a lack of short-term results was due to financial constraints. However, during follow-up interviews, they told the academic team that they had received bank loans after students assisted them with applications, and they have since taken steps to expand their businesses.

Overall, the sponsors were satisfied with the outcomes, and will thus continue to support this program in the ASEAN region. Other SMEs also expressed interest in participating in future programs. Additionally, the team members received requests to introduce the program to other universities. For example, in Malaysia, team members successfully introduced the program at the University Putra Malaysia and the Universiti Malaysia Kelantan.

8.6   STUDENTS' PERFORMANCE AND EXPERIENCES

Students' performance and experiences were assessed relative to team achievement, understanding of business concepts, capabilities demonstrated in their field work, quality of the business analysis, level of confidence exhibited, practical knowledge gained and their entrepreneurial intentions. In terms of team performance, students from multidisciplinary

Table 8.3   Example of the CEE Program Schedule

Steps	Subject	Program description
1	Introduction	• CEE introductory seminar • Application form distribution
2	Candidate selection	• Interviewing students • Student selection • Research team meeting – student selection • Informing successful candidates
3	Orientation	• Explain CEE purpose and outline • CEE program method • Student registration • Briefing on project • Welcome speech • Registration • Kick-off introduction of the industry • Group assignment • Orientation of group members
4	Lecture (in-class preparation)	• Introduction/example of entrepreneurship education • Thailand, Cambodia, Malaysia, Indonesia, Vietnam • SWOT/quizzing • The business environment, SWOT analysis, business consulting • Data collection • Brainstorming
5	Field work	• Data collection • Company introductory meeting • Company field work
6	Seminar	• Brainstorming, idea memoing • Field research/discussion • Consumption chain • Attribute model • Exercise-Attribute model • SWOT presentation • Remarks/feedback
7	Workshop (faculty coaching)	• Discussion of consulting plan • Meeting • Multi-micro planning (short-term actions students will carry out)

Table 8.3   (continued)

Steps	Subject	Program description
		• Student-planning • Presentation of micro planning • Individual activities planning/ distribution of tasks
8	Field work	• Field work at the companies • Data collection • Business plan development • Marketing activities • Design of material & questionnaire for data collection • Market observation • Data collection
9	Work shop (faculty coaching)	• Meeting (progress report) • Survey planning • Business plan development • Data collection
10	Field work	• Collecting data • Marketing activities • Travel • Field operation • Promotion- for the companies • Meeting with company • Preparation for survey
11	Workshop (faculty/expert coaching)	• Meeting (progress report) • Discussion with lecturers and industrial practitioners • Performance assessment
12	Seminar	• Discussion on business plan presentation • Draft business planning • Consumer survey results • Data analysis • Draft report on survey & promotional results
13	Lecture (in-class preparation)	• Lecture on experimental management • Application of IT to business promotion • Lecture • Exercises • Student presentation of progress • Discussion

Table 8.3 (continued)

Steps	Subject	Program description
14	Lecture & field work	• Lecture & discussion • Entrepreneurship assessment feedback • Field visit to related companies • Lecture –competitor analysis • Report on competitor analysis
15	Field work & networking	• Visit companies (SMEs) • Visit related government agencies • Team organized activities
16	Field work & lecture	• Visit Bank Negara (Central Bank) • Lecture • Management by assumption • Milestone planning
17	Field work	• Lecture/field visit/discussion • Evaluation by taskforce • Video – young entrepreneur • Meeting with representative from government agencies • Student presentations of business plan • Evaluation & feedback
18	Field work	• Collaborative work with producers according to the business development plan • Marketing activities • Traveling • Tasks operation
19	Workshop (faculty coaching)	• Meeting & discussion • Marketing activities
20	Seminar	• Discussion on project outcome • Cross-company discussions
21	Program report	• Reflections on the project • Evaluating student progress • Feedback for students
22	Seminar	• Presentation on the outcome of the business development activities • Evaluation and recommendation
23	Seminar	• Finalizing report • Research team meeting

backgrounds showed a high level of cooperation and contributed to group discussions. Students with information technology (IT) skills were given related tasks such as developing a website and PowerPoint presentations. In most circumstances, team performance was emphasized rather than individual performance, enabling close ties among team members. Students managed to learn different skills from each other and they benefitted from the knowledge and skills of multiple disciplines, such as management, statistics and information technology.

Students' understanding of business concepts was significantly enhanced, especially for students who were not from the business disciplines. The students informed the academic team that they had not previously heard of many of the business concepts they were working with. Even if they were aware of some concepts, such as SWOT analysis, consumption chains, and attribute mapping, they had not applied these to real business contexts. Throughout the running of the programs, students were asked to use these tools to analyze the current business operation of the assigned SMEs, and presented the outcomes to the academic team.

The field work emphasized in this program provided a platform for students to communicate with local entrepreneurs, industry players and customers. Students' capabilities in their field work activities, such as in the interviews, observations and information collection, were enhanced by the programs. At the beginning of the programs, some students were not very confident in conducting field interviews; therefore, they were guided by the professors. For students who had never conducted business fieldwork the team approach to these activities encouraged them to interact with the practitioners.

As the activities progressed, it was observed that students became more independent. For example, they arranged to meet with the SME owners by themselves and contacted relevant customers to promote the SMEs' products. The student team from Indonesia even acted as a marketing agent for one of the SMEs and assisted them in setting up a new marketing office. In Vietnam, the students contacted and persuaded more SMEs to participate in future projects. In Malaysia, the students continued assisting the SMEs after the program ended, helping them further to expand their businesses and apply for bank loans.

The CEE program allowed students to perform business analyses of the participating SMEs. In order to do this, the students had to be sensitive to the SMEs' problems, issues, and external and internal environments. Their business analysis skills were enhanced via group work and open discussions. Feedback from team members and the professors encouraged the students to consider the same issue in different perspectives. The business concepts taught in the program helped the students carry out the basic analysis. However, the students were given more responsibilities and freedom to organize their effort, and were more actively involved in planning and conducting business activities.

The students' confidence was reflected in two ways. First, they exhibited confidence in communicating. Given the opportunities they had to interact with business practitioners and make frequent presentations, the students showed more confidence in handling business communications and presentations. Even the rather quiet students managed to express themselves better. Their English communication skills also improved since these programs were conducted in English. Secondly, the students' confidence level increased when they received positive feedback from the SME owners, especially when the business performance of the SMEs improved after their intervention.

At the end of the education program, a few sessions were conducted to understand the students' perception of these programs. The students highlighted the fact that they gained practical knowledge that was different from their usual classroom experience. For example, in these programs, they managed to develop real marketing materials such as brochures. Additionally, they produced packaging designs for products, and suggested pricing strategies that were adopted by the SMEs. In the market surveys they conducted, they learned how to develop basic questionnaires to collect useful information for business decision making. They appreciated these practical experiences very much and suggested that the program should be introduced to other universities. The consulting approach gave them more responsibilities and direct experience with the local SMEs, preparing them well for business communications and problem solving.

Entrepreneurial intentions of the students were enhanced through the program. The majority of the students indicated that they were very much interested in entrepreneurship. Even though they might not immediately venture into business, the intention to become an entrepreneur had started to incubate in their mind. Some disclosed that they would work in a related business and industry first in order to gain experience that would subsequently benefit them in their future business ventures. Moreover, a few students from Indonesia started a business serving as marketing agents for the SME they worked with.

8.7   CONCLUSIONS

The CEE program described in this chapter provides students with the opportunity to work as trainee consultants by connecting universities with local SMEs. Conventional entrepreneurship education programs focus on theoretical concepts and hypothetical case analysis in a classroom setting. The CEE program enables a more practical approach, allowing for learning by doing through experience and experimentation.

An analysis of the program in Malaysia, Indonesia and Vietnam led to several observations. First, consulting-based learning methods can have a positive effect on entrepreneurship education outcomes. Second, programs that utilize research on new educational approaches within a university can have long-term benefits. Such efforts can be administered through a centre of excellence in knowledge diffusion and human resource development. Third, action-oriented CEE programs have a positive effect on the improvement of local SMEs' businesses performance, either directly or indirectly. For instance, they can lead to better planning, new product development and market expansion, particularly in the long term.

A key benefit of the CEE program is its ability to attract students' attention and interest while enhancing their capabilities for handling real business issues and situations. This practical approach also produced active and outgoing students with positive attitudes. Students had to visit the SMEs' owners and staff frequently to explain and discuss their business plan with the owners and potential customers. They promoted the SMEs' products at various locations around the cities. Additionally, they set up temporary counters to promote the SMEs' products at supermarkets, trade shows and universities. Based on the positive feedback and responses received, this program shows potential for application in different locations in ASEAN countries, especially given the similarities of the business environment, while allowing for appropriate local adaptation.

ACKNOWLEDGEMENTS

The authors gratefully acknowledge sponsorship from the Research Institute of Economy, Trade, and Industry in Japan for the program in Malaysia; sponsorship from the Japan Bank for International Cooperation for the progam in Indonesia; and sponsorship from the Association for Overseas Technical Scholarship in Japan for the program in Vietnam. We also would like to thank the participating institutions and members from the Asia Science and Education for Economic Development Institute, Waseda University, Universiti Kebangsaan Malaysia, University of Brawijaya, and the Foreign Trade University in co-implementing these entrepreneurship education programs and providing ongoing support.

NOTES AND REFERENCES

*   Siohong Tih, the corresponding author is an Associate Professor of Graduate School of Business in the National University of Malaysia (sh@ukm.my). Dr Takeru Ohe is a Professor in The Graduate School of Commerce, Waseda University (takeru.ohe@ waseda.jp).

1.   De Faoite, D., C. Henry, K. Johnston and P. Van Der Sijde, "Education and Training for Entrepreneurs: A Consideration of Initiatives in Ireland and The Netherlands", *Education and Training*, 45: 8/9, 2003, 430–439.

2.   Hynes, B., "Entrepreneurship Education and Training-Introducing Entrepreneurship to nonbusiness Disciplines", *Journal of Industrial Training*, 20:8, 1996, 10–17.

3.   Garavan, I.N. and B. O'Cinneide, "Entrepreneurship Education and Training Programmes: A Review and Evaluation", *Journal of European Industrial Training*, Part 1, 18: 8/11, Part 2, 18: 11, 3-11, 1994.

4.   Galloway, L. and W. Brown, "Entrepreneurship Education at University: A Driver in The Creation of High Growth Firms?" *Education and Training*, 44: 8/9, 2002, 398–405.

5.   Johannisson, B., H. Landstrom and J. Rosenberg, "University Training for Entrepreneurship – An Action Frame of Reference", *European Journal of Engineering Education*, 23:4, 1998, 477–497.

6.   Gibb, A.A., "The Enterprise Culture and Education", *Journal Of Small Business*, April/June, 1993.

7.   Fiet, J.O. "Education for Entrepreneurial Competency: A Theory Based Activity Approach", Paper presented at the *Conference: Internationalising Entrepreneurship Education and Training*, IntEnt97, CA, 25–27 June 1997.

8.   Ulrich, T., "An Empirical Approach to Entrepreneurial-learning Styles", Paper presented at the *Conference: Internationalising Entrepreneurship Education and Training*, IntEnt97, CA, 25–27 June 1997.

9.   Jones, C. and J. English, "A Contemporary Approach to Entrepreneurship Education", *Education and Training*, London, 46:8/9, 2004, 416.

10. Lord, M., "Attention, Aspiring Capitalists: B-school students are studying Entrepreneurship", *US News Online*, 1999, available at www.usnews.com.

11. Menzies, T. and Y. Gasse, "Entrepreneurship and Canadian Universities: A Report of a National Study of Entrepreneurship Education", Brock University, St Catherines, 1999.

12. Collinson, E. and L. Quinn, "The Impact of Collaboration Between Industry and Academia on SME Growth", *Journal of Marketing Management*, 18, 2002, 415–434.

13. Klofsten, M., "Training Entrepreneurship at Universities: A Swedish Case", *Journal of European Industrial Training*, 24:6, 2000, 337.

14. Mohd Jani, M.F., Z. Darawi, S.H. Tih, N. Chamhuri, Mohd Radzuan, Ahmad Raflis and M.Y. Ayub, "Research of Entrepreneurship Education in Malaysia", Technical Report prepared for Asia SEED, Japan, 2006.

15. Porter, L., "The Relation of Entrepreneurship Education to Business Education", *Simulation and Gaming*, 25:3, 1994, 416–419.

16. Tih, S.H., Mohd Radzuan Rahid, Norshamliza Chamhuri and Z. Darawi, "Effects of Triangulation Entrepreneurship Training on Trainees' Performance", *Proceeding of SME-Entrepreneurship Global Conference 2006*, Malaysia, 2006.

17. O'Brien, E. and D. Clark, "Graduates – Their Entrepreneurial Role in The Small Firm", *Marketing Education Review*, 7:3, 1997.

18. "Pilot Studies for Knowledge Assistance for Development of Educational Program for Entrepreneurship Facilitator", Final Report for Japan Bank for International Cooperation (JBIC), Republic of Indonesia, 2007.

9. Developing an interdisciplinary social entrepreneurship curriculum

Bonjin Koo, Vathana Duong TE and Joosung J. Lee*

9.1 INTRODUCTION

Social entrepreneurship, as a practice and a field for scholarly research, provides a unique opportunity to solve social problems, meet social demands, and pursue economic profits through entrepreneurship. Social entrepreneurship, as a practice that integrates economic and social value creation, has a particularly long heritage and a global presence.[1] For example, Grameen Bank, established by Professor Muhammad Yunus in 1976, introduced a unique micro-credit system to eradicate poverty and empower women in Bangladesh (http://www.grameen-infor.org). This endeavor has stimulated many social entrepreneurs to start micro-credit businesses globally for the same purposes.

With this point of view, effective social entrepreneurship education in universities has the potential to stimulate global entrepreneurship and create social value that may be missed by traditional entrepreneurship. The global efforts of Ashoka, founded by Bill Drayton in 1980, have provided seed funding for many social entrepreneurs globally. Bill Drayton established Ashoka based on his experience with "Ashoka Table", an interdisciplinary weekly forum in the social sciences which he founded when he was at Harvard University.

Although social entrepreneurship has attracted many researchers and proven its potential in solving social problems worldwide, there exist three problems relative to efforts to introduce this into university entrepreneurship education. First, like entrepreneurship, which even today lacks a unifying paradigm, the term "social entrepreneurship" has taken on a variety of meanings.[2] Second, the concept of social entrepreneurship is still poorly defined and its boundaries to other fields of study remain fuzzy.[1] Third, there has been little discussion of its education methodology.

This chapter addresses these problems, aiming to offer a clear definition of social entrepreneurship, to build a framework for social entrepreneurship education, and to report on teaching methods, student performance, and issues arising around social entrepreneurship lectures at Yonsei University. Also included is a discussion on ways to develop social entrepreneurship education in universities.

A framework for social entrepreneurship education is proposed, consisting of four themes: general entrepreneurship, social devotion, sustainability, and innovation. We also emphasize that general entrepreneurship is a very important issue in Korea, that students prefer practical educational methodologies, and that interdisciplinary curricula are necessary.

9.2   LITERATURE

9.2.1   Definition of Social Entrepreneurship

Social entrepreneurship as a practice has a long history, but its language is relatively new and somewhat perplexing, especially in scholarly research. Although the concept of social entrepreneurship is gaining increased visibility, it means different things to different people. Many associate social entrepreneurship exclusively with not-for-profit organizations starting for-profit or earned-income ventures. Others use it to describe anyone who starts a not-for-profit organization. Still others use it to refer to business owners who integrate social responsibility into their operations.[2]

Due to its vague definition, social entrepreneurship implies a blurring of existing economic sector boundaries, which consist of government and both for-profit and not-for-profit organizations. In order to define social entrepreneurship clearly and its sectoral location, we examine existing definitions of social entrepreneurship and then distinguish these from entrepreneurship through a discussion of keywords.

Some researchers refer to social entrepreneurship as not-for-profit initiatives in search of alternative funding strategies, or management initiatives to create social value.[3][4] A second group of researchers understands it as the socially responsible practice of commercial businesses engaged in cross-sector partnerships.[5][6] A third group views social entrepreneurship as a means to alleviate social problems and catalyze social transformation.[7]

The problem evident across these three groups of researchers lies in attempts to place social entrepreneurship within the span of existing economic sector boundaries. Rather than attempting to place social entrepreneurship in the for-profit or not-for-profit sectors, such initiatives need to be located in a new sector composed of organizations driven by both social purpose and financial promise, thereby falling somewhere between

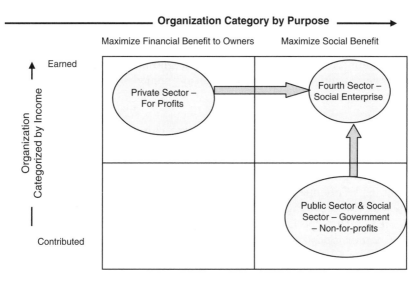

Note: Fourth Sector, "The Emerging Fourth Sector", http://www.fourthsector.net/learn/fourth-sector.

Figure 9.1   Patterns of changes: convergence and emergence

traditional companies and charities (see Figure 9.1). This reflects the fact that participants are creating hybrid organizations distinct from those operating in the government, business and non-profit sectors.[8]

To define social entrepreneurship, we start with some main keywords of entrepreneurship. For example, keywords of entrepreneurship, such as "opportunity", "value" and "willingness", can be adopted to explain social entrepreneurship, but will likely have a different meaning. First, "opportunity" refers to both social opportunity and business opportunity in social entrepreneurship. Social entrepreneurs not only have to find opportunities to solve social problems, which are missed by entrepreneurs or the government, but they must also find the business opportunity in this in order to operate independently without financial constraints.

Second, "value" stands for both social value and economic value in social entrepreneurship. Social entrepreneurs not only pursue social value, by meeting social demands to improve societal well-being; they also create economic value by satisfying a general demand that enables them to secure capital for sustainable growth.

Finally, "willingness" more specifically explains a social entrepreneur's willingness to take risks. While this is similar to general entrepreneurs, it does not stand for willingness to take a risk only for making profits.

Willingness to take a risk for creating a better society is more important than willingness to take a risk for making profits to a social entrepreneur.

Using these keywords, we define social entrepreneurs as those who find opportunities to create social value, and who have a willingness to take risks and an ability to employ general entrepreneurship principles in order to improve society.

9.2.2   Social Entrepreneurs and Enterprises in Korea

Social entrepreneurship is significant in Korea because its government has actively stimulated entrepreneurial approaches to overcoming social problems (e.g. economic polarization – the growing gap between rich and poor; helping low-income groups; creating jobs, etc.). Social enterprise is promoted under a special government branch, the Ministry of Employment and Labor. Social entrepreneurship therefore has a high connection to government and its social support policies, signaling its importance to Korean society.

Korea has a much shorter history of social enterprise than the US and Europe, however. In Korea, the concept has only been formally recognized since 2007, when the Ministry of Employment and Labor started to authorize it. Therefore, it is hard to identify the specific historical role of social enterprise. Clearly, though, there are two distinct differences between the older social enterprises and more recent ones in Korea. Firstly, they have different origins. Most of the older social enterprises started as non-profit organizations, and then turned to social enterprise later. Newer ones, on the other hand, started as social enterprises from the beginning.

Secondly, based on these different origins, their business ideas and models vary slightly. The business ideas of older social enterprises are very similar to non-profit organizations; they are specifically oriented toward solving social problems, and their main income comes from government subsidies. However, newer social ventures have more business elements. They are oriented toward both profit-making and solving social issues, so they have more financial independence than the older ones. In addition, there is no strong relationship between older and newer social enterprises in Korea.

To identify characteristics of social entrepreneurs in Korea, we introduce the results of research on 81 Korean social entrepreneurs.[9] Four results of this research stand out. First, the average age of social entrepreneurs in Korea is 46, which is 13 years younger than the average Korean chief executive officer (CEO). Social entrepreneurs in their thirties or forties occupy over half the age distribution, as Figure 9.2 shows.

Second, they come from various educational backgrounds, similar

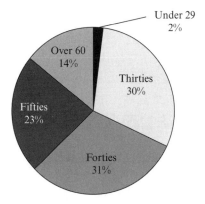

Figure 9.2   Age distribution of social entrepreneurs in Korea

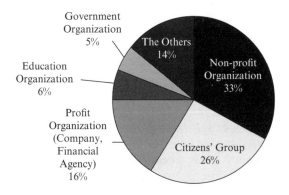

Figure 9.3   Careers of social entrepreneurs in Korea

to general entrepreneurs, but social welfare (20.3 percent) is given more weight compared to other majors. Third, their prior experience has been in not-for-profit social organizations (33.3 percent) and non-profit civic organizations (25.9 percent), but many also have experience in for-profit organizations (16.0 percent), as Figure 9.3 shows.

Finally, social entrepreneurs pursue visionary and future-oriented leadership styles, perhaps because social enterprise in Korea is in an early stage, and therefore needs the guidance of a clear vision.

9.2.3   A Framework for Social Entrepreneurship Education

Based on the previous discussions, we suggest a framework for social entrepreneurship education. This framework consists of four themes:

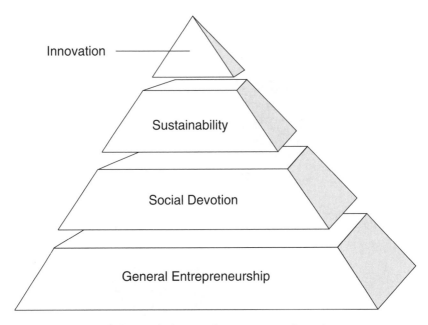

Figure 9.4   The framework for social entrepreneurship education

general entrepreneurship, social devotion, sustainability and innovation (see Figure 9.4).

First of all, general entrepreneurship education is necessary for social entrepreneurship education. A social enterprise is not a not-for-profit organization operating on donations, so a social entrepreneur needs to generate income to survive, just like a general entrepreneur. Therefore, general entrepreneurship education concepts should be part of the core elements of the course.

The social devotion theme is a distinctive factor from general entrepreneurship. Social entrepreneurs must have a considerable commitment to improving their societies. This is the main purpose of their ventures' existence. However, social contexts are very different from country to country, so it is not easy to teach social devotion. Therefore, lecturers must carefully consider how to teach students most effectively how to find unique solutions to problems their particular societies face. There are many effective educational approaches for this theme – e.g. community-based learning, project-oriented learning, problem-based learning and so on – but it is important for lecturers to devise the most effective pedagogies for their particular students and social context.

An organization's sustainability is a critical concern for every company.

In social entrepreneurship, sustainability is considered more important than corporate social responsibility. When teaching sustainability, the lecturer can teach students about virtuous-value cycles (cycle from investment to harvest). More specifically, students should understand how to design a unique business plan that includes virtuous-value cycles. Various educational approaches will be useful in this theme, but detailing how this will be operationalized in a business will be one of the most useful education methods.

The innovation theme is also an important factor in social entrepreneurship. Although a general entrepreneur typically pursues innovation, a social entrepreneur pursues both economic and non-economic innovation. When teaching about innovation, lecturers can introduce cases of social enterprise innovation around the world. Although there are other effective approaches, case studies can be useful in freeing students from prior ways of thinking.

9.2.4 Course Descriptions in General

At Yonsei University, three social entrepreneurship courses were offered as electives in the business school and engineering department. The impetus underlying the initiation of these courses was the belief that social entrepreneurship education is important for universities. Professor Hun-Joon Park in the college of business even visited Columbia University to benchmark its programs before implementing these courses at Yonsei. For the college of engineering, the undergraduate course was introduced as part of a senior design project with a focus on community development. The engineering graduate course was introduced to examine social entrepreneurship from the perspective of academic disciplines. Due to the nature of engineering, the class project had a hands-on focus at both undergraduate and graduate levels.

Interest in social entrepreneurship education has been increasing in Korea. For example, the Korea Advanced Institute of Science and Technology now offers social enterprise management courses for undergraduates and working professionals. Additionally, there are various short-term courses, seminars and forums frequently held at major universities and other institutions in Korea. The number of participants in these classes varies from 10 to 50 students.

Social entrepreneurship was first offered at Yonsei University in the spring of 2009. Enrollment included 30 engineering undergraduates, 10 engineering graduates, and 21 business undergraduates. Because they were not compulsory, the classes thereby attracted students interested in general entrepreneurship, social enterprise and social entrepreneurship.

9.2.5   Social Entrepreneurship Education in the School of Business

The School of Business at Yonsei University first introduced social entrepreneurship in 2007 through the Yonsei Social Enterprise Center (YSEC), led by Professor Hun-Joon Park. The YSEC established the annual Social Venture Competition Korea in 2007. In addition, the YSEC supports social entrepreneurs by connecting them to management mentors and investors, and it develops the curriculum for social entrepreneurship.

As mentioned previously, Professor Park visited Columbia University in 2008 for six months as a research professor to learn about theories and education programs for social entrepreneurship. After he came back from the US, he developed and taught a social entrepreneurship course (called "Social Enterprise and Innovation") for undergraduates. The course consists of four modules. Module one introduces students to "social innovators and entrepreneurs" and their organizations around the world. Module two helps students to understand the potential impact of their financial and business skills on environmental issues. Module three provides answers to the financial questions of social enterprises. Module four helps students to understand the application of financial tools to social problems.

Professor Park's course is highly interactive and depends greatly on student preparation and participation. The participant-centered case learning method employed in this class is not only the most relevant way to learn and apply business knowledge and tools to solve social and environmental problems, but also instills a sense of fun and excitement that comes with being a social entrepreneur.

Additionally, students in the class participate in a Venture Team Action-Learning Project. They develop proposals for social business ideas for a midterm project. This is then expanded to detailed business plans for their final exam. The students are encouraged to find a potential sponsor or investor. Often these investors are the students' friends and relatives. Also, the professor arranges for some mentoring by outside experts. The criteria for evaluating these projects is based on the innovativeness, viability, and detail of their social business idea and plans. As a result, many innovative ideas have been developed and the students have been very satisfied with this practical teaching method.

One favorable result can be seen in the actual launch of a social enterprise in 2008 by one student, Lynn Park, based on her course project. Lynn became a social entrepreneur, launching Ludens Edu (http://www.ludensedu.org) under YSEC's support. This venture focuses on a current social problem faced by Korean children, who do not have enough wholesome play. Ludens Edu comprises a teaching corps of college students

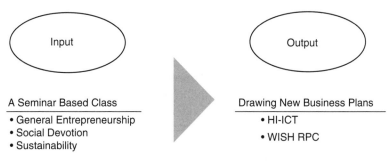

Figure 9.5   Teaching methodology of social entrepreneurship lecture for graduates

and international students who are committed to bring about changes in computer-addicted and socially isolated children. Its ideas are based on the Play Theory of Johan Huizinga, the author of *Homo Ludens, Man the Player*,[10] which discusses the importance of play elements in culture and society. Aiming to end educational disparity and to nurture children's social skills and character, Park's venture runs "Ludens School" and other programs. The school now offers four classes in elementary schools and three nursery school classes and is gaining popularity among parents and children.

9.2.6   Social Entrepreneurship Education in the College of Engineering

In the College of Engineering at Yonsei University, two social entrepreneurship courses were delivered by Professor Joosung J. Lee in the Department of Information and Industrial Engineering, starting in the 2009 spring semester. One course introduced theoretical concepts for social entrepreneurship to graduate students. Social entrepreneurship education is important for graduate students, because they have more skills and specialized knowledge than undergraduate students, so they have a high potential for executing successful ventures.

The teaching methodology is based on a conceptual framework consisting of the four themes previously discussed: general entrepreneurship, social devotion, sustainability and innovation. The class begins by engaging students in a seminar-based class and ends with presentations of innovative business plans (see Figure 9.5).

The main focus of the business plans in the 2009 spring semester was on development in Cambodia. This provided a great opportunity for the students to learn and also create tangible value that can improve the quality of life of the Cambodian people. Every week during the first two months of the semester, the graduate students were required to attend a two-hour seminar class in order to acquire encyclopedic knowledge about Cambodia. This knowledge enabled the students to create their own business projects. The projects covered four main areas: agricultural technology, information technology, medical technology, and technology for developing the culture (leisure) industry.

In order to understand the four areas better, the class arranged a practical workshop with Cambodian students studying in Seoul, the Cambodian Ambassador, and Korean experts from many different fields. The advice received during the workshop helped the students finalize their project designs. The class generated positive results with two innovative business plans: the Wish RPC project and the Hi-ICT project. The WISH RPC project is aimed at enhancing the quality of life of poor Cambodian farmers by providing them with market access and offering micro-credit to help them to increase their output. The Hi-ICT project was initiated with the aim of providing standardized computer and Internet skills for youth in Cambodian high schools, taught by Cambodian undergraduate students with information technology (IT)-related majors and skills.

During the spring semester of 2009, the social enterprise course for undergraduates was also taught by Professor Joosung Lee. The goal of this course was to educate students to carry out projects dealing with real social problems in Korea. Like the graduate class, the teaching methodology was based on the four themes of the conceptual framework (see Figure 9.4). The teaching methods employed various educational approaches, such as theoretical concept-based classes, guest lectures, community-based learning and group activities. In addition, students pursued team-based projects (see Figure 9.6).

During the beginning of the course, students participated in theoretical concept-based classes, which enabled them to learn vital concepts about social entrepreneurship. Then, every two weeks in the first two months, students had the opportunity to study with social entrepreneurs who had started successful social enterprises in Korea. These learning experiences provided students with insights for their projects.

The next step asks students where and how they could put their ideas into action. This question is addressed through a teaching approach called community-based learning. This class involves real social enterprises or organizations related to social enterprise: for example, the Merry-Year Foundation, a Korean non-profit organization that provides micro-credit loans and helps build social enterprises; and the Purme Foundation, which

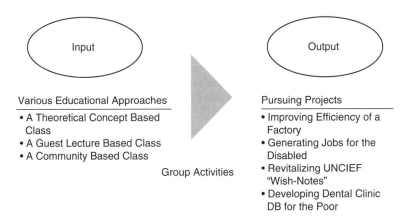

Figure 9.6   Teaching methodology of social entrepreneurship lecture for undergraduates

focuses on improving medical and rehabilitation care for physically disabled people in Korea.

The Yonsei Teaching and Learning Assistance Center helps to make connections to these external organizations. Before the course started, they contacted project sponsors and did initial work in identifying manageable project topics. The professor and the Center then further developed the project topics before the beginning of the course. During the community-based learning activity, students form discussion groups and hold meetings with the organizations and their professors to design their projects and receive feedback.

The following four projects were pursued in the spring 2009 semester: a consulting service to improve the efficiency of a window shade factory which employs only North Korean migrants in South Korea; a business model for establishing a new factory where only disabled persons are employed to make cellphone devices for LG Electronics in Korea; strategies for revitalizing the United Nations Children's (Emergency) Fund (UNICEF)'s "Wish-Note", which connects poor children's needs in developing countries with donors in developed countries; in collaboration with the Purme Foundation, a database system design to manage information for a dental clinic service for the poor in Korea.

These projects are the main outputs of this social entrepreneurship course. Students were evaluated based on the outcome of these projects. The organizational sponsors evaluate the quality of the project, the students' enthusiasm and professionalism, and the extent through which they apply knowledge from their prior courses to actual practice. The professor evaluates progress and performance throughout

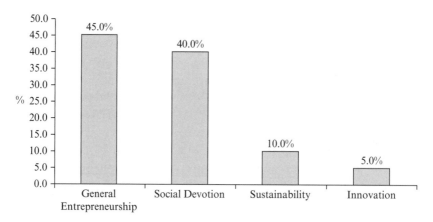

*Figure 9.7   The result of a question: What do you think is the most
important theme in social entrepreneurship education?*

the process, as well as at the end, when the students make their final
presentations.

9.2.7   Issues and Students' Feedback

Thirty-five students enrolled in social entrepreneurship classes in Yonsei
University completed anonymous questionnaires. The results revealed
three key findings.

Students think general entrepreneurship concepts are important for social entrepreneurship education

Many students commented that general entrepreneurship concepts should
be taught before, or together with, social entrepreneurship (see Figure
9.7).

Students prefer practical educational methods in learning about social entrepreneurship

In fact, no one answered that the lecture method is the most effective way to learn social entrepreneurship (see Figure 9.8). They prefer
practical educational methods such as problem-based learning and
community-based learning, because they can experience the satisfaction of creating social value or using their abilities and knowledge to
develop unique business plans. These practical education methods
allow students to apply their own approaches in learning about social
entrepreneurship.

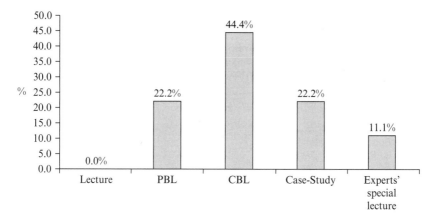

Figure 9.8   The result of a question: What is the most efficient learning method for social entrepreneurship education?

An interdisciplinary curriculum is necessary for effective social entrepreneurship education

Most of the engineering students expressed a need for working with business experts on their projects and gaining professional business knowledge as part of their social entrepreneurship education. Business students commented that their project outcomes could greatly benefit from the expanded perspective gained from having technical experts on their teams.

9.2.8   Next Step to Develop Social Entrepreneurship Education

This initial experience with social entrepreneurship at Yonsei has led to a commitment to establish the Social Enterprise Frontier at Yonsei (SEFY) to advance social entrepreneurship education. The SEFY will develop over three stages, encompassing the education program, interdisciplinary curriculum, and career-supporting programs (see Figure 9.9).

Goals for the education program include raising professors' awareness about social entrepreneurship throughout Korea. The education program for practitioners will focus on increasing executive awareness and abilities as social entrepreneurs. The plan for developing an interdisciplinary curriculum includes co-developing an integrated engineering and business curriculum for social entrepreneurship education. The third step involves the creation of career-supporting programs.

The SEFY's objective is to create a unique and practice-focused curriculum. One example is the plan to create a world experience program to enhance global social entrepreneurship learning for students. This

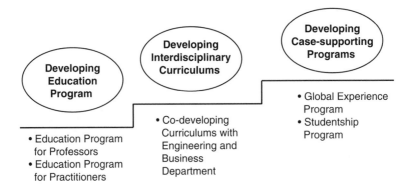

Figure 9.9   The plans for developing social entrepreneurship education

will call for relationships with social entrepreneurs in other countries, and enable students to expand their range of understanding by working in real social enterprises abroad. In addition, SEFY will design student internship programs to provide work experience to students and practitioners.

9.3   CONCLUSIONS

This chapter started with a definition for social entrepreneurship and a framework for social entrepreneurship education based on literature in the field. Following this, we discussed Yonsei University's experience with developing social entrepreneurship curriculum for both undergraduate and graduate levels. This effort, however, was not without challenges. First, it is hard to evaluate learning outcomes for social entrepreneurship. The output of the business plans and observed performance of students provided a basis for this evaluation, but because there are other important factors in understanding social entrepreneurship, this assessment may be imperfect.

Second, it was difficult to find sponsors for the graduate course, which focused on development in Cambodia. If actual sponsors could be found for launching the best business ideas from the class, this would increase practical impact and student satisfaction. Third, the community-based learning approach requires establishing and maintaining relationships with external organizations, and this calls for dedicated resources. The students evaluated this approach as highly effective, but this was only made possible through the assistance of the Yonsei Teaching and Learning Assistance Center.

Finally, teaching students to find and evaluate a social entrepreneurship opportunity is difficult. While this is also a challenge in general entrepreneurship courses, a social entrepreneurship opportunity has to create both social value and economic opportunity. In addition, social entrepreneurship requires curriculum and faculty experience with general entrepreneurship, practical educational methods and interdisciplinary curriculum.

Altogether, social entrepreneurship educators are encouraged to use various practical educational methodologies, which can help students apply their knowledge and skills to address social problems and work with real social enterprises. Educators also need to think about how to integrate general entrepreneurship principles into a social entrepreneurship course. Finally, interdisciplinary curricula are recommended for the design of social entrepreneurship education.

Entrepreneurship education is not very common in Korean universities, but it has been continuously increasing. Social entrepreneurship has become more and more important in Korea, however, in part because the government strongly wants to stimulate it. However, social entrepreneurship education is still in a very early stage of development. Thus, further efforts will be needed to develop social entrepreneurship education in Korea, and likely in other countries with similar conditions.

NOTES AND REFERENCES

* Bonjin Koo the corresponding author is a PhD Candidate in Department of Management Engineering KAIST Graduate School of Management (bonkoo@business.kaist.ac.kr). Vathana Duong is a MS in Information and Industrial Engineering, Yonsei University (teduongsun@yahoo.com). Joosung J. Lee is Assistant Professor at KAIST Graduate School of Innovation and Technology Management (jooslee@kaist.ac.kr).
1. Mair, Johanna and Ignasi Marti, "Social Entrepreneurship Research: A Source of Explanation, Prediction, and Delight", *Journal of World Business*, 41, 2006, 36–44.
2. Dees, G., *The Meaning of Social Entrepreneurship*, 1998, http://www.caseatduke.org/documents/dees_sedef.pdf.
3. Austin, J., H. Stevenson and J. Wei-Skillern, "Social Entrepreneurship and Commercial Entrepreneurship: Same, Different, or Both?" Working paper series no. 04-029, Harvard Business School, 2003.
4. Boschee, J., "Merging Mission and Money: A Board Member's Guide to Social Entrepreneurship", 1998, http://www.socialent.org/pdfs/MergingMission.pdf.
5. Sagawa, S. and E. Segal, "Common Interest, Common Good: Creating Value Through Business and Social Sector Partnership", *California Management Review*, 42:2, 2000, 105–122.
6. Waddock, S.A., "Building Successful Partnerships", *Sloan Management Review*, 29:4, 1988, 17–23.
7. Alvord, S.H., L.D. Brown and C.W. Letts, "Social Entrepreneurship and Societal Transformation," *Journal of Applied Behavioral Science*, 40:3, 2004, 260–282.

8. New York Times, "Businesses Try to Make Money and Save the World", 6 May 2007, http://www.nytimes.com/2007/05/06/business/yourmoney/06fourth.html.
9. HERI 2nd Review, "Deep Analysis of Social Entrepreneurs in Korea", http://www.heri.kr/dev/board/listbody.html?h_gcode=board&h_code=2&page=9&po_no=42 [헤리리뷰2호] 비영리기관·시민단체 출신의 40대가 '표준형'(2008), 한겨레경제연구소.
10. Huizinga, J., *Homo ludens: A study of the play Element in Culture*, Boston, MA: Beacon Press, 1955.

10. Microfinance field study projects in Asia

George Abe, David Chang and Priya Mohan*

10.1 INTRODUCTION

The University of California has a thesis requirement for all students in the ten campus systems who are candidates for a Master's degree. At the Anderson School of Management at the University of California, Los Angeles (UCLA) the thesis requirement is fulfilled by a mandatory two-quarter field study assignment, which provides two full course credits for the students.[1]

A field study consists of a team of four to six students, a faculty adviser and a client working together for 20 weeks. Two weeks are typically spent in-country by the students. During this time, students conduct secondary research, making primary research calls in the US and consulting with their adviser. There is no classroom work specific to the field study. The students must fit their field study work into their regular course load. They will have, contemporaneously, two or three additional courses not related to the field study.

The objective of a microfinance field study project is to bring together students and microfinance clients together to solve a strategic business problem for the client and render a worthy educational experience for the student.

For the academic year 2008–2009, UCLA had 126 field study projects, eight of which were microfinance and another 14 that were not-for-profit. This program requires an administrative office to recruit clients, coordinate team selection, recruit and qualify faculty advisers, match teams with clients and make sure deliverables are on time.

Since Professor Muhammad Yunus visited UCLA on 22 October 2007, there has been an upsurge of interest in microfinance, and social entrepreneurship in general, among UCLA management students.[2] In addition, the UCLA Center for International Business Education and Research (CIBER) is actively engaged in microfinance projects as part of its regular program in international education and research. CIBER is a consortium of 33 member-universities, administered by the US Department of Education.[3] Microfinance projects include lending programs, insurance, financial infrastructure for microfinance institutions and banking. The CIBER funds defray student travel expenses. Students receive no stipends and the client organizations pay no fees.

Microfinance clients are government organizations, non-governmental organizations (NGOs), and banks operating in developing countries, as well as cooperatives and private institutions. Microfinance projects for the 2008–09 academic year at UCLA include:

- Wheelchairs in Guatemala. UCLA, in conjunction with mechanical engineers from the California Institute of Technology, is developing a business plan for an NGO to build wheelchairs from recycled bicycle parts and other recycled metal parts. The demand for wheelchairs is large, and manufacturing can provide a source of trained local employment.
- Cellphone web server to facilitate microfinance loan processing. Oracle, a large US software provider, has developed web server software that can be installed in cellphones. They question whether this software can reduce the cost of loan processing in rural India.
- Capitalizing on remittances in Paraguay. Worker remittances from Spain, Brazil and Argentina are a major source of foreign currency reserve in Paraguay. The institutions receiving these remittances, however, do not have strong banking practices. The question addressed is how a small, local financial institution can capitalize on this flow of funds to encourage borrowing and lending in rural Paraguay.
- Microfinance lending in Los Angeles by Grameen Bank. Grameen Bank posed a very interesting question: can its microfinance model be used in urban areas of the United States? UCLA was asked by Grameen to determine where microfinance lenders should locate in Los Angeles and what the lending policies should be.
- Microlending to migrants in Beijing. Beijing is home to many migrants from the countryside. Often these migrants become entrepreneurs, running businesses such as light manufacturing and restaurants. These people are outside the regular banking system. The question raised is how a microfinance lending model can be used for this population.
- Youth employment in Ghana. A local non-profit start-up is currently in the process of developing an implementation plan for a pilot youth employment program. The question faced is how to

finance the new business venture using a combination of local and donated international funds.

- Microinsurance in Vietnam. Despite the rapid pace of economic development in Vietnam, risk management is still in its early stages. The question raised by a commune in the northern part of the country is whether and how insurance, particularly crop insurance, can or should be introduced.
- Microfinance lending in Shaaxi province, China. Shaanxi is home to Xi'an, the ancient capital of China; the concept of economic development, however, is relatively new there. The question raised is how microfinance lending can be implemented there.

The final two projects are discussed in sections 10.3 "Vietnam Microinsurance" and 10.4 "Microfinance Lending in Shaanxi Province", below.

10.2   THE FIELD STUDY PROCESS AT UCLA

10.2.1   Client Recruitment

The first step in the field study process involves client recruitment. How does an American university get access to the real microfinance cases? Deal flow can happen in a number of ways. First, students can find the project themselves and propose it to the AMR Office. Second, individual faculty members may become aware of projects through their research activities. Third, projects can come from CIBER; for example, there is an annual CIBER conference, a part of which showcases microfinance projects. Fourth, the university may have cooperative relationships with government or NGO entities in developing countries, although more generally targeted toward the recruitment of field study projects of all types, not just microfinance. Finally, client institutions may contact the university directly through an alumni network or other means of contact.

10.2.2   Student Team Formation

Once a set of potential projects is identified, students decide if they want to pursue a microfinance project at all, and if so, who should be on the team. Students engage in a microfinance project because of their own personal interest in social entrepreneurship or their interest in the developing country. Sometimes the student may be a citizen of that country and wants to return. Most microfinance projects involve travel, which has its own appeal. Because of the need to do primary research in a foreign country, there is the requirement that at least one team member be fluent in the language of the client.

Once students decide that microfinance is the right type of project, then they self-assemble into teams. The advantage of self-assembly is that students generally know with whom they have worked successfully with in prior classes. The problem with self-assembly is that they tend to team up with friends. This raises the serious problem of an imbalance of skills. It would be a mistake for the team and client to have five finance specialists on the team, for instance, or five of any specific discipline, for that matter. That is why some universities put the teams together administratively, in order to have a mix of specialties. Our view is that team formation is a real-life exercise and that students should cope with the problems.

The process of team formation takes about a month. Once a team has formed, its students are required to formalize a set of team norms. They should openly discuss, and commit in writing, their individual interests, what each student wants to derive from the project, their work schedules, when they should have meetings, and who will be responsible for what parts of the project.

Note that at the time the teams are formed and norms decided, the project is still not identified. Part of the group norming process is to get clarity on the project and the adviser.

10.2.3   Faculty Adviser

Each team will then select a faculty adviser. Many institutions will assign the adviser to the team.[4] Our policy is that the team finds the adviser. This puts responsibility on the students.[5] The administrative problem is that the faculty member does not know in advance how many teams he/she will advise.

Students generally select microfinance faculty advisers who have demonstrated a research or teaching interest in social entrepreneurship and microfinance in prior work. Students are counseled to select an adviser with the following characteristics:

- An ability to assist in resolving intra-team student problems. Teams are together for six months. Problems arise among the students. The adviser is the first resort.
- An ability to assist in resolving client problems. Clients pose their own problems. Occasionally, they do not provide enough data; they change scope; there is staff turnover; or there are logistical problems related to communicating in a developing country. These all impede

the progress of the project. The adviser must be competent in client management.

- Assistance in revising the scope as needed. Often, the original scope of work proves to be impractical. What then? The students are still required to write a thesis. In December 2007, a project that involved writing a business plan for a medical facility in Nairobi, Kenya, required a site visit. Just at that time, civil strife occurred in the country and the safety of the students could not be guaranteed. The original scope of work was scrapped midway through the project. The faculty adviser, in conjunction with the AMR Office, was key in revising the scope of work. In this case, a disaster recovery plan for the hospital was written. The students addressed a question concerning how a hospital should plan for civil strife and natural disasters.

- An ability to refer students to other sources of information. In the Nairobi case, it was important for the adviser to have the resourcefulness to reconfigure the project and contacts, and find information sources quickly.

While domain knowledge is useful, it is more important for the adviser to have a background similar to consulting. Field study projects are consulting engagements. The adviser is expected to make key contributions in helping teams with client management, project management and team dynamics.

Faculty advisers are given course relief for this role. Advising four teams is equivalent to one course. There is never a shortage of advisers; faculty members are happy to advise field study teams. They see their teaching being applied toward solving a real-world business problems, which often nourishes their classroom work.

10.2.4 Scope of Work

In the first month of the project, the students, adviser and client agree on a scope of work. Inasmuch as the client and students have not engaged in such an assignment previously, particularly a microfinance project, the role of the faculty adviser is particularly important in deriving the right scope of project. Projects tend to be overambitious at the beginning. It is critical that the faculty adviser provide guidance to make sure the scope of work is of sufficient interest to the client and of sufficient scale to justify five persons receiving Master's degree credit. Yet it must also be realistic, given constraints on time, money and expertise.

During the primary research stage, it is common for the scope of work to change. This should be expected and accommodated. Projects change in real life. It is an important teaching point for students to learn the difference between flexibility and random changes. The faculty adviser, client and each student sign off on the scope of work. Included in the scope of work is a budget, a timeline, an agreement on the primary research sources and deliverables, and the location of the final presentation.

10.2.5   Deliverables

After ten weeks of the program, the students present their midpoint findings. This is a one-hour presentation to the AMR Office to review progress to date. The main purpose of the presentation is to inspect the primary research and uncover any client or team issues. It is a stated intent that all secondary research and most primary research be completed by the midpoint of the program. This presentation provides the impetus for students to meet that milestone.

Sometimes the students have completed their travel by this time, sometimes not. Travel schedules are determined during the scope of work, but logistical difficulties may cause a change in travel plans. If travel is not completed by the midpoint, then precise travel plans should be presented, tickets in hand.

The final deliverable consists of a presentation to the client and a written report, which is the student's masters' thesis. The report and presentation are completed by the teams. However, each student is graded individually, based on: peer review by other members of the team; individual evaluation by the faculty adviser; and the nature and quantity of primary research conducted.

The final presentation is made either on campus, at the client site or via Webcast. It is important to have a face-to-face presentation to serve as a student learning experience and give the opportunity for the client to ask questions. How the students respond to the questions is a part of the grading process.

Some clients do not want or need the final report. This does not remove the responsibility of the students to write one. It is their thesis requirement, which could be independent of the client's needs.

The average length of the final paper is 30–50 pages, not including appendices. Total work is typically over 100 pages. The faculty adviser grades the deliverables, with input from the Faculty Director of the AMR Program. Financial prizes are awarded for the best papers, with funds donated by interested community members. A handful of papers fail each year and must be rectified after graduation. The client has no input into the grading process since there are elements of the grading invisible to the client, such as student teamwork. Student peer review is an important part of the grade. Also the AMR program is rigorous in applying academic standards, with which the client may not be familiar.

Given this general background on microfinance field studies, two specific projects are discussed in the following sections. The first is a plan to develop a microinsurance business in rural Vietnam; the second involves writing a plan for a microfinance lending institution in Xian, China.

10.3   VIETNAM MICROINSURANCE

10.3.1   The Problem

Despite the rapid pace of economic development in Vietnam, risk management is still in its early stages. The primary risk mitigation product available to rural Vietnam is credit life insurance. Credit life provides that a loan be paid in the event of the death of the borrower, thereby relieving the borrower's family of the burden of loan repayment. This is essentially a term life insurance policy. A variant of this type of insurance, called credit life plus, provides minor additional coverage to the decedent's family. But other forms of insurance are not widespread, although hypothesized to be potentially profitable, particularly crop insurance. Vietnam is subject to intense meteorological events that can ruin crops. Major institutions in Vietnam have access to major US and European carriers. But what about villagers, small farmers and entrepreneurs?

A client called Chi Em was identified. Chi Em provides microfinance lending services to the 340 000 people in Dien Bien province. Dien Bien is located in the north of Vietnam, about an hour from Hanoi. The question addressed in this project was whether Chi Em could or should diversify into insurance, particularly crop or livestock insurance.

10.3.2   Team Formation and Research Planning

A team of five students chose this project. No students were conversant in Vietnamese. The coordination of the logistics in the country was arranged through the assistance of a bilingual American who was working with Chi Em. The American intermediary was responsible for language translation, including written materials and questionnaires. Arrangements were made for all five to visit Dien Bien province.

The students spent the first two months scoping the project, developing a field research plan, which included questionnaire development, and completing their secondary research. Upon arriving in the country, interviews were held with local insurance professionals, NGOs, microfinance borrowers and local officials. Once the students returned from their trips, they used analytic tools learned in class and performed additional research as needed.

10.3.3   Findings

Due largely to the young population of Vietnam, any life insurance product, credit life in particular, is highly profitable. For credit life, less than 25 percent of premiums are paid out in claims. This creates optimism that the general concept of insurance would work. European insurers, like Munich Re and Prevoire, are showing interest in providing new insurance products. In particular, Munich Re announced a crop insurance program for Indonesia in May 2009.[6] Accordingly, there is a pilot project in Ninh Phuoc province, neighboring Dien Bien.

On the other hand, the government sets most insurance products and policies. Insurers do not perform their own actuarial calculations. Pricing is set within regulated ranges by the government. In addition, actuarial experience is key to the development of an insurance industry in a region. For crop insurance, historic weather data is crucial and there is a substantial potential for mispricing risk.

The lack of a sophisticated insurance industry in Vietnam makes partnership with non-local carriers a must. Technical advisers can help fill the gap in education and the administration of insurance programs promulgated by local finance organizations, such as microfinance lending institutions.

10.3.4   Recommendations

The students developed an action plan that targets the sale of crop insurance in two years. The transition plan identified four areas for development. The first involves educating both the carriers and the insured. Second is the development of a rudimentary notion of underwriting risk. This requires organizing weather data and other loss provisions. Third is the scale-up of the current microlending practices to provide support for an insurance product. This means there should be enough borrowers from Chi Em to provide both the cash flow and the potential market for insurance products. Fourth, staffing must be augmented, particularly among ethnic minority Muong people in the province. Along with staffing, there need to be systems and processes in place.

Key problems remain, mainly the lack of a reinsurance infrastructure. However, the demand, price elasticity and the availability of capital make such a venture worthwhile.[7]

10.4 MICROFINANCE LENDING IN SHAANXI PROVINCE

10.4.1 The Problem

Although microfinance lending was established in the 1980s in mainland China, the vast majority of microfinance institutions experience low utilization of capital and the inability to attract outside depositors. If capital utilization is low (that is, the ratio of borrowing to assets), there is little incentive to invest in banks. This is especially true in rural provinces like Shaanxi, despite its population of nearly 40 million.

The UCLA team was recruited to analyze the prospects of a particular microfinance institution in Shaanxi to recommend solutions. The client is run largely as a family-owned bank that conducts business with people they are familiar with. The question is how to break out of the "friends and family" mode and move on to growth within the province.

10.4.2 Team Formation and Research Planning

A team of five students chose this project. Two students were fluent in Mandarin. Arrangements were made for all five to visit the province from 11 December through 21 December 2008. This was approximately nine weeks after the project began. The students had banking experience and all were interested in microfinance. The initial nine weeks were used to scope the project, develop a field research plan (including questionnaire development), and complete the secondary research.

Upon arriving in Shaanxi, the students conducted interviews in Mandarin with employees of the client, government officials, potential borrowers and investors. Appointments were arranged in advanced by a combination of cold-calling, the use of university resources, which included alumni and introductions from faculty, and through government agencies and other microfinance organizations.

The scope, as originally envisioned, was broad and needed constant review. In the end, a strategic direction was chosen, along with specific tactical items.

10.4.3 Findings

The students identified a number of factors that made for a favorable banking environment in Shaanxi. Among these were high demand for loans among small and medium-sized businesses (SMEs) and the so-called *getihu* or individual entrepreneurs, low competition and relatively high barriers to entry for new microfinance institutions in the province, due to regulatory restrictions. The potential loan volume in the province was estimated at 24 billion RMB annually. SMEs often borrow through an informal lending network, which does not have usury laws around the charging of interest. SMEs are thus looking for alternatives.

On the other hand, there is a high degree of risk aversion by banking officers, a result of misaligned compensation policies. For example, if a particular loan officer made a loan that eventually went into default, a portion of the loan loss would come out of the loan officer's compensation. This creates a high degree of risk aversion. As a result, there is the perception among borrowers that it is too difficult to borrow from the bank. Additionally, there is a lack of standard (i.e. familiar Western) banking practices such as formalized credit scoring; low awareness by borrowers of their funding options; an over-reliance on friends and family for loan volume and investment capital; and operational problems due largely to inexperience. Finally, the regulatory environment for small banks is unpredictable, which creates challenges for a small, undiversified bank.[8]

10.4.4 Recommendations

The students addressed the following strategic problems. Should the client concentrate on agricultural loans or small business and *getihu* loans in urban areas? Should the bank expand its investment capital by attracting private investment, expanding its deposit base, or should it rely on institutional borrowing, primarily from the central bank? How much rigor and formality should it institute in lending practices? In what ways should the client upgrade its human resources, e.g. more training, different hiring, different incentives? How should the client segment its potential markets (apart from the rural/urban choice) and how should it market itself to these segments?

In the end, the students concluded that the bank should opt for SME/*getihu* clients in urban areas, formalize lending practices, particularly credit scoring, change the compensation plan to provide some reward for successful borrowings, opt for private capital and therefore provide greater transparency in financial reporting. In addition to these recommendations, the students crafted elements of a prospectus and a detailed credit scoresheet.

10.5 CONCLUSIONS

Microfinance projects afford excellent educational opportunities for students. Microfinance organizations are small enough so that a team of graduate students can have a major impact on the client. This is a key attraction for students. They like the idea of having their coursework create a real impact on a business problem.

Outlined are the following challenges and considerations. First, there is a high requirement for primary research from unconventional sources. Students are confronted with unfamiliar social and business cultures and are expected to respond professionally.

Second, projects like these require a sophisticated student that is able to travel and conduct business in a foreign country. Extensive preparation is needed for the trip, such as in the selection of interviewees and the preparation of questionnaires, to say nothing of logistical issues around travel, schedule and expense management.

Students working in such projects find that their experience is applicable to normal career opportunities and are therefore empowered to think strategically. The challenges for an educational institution creating an experienced-based program lie in finding deal flow and faculty advisers who are willing and able to provide consulting management. With respect to the latter, domain knowledge is not sufficient. Faculty should provide team mentoring, project management and client management support to the students.

There is an opportunity for further collaboration between Western and Asian universities to extend their respective field study programs by incorporating more microfinance projects. Collaboration can involve sourcing of projects, providing data sources, providing students, and sharing information, such as regional social and business practices. There is also a demand from microfinance institutions, substantial educational opportunities, and positive social benefit. In addition, students responded positively to their projects. In the 2009/10 academic year, it was anticipated that ten microfinance projects would be sponsored by UCLA.

ACKNOWLEDGMENTS

The author would like to recognize the outstanding students who worked on these projects. For the microinsurance project, they were Celia Adelson, Chase Cairncross, Matt Craig, Kyle Villegas and Casey Winn. For the ShaanXi project, the students were Christopher Bishop, Oksana Hickok, Jaehee Song, Joanna Yuan and Xi Wang.

NOTES AND REFERENCES

  * George Abe (correponding author) is Lecturer and Faculty Director, Applied Management Research Program (AMR), Anderson School of Management, University of California, Los Angeles (amr@anderson.ucla.edu). David Chang is associate director, UCLA, AMR (amr@anderson.ucla.edu). Priya Mohan is associate director, UCLA, AMR (amr@anderson.ucla.edu).
1. The program is defined at http://www.anderson.ucla.edu/x911.xml.
2. For more information on Prof. Muhammad Yunus visit to UCLA, see www.anderson. ucla.edu/x18870.xml.
3. For more information on CIBER, visit http://ciberweb.msu.edu.
4. Raymond, Corey, *MBA Field Studies*, Boston, MA: Harvard Business School Publishing, 1990.
5. UCLA Applied Management Research website, http://www.anderson.ucla.edu/x911. xml.
6. *Financial Times*, 4 May 2009, p. 15.
7. *Microinsurance in Dien Bien, Vietnam*, Student project in the UCLA AMR program, 30 May 2009.
8. *Xinchang Microcredit, LLC (ShaanXi)*, Student project in the UCLA AMR program, 30 March 2009.

11. Teaching entrepreneurial business strategies in global markets: a comparison of cleantech venture assessment in the US and China

Peter Adriaens and Timothy Faley*

11.1 INTRODUCTION

Investment in clean technologies has been identified by governments around the world as a strategic priority to combat global warming and to differentiate economic development in a technology domain that is often likened to the information technology (IT) revolution. As with the IT revolution, the center of innovation has shifted from the US to Asian economies, whereby US start-ups are focused on technology de-risking and prototyping, and Chinese start-ups are focusing on growth and scalability. Though both are part of the innovation continuum, these differences are often ignored by scholars, and yet both are essential to jump-start a cleantech entrepreneurial economy.

We describe here the educational platforms necessary for preparing US and Chinese engineering and MBA students for a global cleantech economy. The goal of integrating global entrepreneurial business strategies in US and Chinese engineering and business curricula is to discuss and identify differences in these strategies and global opportunity shifts in response to economic disequilibria. The specific objectives are to: understand the enabling technological and social drivers that render entrepreneurship successful, teach entrepreneurial business tools for technology venture assessment, and apply these tools and drivers to the cleantech opportunity space. The programs have resulted in student exchanges between Chinese institutions and the University of Michigan (UM); a cleantech joint venture between a US and a Chinese business and joint US–China CleanTech Entrepreneurship workshops.

11.2 BACKGROUND

11.2.1 Economic Drivers for Global Cleantech

Two major economic forces are shaping China's economic growth. The first one is characterized by ever-increasing demands for energy, water and raw materials, escalating carbon and waste emissions, and the mounting consumption needs of industry and a rapidly growing urban population. In order to achieve sustainable economic development and to help achieve the central government's impressive energy efficiency, emission reduction and resource consumption targets, the successful introduction and adoption of leading, scalable cleantech solutions across industrial and consumer sectors are essential.[1]

The second is that China's long-term growth strategy plan is framed by innovations up the value chain, rather than by outsourced manufacturing alone. In fact, outsourcing (i.e., exports) is responsible for only 10 percent of all jobs in China, and 18 percent of value-added.[2] These innovations are increasingly focused in the cleantech opportunity space, with a focus on energy efficiency, alternative energy production and clean water. Energy and water security are at the core of China's continued social, economic and political development, and China is well on its way to being the most important energy market in the world. Massive amounts of capital will be required to finance the deployment and development of cleantech in China. The Pew Environment Group[3] estimates that China will spend \$738 billion on domestic renewable energy capacity over the next decade, having surpassed the US in 2009. This compares to global cleantech stimulus programs (2008–10) totaling over \$500 billion.[4]

So, whereas China is dominant in the investment in (and deployment of) clean energy (and other green) technologies, its business model innovations have focused on how to make the technology cheaper by learning from economies of scale. For China to move up the value chain (Figure 11.1) and control technological innovation, its entrepreneurs need to learn to take on the risks associated with entrepreneurial ventures. A number of social and technical enablers for entrepreneurial value creation need to be in place.

A recent article in *The Economist* highlighted the social and technical enablers that allow for the emergence of entrepreneurial economies.[5] Social enablers include:

- the breakdown of managed capitalism, resulting in a shift in risk and security attitudes;

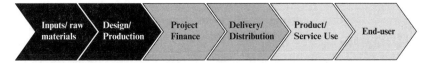

*Figure 11.1   Illustration of shift from manufacturing to product innovation
on a generic value chain*

- institutional support (e.g. universities), resulting in shifts towards value creation and innovation;
- a shift in entrepreneurship from a niche occupation to mainstream activity (e.g. 'naming and shaming' competition; World Bank Report);[6] and finally
- government support for broad-based (across the political spectrum) pro-business regulatory and credit access.

The technological enablers, which are in place in China, include:

- cheap Internet-based platforms for interactive businesses;
- dynamically scalable (and often virtualized) Internet service resources (e.g. cloud computing), and mobile access to regulated markets such as telecom, particularly those driven by touch-screen technology and fast wireless networks.

It is generally accepted that the pre-eminence of entrepreneurship in the US is enabled by social elements such as the acceptance of risk taking, the freedom to hire/fire, exposure to rewards for success (meritocracy), and a mature venture capital industry. The close relationships between universities and industry, transparent intellectual property processes, open immigration policies (25 percent of US start-ups and 52 percent of Silicon Valley start-ups were started by immigrants)[5] 'Venturesome consumers' (i.e. early adopters) further enable an entrepreneurial economy. Hence, lessons can be drawn not only from developing economies, but also by states that were previously heavily reliant on manufacturing (e.g. Michigan), and who have learned to move up the value chain in terms of investments, policies, and cultural shifts that needed to take place (see Figure 11.1). Conversely, business models originating in emerging economies (characterized as 'frugal innovation') increasingly have the potential to make inroads into Western economies, resulting in product differentiation and the creation of new markets.[7]

Testimony to China's move up the value chain are the construction of sprawling science and technology parks throughout the country,

Figure 11.2　　Ecological Science Hub, Suzhou Industry Park

adaptations in business and engineering curricula to address this new paradigm, and the availability of government-underwritten venture funds for start-up companies in high-tech, biotech and cleantech.

11.2.2　Technological and Social Drivers for Successful Entrepreneurship: Application to China's Emergence as a Cleantech Innovator

As indicated earlier, strategies for developing countries (or states) to move up the value chain and transition into a more entrepreneurial economy require a number of key enablers in place. US students learn of the impact these enablers have on driving innovation in the cleantech space, and compare the US to China.

University–industry relationships
One of the largest technology parks developed to date in China is the Suzhou Industry Park (SIP, http://www.sipac.gov.cn), near Shanghai, in Jiangxu province. Initiated in 1998, in cooperation with Singapore, the SIP has attracted 12882 projects from foreign-owned and domestic companies since 2006, including 66 Fortune 500 companies. Its Ecological Science Hub (Figure 11.2) has already brought in 42 companies from home and abroad in the field of eco-environment protection and energy conservation, which cover businesses relating to water treatment, new energy materials, air purification, environment testing, monitoring and relevant software development. In addition, the SIP is supported in part by a $2.5 billion venture fund in syndication with domestic and global venture capitalists. One of the reasons for its successful syndications is the 40 percent matched funding that the park offers to foreign investors, in addition to other risk-sharing guarantees and services.

The technical and business innovation pipeline for SIP is derived, in part, from a higher education initiative (Dushu Lake Innovation District of Science and Technology) comprising 14 renowned universities and 98 research and development institutions, with students exceeding 40 000 in number (e.g. University of Science and Technology of China, University of Liverpool, National University of Singapore, Hong Kong University, Cornell University). In addition, within a radius of 250 km from SIP, there are over 200 universities and higher education institutions with a total output of 260 000 graduates every year. Annually, over 30 000 professionals join the SIP for their career development. The new industries supported within the SIP by domestic and foreign inventions (intellectual property can be held in China, US or Europe) account for 60 percent of the SIP's total industrial output. Approximately 20 percent of the companies are focused in the cleantech space, including drinking water and energy production for Shanghai; sustainable aquaculture, which makes up 28 percent of economic output in the Yangtse River Delta; and green infrastructure (building) technologies.

Government policies

Establishing reliable supplies of domestically sourced renewable energy will be a major challenge and opportunity for China going forward. Biomass-generated biodiesel and bioethanol, wind, hydropower and solar energy are all part of this mix; however, they vary in their respective stages of technological and commercial development and their relevance in meeting China's social, economic and environmental challenges. By 2020, Beijing has mandated that 15 percent of the nation's power come from renewable energy sources. In addition, by 2010, mandates for 20 percent reductions in energy intensity, 10 percent reductions in key pollutants such as sulfur dioxide, and a 20 percent reduction in water consumption are to take effect.[8]

China's government is providing a favorable policy environment by granting feed-in tariffs[9] for renewable power, and targeting energy-intensive enterprises for significant and documented energy efficiency improvements (supported by the Chinese stimulus plan). In addition, water is an increasingly scarce resource with supply constraints set against rising consumption. Pollution is aggravating the shortage, contaminating supplies. Significant growth in private sector ownership and management of water infrastructure is expected. Lastly, the role of agencies charged with energy policy and environmental protection is strengthened, allowing for a more open debate around the environmental impacts that rapid industrialization has had on the country.

Venture investment

Global investment in cleantech in 2008 stood at $8.4 billion, but has decreased with the recent downturn, making it the third-largest investment space.[10] Chinese companies raised $430 million in venture capital (5.1 percent of global), as compared to $4.6 billion in the US.[11] Solar companies accounted for more than half of the investments in China. To date, public markets have exhibited a strong appetite for cleantech offerings from China's solar photovoltaic manufacturing sector. The exit market for domestically developed technologies, energy efficiency plays, or developers of domestic clean energy capacity may reemerge along with advances in the broader initial public offering (IPO) markets as the global economy improves. That said, most investment has been in the business expansion stage of cleantech companies, rather than in early-stage ventures.

At the 2008 China CleanTech Investment Forum in Shanghai, discussions centered around opportunities and differentiation for Chinese innovations in cleantech. The current emphasis on low-cost manufacturing alone is not sustainable, necessitating a move toward technological differentiation and high-margin products (as opposed to low-margin volumes). Since cleantech in China is dominated by private equity, investors have high expectations for "A round" venture capital investments and generally low risk tolerance for technology and market uncertainties. Excitement about investing in China's cleantech industry is high because of its clear policy signals, China's stimulus package, and government support in this space, according to a recent Deloitte report.[12] In 2009, the Obama administration was lauded for a major policy change (encapsulated in its own stimulus bill) to ensure that the US will not be left behind in the global drive to 'green the economy' and create jobs.

Dr Xijun Zhang, Business Development Director of the SIP, identified that one of the major challenges in incubating start-up companies in China's industry parks is the absence of a core competence for entrepreneurs and investors in screening entrepreneurial venture opportunities for attractive exit strategies. This is in part due to the current emphasis on later-stage companies, which are in growth mode and are profitable in China. If China wants to move up the value chain, venture capital has to acquire the expertise to vet early stage companies. This is particularly true in cleantech, because of the challenges associated with successful venture deals in this space:

- long development and investment cycles;
- large-scale infrastructure investment;
- dependence on uncertain energy and environmental policies; and
- immature knowledge and connectedness of entrepreneurs and investors in the industry.

For the last year or so, the SIP in general and the Suzhou Institute of

Sichuan University (SISU) and Shanghai University have been reaching out to US and European institutions, and have initiated the development of 'enterprise institutes' to help develop core expertise in entrepreneurial business fundamentals and to support competitive strategic opportunities for China, and Suzhou more generally, with target applications in the cleantech space in particular.

11.3 DESIGN OF AN INNOVATIVE INTERNATIONAL ENTREPRENEURSHIP EDUCATION PROGRAM

11.3.1 Program Description

Since 2008, the Zell Lurie Institute at the UM and SISU have been piloting a joint educator-initiated entrepreneurship education program that engages engineers, scientists, MBAs and start-up companies. The program responds to the need for global entrepreneurial business development in the cleantech space, and to better understand the impact of, and opportunities resulting from, greening the economy. China is motivated by the resource constraints impacting its economic growth as well as the opportunity to position itself as a major exporter of innovations in energy, water and batteries. The US is motivated by the competition resulting from the changing strategic role of China in the automotive and energy space, global industrial supply chains, and by the opportunity to leverage its entrepreneurial edge in cleantech.

At the time of this writing (late 2009), the program is not integrated in the MBA programs at either school, but the courses constitute electives at UM, and modules (i.e. individual lectures) as part of the evening MBA program at SISU.[13] The following courses are relevant to this program: "Entrepreneurial Business Fundamentals for Scientists and Engineers" (ENGR 520; 3 credits), "CleanTech Entrepreneurship" (ENGR 521; 3 credits), and "CleanTech Venture Assessment" (ES 520; 1.5 credit). The first two courses capitalize on the core expertise of engineers who tend to address technological uncertainties while ignoring the business model that enables a path to market. "CleanTech Venture Assessment" leverages the MBA background in corporate strategy and business finance to work with entrepreneurial start-up companies in this space. In the US, "CleanTech Venture Assessment" is a 1.5 credit course (seven weeks), whereas at SISU it represents a subset of lectures in the MBA core. The lectures for SISU students are given during the academic term in the US; global entrepreneurship lectures for US students are taught remotely and interactively using Skype and YouTube technology.

The challenges of the program are derived from the fact that entrepreneurship education, until recently, was not central to the core of business schools in the US and definitely not in China. Cleantech entrepreneurship in particular is nascent, and even in the US is only taught at a few schools, despite the popularity of cleantech business plan competitions, which have become quite lucrative. Bridging the cultural gap is challenging for any program, not the least because of the differences between government- and market-driven approaches to investing in ventures and the protection of home-grown technologies. Recruitment of MBA (and engineering) students with appropriate backgrounds in the US is strong, as compared to the generalist background of many Chinese MBA students. Hence, we have to demonstrate the value of the proof-of-concept to the target market of paying students, before this program will be integrated into global business programs.

11.3.2   Entrepreneurial Business Tools for Technology Venture Assessment

Technology-based entrepreneurship, regardless of the opportunity space, requires a mixture of technological and business skills. Our aim in teaching global entrepreneurship, which focuses on cleantech, is to enhance the blended strengths of engineering and business students, not turn each into the other, and to provide the students with the flavor of the impact of regional cultural and policy incentives on the business design.

The innovation continuum
It is valuable to think of the continuum of new venture formation and growth as a series of development phases: identifying opportunities and shaping them into business concepts; feasibility analysis and assessment; creating an actionable business plan; launching the business; and growth and exit strategies (Figure 11.3).

Structuring the program along this continuum not only allows us to focus on specific phases where student skills are complementary, but it also allows us to draw a comparison between the US and China. For example, the complementary skills of both the engineers and the business students are crucial in the early phases where innovation opportunities are honed. Opportunity identification, for example, takes two forms: finding an optimal market opportunity for a given technology; and identifying an emerging market opportunity and determining what technology may be necessary to exploit it.

As indicated earlier, the Chinese focus on growth stages, rather than opportunity identification, draws on different skill sets of the

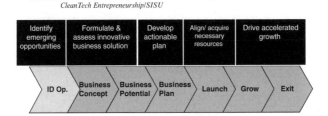

Figure 11.3 *Business development phases, and alignment of core courses for UM-SISU partnership*

entrepreneurs, as well as the investors. By differentiating the earlier and later stages of entrepreneurial business development, and by drawing comparisons between government- and market-driven cleantech investment policies, the students learn to appreciate the different value-creating paradigms between China and the US.

Motivation

Most entrepreneurship curricula begin with a course on some form of writing a business plan. The message to students is that all their ideas are worthy of converting into detailed operating documents. They are not. These ideas must be screened and assessed. The entrepreneur's time, after all, is the most precious resource of all. There is no sense wasting it on an idea that is unlikely to be economically successful, based on business fundamentals. Similarly, many start-ups, even those that have received funding, are often searching to articulate the value proposition, in part because they have been (at least in the early stages) too technology-centric. The good news is that there is increased attention being paid to determining the feasibility of the business. More and more institutions are thus beginning to look at teaching methodologies to assess the feasibility of a proposed new business.

Teaching modules (within a course)

To address the need for having the student understand the value of early entrepreneurial business assessment, and to allow the engineering student to de-emphasize the technology-based perspective of entrepreneurial business development, we have developed a series of teaching modules. These modules systematically test the business hypothesis formulated by entrepreneurial ventures in their business plans, and help to reposition the company and its product development. The modules include value chain assessment, sustainable differentiation,

Table 11.1   Course modules, tools and assessment

Module	Tool	Evaluation	Timeframe
1. Value chain assessment	EBITDA Margin analysis (public sources)	Team	Weeks 1–3
2. Micro-industry (product assessment)	Differentiation (intellectual assets, complementary assets)	Team	Week 4
3. Macro-industry (industry assessment)	Porter's 5 Forces (across value chain segments)	Team	Week 5
4. Business vehicle assessment	How do complementary asset needs influence your business structure [13]?	Team	Week 8
5. Market needs (target market)	Persona (specific target customer) analysis	Team	Week 9
6. Market segmentation (macro-market)	Influence diagrams	Team	Week 10
7. Revenue models	Revenue stream analysis, pricing, income statement, cash flow	Team	Week 12
8. Entrepreneurial finance	Capitalization tables and enterprise valuation	Individual	Throughout the term

entrepreneurial marketing, entrepreneurial finance, and determining the optimal business vehicle. Content-specific lectures are supplemented by live cases of early start-up companies, culminating in a student-team based assessment, analysis and design of a new business (ENGR 520) or repositioning of an existing cleantech business model (ENGR 521 and ES 520). In China, the course modules are taught as individual lectures focusing on theory and practice to demonstrate the value of a rational approach from idea to enterprise.

The tools that are taught and used are illustrated in Table 11.1, exemplified for the "Business Fundamentals" course (ENGR 520). Similarly, Figure 11.4 shows the sequence of activities across the opportunity and solution space, aligned with the tools needed to get to the next step, as it would be implemented. There are some modifications in the sequence between ENGR 520 and ENGR 521/ES520 because the former starts with an opportunity space (e.g. water, solar, transportation) in which the students seek and design an investable venture, and the latter starts with an existing venture that has a prototype design of its product.

The divergence/convergence diagram allows the students to analyze a proposed business concept for a start-up company in the context of

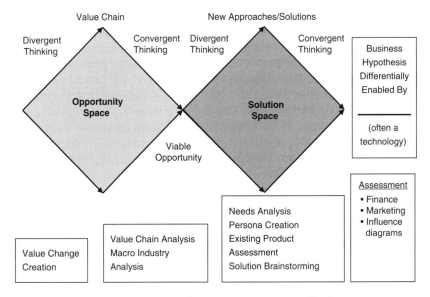

Figure 11.4   Course structure: from opportunity to technology

the opportunity space the company is attempting to enter, and the need addressed by the company to capture value. At the end of this iterative analysis of the company, the business hypothesis is modified for optimum theoretical value capture. The top companies are considered for angel or venture investment by two funds managed by the Ross School of Business: the Frankel Commercialization Fund and the Wolverine Venture Fund.

Business fundamentals and technology entrepreneurship
The students need to understand that for a technological solution to become valuable, business (How are you going to make money?) and market (How do you strategically position your business?) uncertainties need to be addressed. Following the participating company pitch, the students articulate the business hypothesis they will test using the tools taught during the content lectures. The hypothesis is based on the answers to the following questions as they understand it from the company's business plan: What is the product or service? Who are your users? Why will they use your product? How does your business make money? They then set out to conduct a number of 'tests'. The first test analyzes the operating margins of the industries currently operating in the value chain segments of the opportunity space the company is addressing. The students will compare the segment that the company is positioned in to the highest-margin segment, and analyze the reasons for the margins. The

next step involves an analysis of the challenges and pains in the actual industry segment based on credible referenced reports, and compares the company's solution to the incumbent and alternative solutions.

Using a product analysis (from a differentiation perspective), the students will conduct a competitive strategy analysis on the solutions segment, and identify means to sustain its differentiation. We consider here that all segments operating along a value chain are in a continuously changing equilibrium, and ask the students what the company could do to shift the equilibrium in their solution's favor. At this point, the students will evaluate the strength of the actual intellectual assets of the company (patents, knowledge, trademarks, etc.) and the type of complementary assets required (generic or specialized) to decide on the optimal business vehicle (product, service, license, partnership, etc.).[14]

The question then becomes whether this is a venture-backable company from the perspective of returns for investors and valuation of the company. The students learn to apply the levers in a custom-developed Excel-based capitalization table tool, and a valuation tool (based on the analysis of the enterprise value of the company using pure-play proxy companies). Pending the outcome of this analysis, the company may or may not be attractive to investors based on the current business hypothesis. The final outcome of the project iterates on the hypothesis, accompanied by suggestions of how the company or product can be repositioned to capture value and represent an attractive investment.

11.4 CONCLUSIONS: TEACHING GLOBAL CLEANTECH ENTREPRENEURSHIP

One of the objectives of the joint entrepreneurship education program is to identify and communicate the impact of Chinese investment in entrepreneurship and cleantech on global opportunities. The course modules are aimed at educating US engineers and MBAs on the one hand, and MBAs at the SIP on the other hand, about entrepreneurial business development skills in general, and their application to the cleantech space in particular. Differentiating elements between China and the US include the business and policy environment, the investment culture, and the strength of the intellectual property.

To date, over 100 engineering students and 60 MBA students have taken the courses at the UM, and approximately 350 MBA student hours have been taught at SISU. In ENGR 521 and ES 520, 34 early-stage companies have been assessed and recommended for repositioning. These companies span the energy, water, energy efficiency, green grid, and automotive spaces. Three companies have been recommended for investment, and two have received seed rounds totaling $220 000. In China, the educational modules are largely disconnected from the SIP investment decision-making because the higher education authority (Dushu Lake Innovation District of Science and Technology) is a separate entity from the business management authorities of the SIP. However, it is expected that one joint venture between a US company and a Chinese company will receive investment to locate in the Ecological Science Hub.

Infrastructure Challenges

As part of the UM–SIP–SISU interaction, for the Chinese MBAs there is a focus on the specifics of the entrepreneurial cleantech venture enablers in China in general, and on the specific incentives at the SIP in particular. For example, the park has a US$2.5 billion government-underwritten venture capital fund, and a strong investment team, but no formal structure in place for performing due diligence on the companies applying for the funds. Particularly due to the steep growth in cleantech investment, and the lack of knowledge in this investment domain, the quality of the deals has dropped significantly. Hence, the focus in the SISU course modules is on pre-money company valuation methods, and structuring investment rounds using capitalization tables. Specific questions include, for example: How does foreign intellectual property influence investment rounds and exits? How does the deal quality compare to US ventures and how does this influence valuation?

As noted before, the business model of the SIP and other technology parks is investment through syndication, whereby the government-backed venture capital fund invests in first rounds, and the park provides building lease payment deferrals, and may offer a co-investment for private investors (domestic or cross-border). Currently, there is a lack of exposure of the SIP-backed companies to global cleantech investors, and a lack of knowledge about cleantech company quality for foreign investors, a need we address by teaching the screening process and tools described earlier. As more data and information becomes available on the SIP-based companies, the course modules at SISU will increasingly be based on 'real-life' cases developed from the SIP experience.

The global component in this teaching program comes through in-class discussions of how business environment parameters (e.g. policy, strength of intellectual property, investment strategies, government support, cross-border partnerships and license agreements) influence the business model and attractiveness of the industry segment in which the company is attempting to create value. At UM, we have looked at US-based start-up

companies based on the availability of business plans, engagement opportunities with the entrepreneurs, and language issues. As indicated earlier,
two companies have received investment from the Wolverine Venture
Fund and the Frankel Commercialization Fund following this analysis, and nine cleantech-based business plans submitted by students that
took the courses have won top-three prizes in national business plan
competitions.

At SISU, we have focused on learning from cleantech business development workshops that connect Chinese entrepreneurs with Chinese and US
investors. This has helped to provide an understanding of the context of
the Chinese business environment and policies that drive investments and
technology development. Interesting differences with the US include the
lower expectations for investor returns (in part because most investments
are later-stage), the lack of available venture risk capital, the lesser focus
on intellectual property strength, and the lack of transparency for cross-
border partnerships, which impacts the ability of foreign investors and
entrepreneurs to calculate their risks and returns. To date, we have not yet
been able to connect course-based venture assessment and SIP investment,
but are working toward this goal, similar to our current collaborative
practice between ENGR 521 and the UM's Frankel Pre-Seed Fund and
Wolverine Venture Fund.

NOTES AND REFERENCES

*   Peter Adriaens is a Professor of Civil and Environmental Engineering and
    Professor of Entrepreneurship, Ross School of Business, the University of
    Michigan; Distinguished Professor of Entrepreneurship, Sichuan University (Suzhou
    Institute), Suzhou, China. Timothy Faley is a Managing Director, Samuel Zell
    & Robert H. Lurie Institute for Entrepreneurial Studies, and Adjunct Professor
    of Entrepreneurship, Ross School of Business. The corresponding author is Peter
    Adriaens (adriaens@umich.edu).
1. P. Adriaens, "Leading Innovations: CleanTech", *Encyclopedia of Sustainability,
    Volume 2: The Business of Sustainability*, Great Barrington, MA: Birkshire Publishing,
    292–297, 2010.
2. *The Economist*, "Bamboo Shoots of Recovery", 16 April 2009.
3. The Pew Environment Group. "Who's Winning the Clean Energy Race?" Washington,
    DC: The Pew Charitable Trusts, 2010.
4. Edenhofer, O. and N. Stern, "Towards a Global Green Recovery: Recommendations
    for Immediate G20 Action", 2009, http://www2.lse.ac.uk/granthamInstitute/publica
    tions/GlobalGreenRecovery_April09.pdf.
5. Wooldridge, A., "Global Heroes. A Special Report on Entrepreneurship", *The
    Economist*, 12 March 2009.
6. World Bank, "Doing Business: Measuring Business Regulations", 2010, http://www.
    doingbusiness.org/economyrankings/.
7. *The Economist*. "A special Report on Innovation in Emerging Markets", 15 April 2010.
8. Dewey & Leboeuf, LLP, "China's Promotion of the Renewable Electric Power

Equipment Industry: Hydro, Wind, Solar, Biomass", Washington, DC: National Foreign Trade Council, 2010.

9. Under a feed-in tariff, eligible renewable electricity generators (which can include homeowners and businesses) are paid a premium price for any renewable electricity they produce. Typically regional or national electric grid utilities are obligated to take the electricity and pay the suppliers. This policy instrument is aimed toward encouraging the adoption of renewable energy sources and to help accelerate the move toward grid parity.

10. Cleantech Group, "The 2008 Annual Review and 4Q08 Investment Monitor", *CleanTech Investment Monitor*, 7:4, 2009, Available at www.CleanTech.com.

11. CleanTech Group, "Cleantech Venture Capital and Private Equity Investing in China", 2008, http://www.Cleantech.com.

12. DeWoskin, K. and J. Mahoney, "Cleantech in China", *The 2009 Research Agenda*, http://www.Cleantech.com, 2009.

13. The program described in sections 11.3 and 11.4 between SISU and UM was discontinued in late 2010 because of funding. As this volume goes to print in late 2011, UM plans to restart in 2012 a similar program with Shanghai University.

14. Teece, D.J., "Capturing Value from Knowledge Assets: The New Economy, Markets for Know-how, and Intangible Assets", *California Management Review*, 40:3, 1998, 55–79.

Index